D1124564

SHAKESPEARE'S
TRAGIC HEROES
SLAVES OF PASSION

SHAKESPEARE'S
TRAGIC HEROES

SLAVES OF PASSION

by LILY B. CAMPBELL

With Appendices on Bradley's Interpretation
of Shakespearean Tragedy

BARNES & NOBLE, INC., NEW YORK

PUBLISHERS • BOOKSELLERS • SINCE 1873

Published in 1930 by the Cambridge University Press

Reprinted by Barnes & Noble, Inc.
by Special Arrangement with the Cambridge University Press

Eight Printing, 1968

PRINTED IN THE UNITED STATES OF AMERICA

The VSE of
PASSIONS
(Written in French by
J. F. Senault.
And
put into English
by
Henry Earle of
Monmouth
1649.

Divine Grace

Reason

Joy

Feare

Despaire

Sorrow

Choller

Hope

Boldnesse

Eschewing

Love

Hatred

Desire

Passions araing'd by Reason here you see,
As they'r Advis'd therein by Grace Divine:
But this (you'll say) is but in Effigie!
Peruse this Booke, and you in ev'ry line
Thereof will finde this truth so prov'd, that you
Must Reason contradict, or grant it True.

W.M. sculp

PLATE I. Title-page from Senault, *The Use of Passions*.

The first Design of Dramatic Poetry, was to amend the Heart, improve the Understanding, and, at the same Time, Please the Imagination. To Tragedy, one Species of the Drama was allotted, the Description of those Passions, which, when loose and ungoverned, are productive of the most terrible Consequences on the one Hand; but if, on the other, they are kept within their proper Limits, and chuse Reason for their Guide and Director, they become Highly conducive to the Happiness of Mankind. To Comedy was assigned the Correction of Vices and Follies of an inferior sort.

In the first Instance, we are taught, by a Collection of fatal Events, to avoid Ruin and Misery; in the last, by a Representation of fashionable Foibles, and particular extravagant Humours, to shun Ridicule and Absurdity.

SAMUEL FOOTE, The Roman and English Comedy
Consider'd and Compar'd. 1747.

PREFACE

IT was in 1898 that Sir Sidney Lee summarily disposed of future Shakespearean interpreters in the preface to his *Life of William Shakespeare*: "Aesthetic studies of Shakespeare abound, and to increase their number is a work of supererogation". But in spite of this anathema the end was not yet. And in the criticism of the intervening thirty years there are two lines of interpretation that are to be specially remarked. In 1904 Professor A. C. Bradley's interpretation of Shakespearean tragedy, partly psychological and partly metaphysical, was to serve as a new landmark and a new point of departure in Shakespearean criticism— one may almost say in literary criticism. In 1907 Professor Dowden published in the *Atlantic Monthly* a paper on "Elizabethan Psychology", which pointed toward an ideal of criticism on the basis of contemporary thought.

Professor Bradley began his analysis of Shakespeare's conception of tragedy by a discussion that implicitly accepted Aristotle's *Poetics* as the basis for differentiation. He questioned the mediaeval idea of tragedy, "a story of exceptional calamity leading to the death of a man in high estate", as inadequate to explain Shakespeare in full, and he specifically affirmed that "the tragic world is a world of action, and action is the translation of thought into reality". He concluded: "The tragic suffering and death arise from collision, not with a fate or blank power, but with a moral power, a power akin to all that we admire and revere in the characters themselves". It is this conception of tragedy as action, and of the plot of tragedy as a statement of metaphysical belief that has so much interested later critics. A further quest along these lines is to be seen in the recent work of Professor Farnham in connection with *A Mirror for Magistrates*.

The line of inquiry launched by Professor Dowden called attention to the need for understanding Elizabethan psychology if we were to interpret Shakespeare's characters aright. And although Hamlet and Othello, Lear and Macbeth, are still psycho-analysed or enrolled with pro-Germans or classified with the Rotarians according to the preconceptions of the critic, yet since the Dowden paper there have been spasmodic attempts to study one or other of the Shakespearean characters in something of the light in which Shakespeare must have thought of them. In the papers of Professor Stoll this desire has been particularly apparent. Further studies by Professor Hardin Craig and Professor M. W. Bundy have indicated a tendency to go more curiously into the matter. A recent thesis by Miss Ruth Anderson, which I have only seen since completing this manuscript, carries the study further.

I myself had thought to claim at least the negative distinction of not contributing any supererogatory interpretations of Shakespeare. But each time that I read and taught the tragedies of Shakespeare I became more dissatisfied with my interpretations. I became convinced that Shakespeare in all his tragedies was primarily concerned with passion rather than with action. I determined to find what was known and thought about passion in the sixteenth century. I went trustingly to my philosophical friends and asked for guidance, only to be told that the researches of the historians of philosophy ended with the Middle Ages and began again with Descartes. I perceived, therefore, that my task was to take on the nature of an adventure in searching for the philosophy that was moulding the thinking of men in England during the great humanistic period.

Gradually, therefore, my work seemed to call for three separate studies: a study of the philosophical thinking of

Shakespeare's day in regard to passion; a study of the way in which this thinking was related to the current conceptions of literature and the purposes of literature; and a study of Shakespeare's incorporation in his tragedies of the prevailing ideas of the humanists in regard to passion. This book is accordingly divided into three parts: I have put first the consideration of the purposes to be served by literature as Shakespeare's contemporaries thought of such purposes; next I have tried to show how the passions were understood and why the passions were the pivotal point for discussion by physicians and philosophers of the period; and finally I have discussed the embodiment of passion in the four great tragic heroes of Shakespeare, in each of whom a dominating passion is analysed in accordance with the medical and philosophical teaching of the period. The result of my research has been the conviction that Shakespeare, much more than has generally been thought, was a man familiar with the learning of his day, a student of philosophy, and a purposive artist.

To trace the history of Shakespearean scholarship is a task of a lifetime. The student of Shakespeare, therefore, who would add to the comments made through the centuries is forced almost to the necessity of seeming to ignore the mass of material already contributed; he must indeed fix his eyes upon Shakespeare as though there had been no others gazing upon the sun. This is my reason for trying to present my theory of the central design in Shakespearean tragedy without specific mention of the common thought that has appeared in the comment of Shakespearean critics for two centuries. To correlate my own hypothesis fully with what has gone before would necessitate, I believe, losing sight of Shakespeare in the confusing assembly of his commentators. This is my apology as I bring my bucket to the sea.

The great riches of the Henry E. Huntington Library have afforded me my chief material for study. My indebtedness to Mr Cecil K. Edmonds and to Mr Robert Schad or this library is beyond possibility of definite acknowledgement, for without their help I could not have established the necessary bibliography. To the Library of Congress I am also indebted for the loan of necessary books. To the British Museum I owe gratitude for the kindness which is the common experience of students. To Mr Paul Jordan-Smith I am indebted for generous help in many difficulties, particularly in the second part of this work, where his experience in the editing of Burton's *Anatomy of Melancholy* was of invaluable service. To Professor John M. Manly, who has read the manuscript in its entirety, I am once more indebted for counsel and advice as I have been indebted throughout my life as a student. And finally, to Mr Merritt Williams, my pupil and friend, I owe the assistance that has made possible the completion of my work.

I have quoted much in the course of this study, and I have tried to make quotations accurately represent the works from which they were taken. I have not modernized quotations save that I have interpreted the old type-forms, *j, s, u, m*, etc., in accordance with modern usage; punctuation and spelling otherwise appear as in the original works. I have used uncritically the Cambridge edition of Shakespeare with its basic acceptance of the Globe numbering of lines.

L. B. C.

CONTENTS

SECTION I

THE PURPOSE & METHOD OF TRAGEDY

SECTION II

MORAL PHILOSOPHY IN SHAKESPEARE'S DAY

SECTION III

MIRRORS OF PASSION

PLATES

SECTION I

*The Purpose and Method
of Tragedy*

CHAPTER I

The Mirrors of Fortune   The Problem of Evil
The Problem of Justice   How God Revenges Sin

THE problem of tragedy has always been the problem of evil in the world. The presentation of the evil that befalls men is but one of the concerns of tragedy; the other and the more important is the explanation of the why of the evil so presented. Thus it is that tragedy and philosophy, tragedy and religion, must always have much in common. And if we are to find the meaning of Shakespeare's tragedies, we must find how men looked at this problem of evil in the day when these tragedies were first played to English audiences. We must, therefore, look to such explanations as were given both by writers of tragedies [1] and by philosophers in Shakespeare's time, but these explanations will best be understood when we can trace them from their mediaeval origins through their period of modification by the re-born classical philosophy and classical literature.

Chaucer's *Monk's Tale* testifies to the fact that tragedies were considered as *exempla* to warn men of the fickleness of fortune and of the causes why men fell from weal to woe. The Monk begins:

> I wol biwaille, in manere of tragedie,
> The harm of hem that stoode in heigh degree,
> And fillen so that ther nas no remedie
> To brynge hem out of hir adversitee;
> For certein, whan that Fortune list to flee,
> Ther may no man the cours of hire withholde.
> Lat no man truste on blynd prosperitee;
> Be war by thise ensamples trewe and olde.

[1] In this first chapter I have confined my study to non-dramatic tragedies, in which the tradition is carried over directly from the mediaeval period. In the second chapter I shall discuss this theory of tragedy as it was applied to the dramatic tragedies of the Renaissance.

Moreover, the Monk not only speaks *de Casibus Virorum Illustrium* but points out in every instance the sin which led to the destruction described in the tragedy.

Lydgate followed his master, taking up the same theme in his *Fall of Princes*:

> My maister Chaucer, with his fresh comedies,
> Is ded, allas, cheeff poete off Breteyne,
> That whilom made ful pitous tragedies;
> The fall of pryncis he dede also compleyne,
> As he that was of makyng sovereyne,
> Whom al this land sholde off riht preferre,
> Sithe off oure language he was the lodesterre.
>
> Senek in Rome, thoruh his hih prudence,
> Wrot tragedies of gret moralite;
> And Tullius, cheeff welle off eloquence,
> Maad in his tyme many fressh dite;
> Franceis Petrak, off Florence the cite,
> Made a book, as I can reherce,
> Off too Fortunys, welful and perverse.[1]

Explicitly he stated the theme of his own work as well as that of his great original, Boccaccio:

> And thus in cheef thes causes affor told
> Meved the herte of Bochas to writyng,
> And to remembre be many story old
> Thestat of pryncis, in chaieres hih sittyng,
> And for vices ther unwar fallyng,
> Yiving exaumple, as I afferme dar
> Of fals Fortune how thei shal be war.[2]

---

[1] E.E.T.S., Ex. Ser. vols. CXXI, CXXII, CXXIII. Ed. by Dr Henry Bergen. Cf. vol. CXXI, pp. 7, 8. Prologue, ll. 246–59.

[2] *Ibid.* vol. CXXII, p. 477. Bk. IV, Prologue, ll. 155–61. *The Fall of Princes* was a paraphrase of Laurence de Premierfait's second amplified version in French prose of Boccaccio's *De Casibus Virorum Illustrium*, of which Dr Bergen says: "It is a collection gathered throughout the centuries describing the most memorable and crushing blows dealt by fate to the illustrious personages of mythology and history, and written, as the author himself said, with the object of teaching princes the virtue of wisdom and moderation by holding up to them the example of misfortunes provoked by egotism, pride, and inordinate ambition".

PLATE II. Illustration from the 1554 edition of Lydgate, *A Treatise excellent and compendious, shewing and declaring in maner of tragedye, the falles of sondry most notable Princes and Princesses with other Nobles, through ye Mutabilitie and change of unstedfast Fortune together with their most detestable & wicked vices.*

PLATE III. Illustration from the 1554 edition of Lydgate, *The Falles of Princes*.

Lydgate's main theme is thus seen to be, as it is in Chaucer and in the common inspirer of both, Boccaccio, the uncertainty of prosperity, but the theme which is not less insistent is that of the vices which cause the fall of princes. As Professor Farnham has pointed out, however, Lydgate was not thoroughly consistent in his relating of misfortune to desert, and "dwells lovingly on the evidence that even the valiant and the virtuous come to grief".[1] But in spite of this inconsistency, it is quite clear that the tragedies which he retold were offered as warnings, not only of the fickleness of "fals Fortune", but also as evidence that the "pryncis, in chaieres hih sittyng" must be considered "for vices ther unwar fallyng".

This traditional view of tragedy was most conspicuously carried over into the Renaissance in the series of tragedies which were first published in 1559 under the title of *A Myrroure for Magistrates. Wherein may be seene by example of other, with how grevous plages vices are punished: and howe frayle and unstable worldly prosperitie is founde, even of those, whom Fortune seemeth most highly to favour.*[2]

It is significant that it was to the William Baldwin whose *Treatise of Morall Philosophy*, published in 1547, continued for more than a century to be the popular book of moral philosophy in England, that the printer went to secure the continuation of the *Fall of Princes*, which he was proposing to print. Baldwin says in his address "To the nobilitye and all other in office" that they can see in Boccaccio's book how God has plagued evil rulers in other nations, and he continues:

[1] Cf. Professor Willard Farnham's article on "*The Mirror for Magistrates* and Elizabethan Tragedy", in *Jour. of Eng. and Ger. Phil.* vol. XXV, pp. 66–78, for interesting though tentative comment.

[2] For an account of the history of *The Mirrour for Magistrates*, see the article by Professor J. W. Cunliffe in the *Camb. Hist. of Engl. Lit.* vol. III, pp. 216–26; W. F. Trench, *A Mirror for Magistrates: Its Origin and Influence*, 1898; and the article by Professor Farnham already instanced.

Howe he hath delt with sum of our countreymen your auncestors, for sundrye vices not yet left, this booke named *A Myrrour for Magistrates*, can shewe: which therfore I humbly offre unto your honors, beseching you to accept it favorably. For here as in a loking glas, you shall see (if any vice be in you) howe the like hath bene punished in other heretofore, whereby admonished, I trust it will be a good occasion to move you to the soner amendment. This is the chiefest ende, whye it is set furth, which God graunt it may attayne.

Yet Baldwin was forced to admit that it was not only evil men who suffered misfortune:

And although you shall finde in it, that sum have for their vertue been envied and murdered, yet cease not you to be vertuous, but do your offices to the uttermost: punish sinne boldly, both in your selves and other, so shall God (whose lieutenauntes you are) eyther so mayntayne you, that no malice shall prevayle, or if it do, it shal be for your good, and to your eternall glory both here and in heaven, which I beseche God you may covet and attayne.

In his address "To the Reader" Baldwin extends his moral purpose as he explains that the printer came to him

to procure to have the storye contynewed from where as Bochas lefte, unto this presente time, chiefly of suche as Fortune had dalyed with here in this ylande: whiche might be as a myrrour for al men as well noble as others, to shewe the slyppery deceytes of the waveryng lady, and the due rewarde of all kinde of vices.[1]

In 1574 this work was reprinted as *The Laste parte of the Mirour for Magistrates*, for the printer was publishing in 1574 also a collection of tragedies antedating in their stories

[1] These quotations are taken from the first edition of 1559, but Baldwin is himself the authority for the book's having been partly printed in 1555. The purpose of the work was restated in the well-known *Induction* of Sackville in the 1563 edition:

"That musing on this worldly wealth in thought,
Which comes, and goes, more faster than we see
The flickering flame that with the fire is wrought,
My busy mind presented unto me
Such fall of peeres as in the realm had be;
    That oft I wished some would their woes describe,
    To warn the rest whom fortune left behind."

the stories collected in the original publication and now to be published as *The First parte of the Mirour for Magistrates, containing the falles of the first infortunate Princes of this lande: From the comming of Brute to the incarnation of our saviour and redemer Jesu Christe.* The author of this group of tragedies was John Higgins, and in his address "To the Nobilitie and all other in office" he brings the whole discussion of tragedy and of reward and punishment over into the realm of moral philosophy. I quote from this address at length because Higgins gives here, somewhat wordily it is true, the philosophy that was more often concerned in forming tragedy than is usually recognized:

Amongst the wise (right Honorable) whose sentences (for the moste parte) tende either to teache the attaining of vertue, or eschuing of vice: Plotinus that wonderfull and excellent Phylosopher, hath these wordes: The propertie of Temperaunce is to covet nothing which may bee repented: not to exceade the bandes of measure, and to keepe desire under the yooke of Reason. Whiche saying if it were so well knowen, as is needefull: so well imbraced, as hee wyshed, or so surely fixed in minde, as it is printed in his woorkes: then certis manye Christians might by the instruction of an Ethnicke Phylosopher, shunne great and daungerous perils. For to covet without consideration: to passe the measure of his degree: and to lette will runne at randon, is the only destruction of all estates. Else howe were it possible, so many learned, politike, wise, renoumed, valiaunt and victorious personages, might ever have come to such utter decaye. Will you that I rehearse Alexander the great, Caesar, Pompey, Cyrus, Hannibal, etc. Al which (by desire of glorie) felte the rewarde of their immoderate and insatiable lustes.... But you wil say, desire of fame, glorie, renowne, and immortalitie (to which al men wel nighe of nature are inclined especially those which excel or have any singuler gift of Fortune or of the body) moved them to such daungerous, great and hardy enterprises, which I must nedes confesse as an infallible veritie: but for so much as the above named vertue by Plotinus his judgement hath such excellent properties, it is so fit in a Magistrate, that I surely deme those Princes above specified (considering their factes, estates, fortunes, fame and exploytes) had never come to suche ende, but for wante of temperance. Yet sithe there are three other Cardinall vertues whiche are requisite in him that should be in authoritie: that is to saye, Prudence, Justice, and Fortitude, which so wonderfully adorne and beautifie all estates, (if Temperaunce bee with them adjoyned that they move the very enemies with admiration to praise them) some peradventure as affection leades: will commende one, some another. Yea, and though Aristotle prince of Phylosophers name Prudence, The mother of vertues. And Cicero define hir the knowledge of thinges which ought to be desired and followed: and also of them which ought to be fled and eschewed, yet shall you finde that for wante of Temperaunce, those which were counted the wisest that ever were, fel into wonderfull reproche and infamie. Yea and though Justice that incomparable vertue, as the auncient Civilians define hir, be a perpetuall and constant will which geveth to every man his right. Yet if she be not constant, which is the gift of fortitude, nor equal in discerning right from wrong, wherin is prudence: nor use proportion in judgement and sentence which per- taineth to temperaunce, shee can never be called equitie or justice, but fraude, deceate, injustice, and injurie. And to speake of Fortitude which Cicero definith, A consyderate undertaking of perils, and enduring of labours. If hee whom we suppose stoute, valiaunt, and of good courage, want Prudence, Justice, or Temperaunce, he is not counted bolde, manly and constant, but made beastly and desperate. I will also sith I have gone so farre with the vertues (and the place so urgeth) lastly set downe the definition of Temperaunce, according to Cicero his opinion, Temperaunce (saith he) is of reason in lust and other evill assaultes of the minde, a sure and moderate dominion and rule. This noble vertue hath three partes, that is continence, clemencie and modestie, which well and wisely observed and kept (if grace be to them adjoyned) it is impossible for him that is endued with the above named vertues ever to fall into the unfortunate snares of calamitie or misfortune....I have here (right honorable) in this booke (which I am so bolde to dedicate to your honors) only reproved foly in those which are heedelesse: injurie in extortioners, rashness in venterers, and excesse, in such as suppresse not unruly affections.

It is evident that to Higgins the virtues are the only means to avoid misery and to secure happiness:

> We ether are rewarded, as we serve:
> Or else are plaged, as our deedes deserve.[1]

But Higgins wrote of punishments ingeniously fitted to the vices they rewarded. Thus Manlius, minded to kill his

[1] From the story of Manlius, *op. cit.* fol. 36.

brother, was by him slain: Bladud, practising by curious arts to fly, fell and broke his neck; Kimarus, hunting, was slain by wild beasts. It is the kind of punishment described by the phrase "the biter bitten". And bewilderment as to the ways of Fortune or of divine justice is lacking.

In 1578 was published by Richard Webster *The Seconde part of the Mirrour for Magistrates, conteining the falles of the infortunate Princes of this Lande. From the Conquest of Caesar, unto the commyng of Duke William the Queror.* This work, not originally intended for the public, was published while the author, Thomas Blener-Hasset, was abroad. There are interesting suggestions of changes in the permanent theme of the mutability of human life and the relation of the fall of princes to their deserts. Thus we find: "How Guidericus refused to pay tribute unto Claud-Caesar.... This historie is a singuler example of Gods vengeance against pride and arrogancye". And the motto of the whole which is appended, *Goe straight and feare not*, is summed up in the closing words of the story of Harolde:

> Let no man thinke by fetches finely filde,
> By double driftes convayed cunningly,
> To get or gayne by any craft or guile,
> A good estate with long prosperitie.
> His lust obtaynde, he lives in miserie,
> His guilty ghost dooth see his plague appeare,
> Who goeth straight he needeth not to feare.

In the same tradition should be noted particularly *The reward of Wickednesse* by Richard Robinson, the prefatory letter to which is dated 1574. The purpose of the author was explained in his words of "The Aucthour to the Booke", bidding the book

> reveale abroade the woe
> That is among the sillie soules, in Plutos ouglie lake,
> For wickednesse done on the Earth, howe Jove doth vengeance take.
> Blushe not my booke, to thunder foorth, the tormentes thou hast seene,
> Tell wilfull wits, and hatefull hearts, what just deserved teene.

One of the interesting features of this book is the marginal notes which accompany the stories, for they are in the nature of moral aphorisms: "Vertue is the beautie of man and woman"; "Olde pleasures brede new sorrowes"; "Wickednes destroyeth it selfe", etc.

Also there must be noted the significant work of Antony Munday printed in 1579: *The Mirrour of Mutabilitie, or Principall part of the Mirrour for Magistrates. Describing the fall of divers famous Princes and other memorable Personages. Selected out of the Scriptures....* The author explains:

> Marcus, Tullius, Cicero, that flourishing floure of all Eloquence, hath in divers and sundry places prescribed the direct rule of a verteous life, declaring many excellent exhortations to avoyd the vices which are incident to the weakned minde. As the Pride of life. The Envy of the minde at the prosperitie of an other. The Wrath which wasteth and molesteth the hart. The Gluttonous excesse of belly Gods and pampred paunches, in their daintie fare and drunken delights. The lascivious and unlawful desire of the flesh. The Covetous consciences of welthie worldly misers. And lastly the sluggish Sloth and idle life, enemye to all verteous actions. The consideration wherof: caused me to write this Discourse, as a plain and sufficient example to all in generall, wherin they may see, the dissolute life of divers personages forepassed, as the Scripture by credible authoritie maketh deliberate mention.

Munday embodies in his selected tragedies examples, not only of the seven deadly sins, but also of cruelty, rashness, incontinence, voluptuousness, wilfulness, etc.

In 1597 there was published *The Theatre of Gods Judgements: or, a Collection of Histories out of Sacred, Ecclesiasticall, and prophane Authours, concerning the admirable Judgements of God upon the transgressours of his commandements. Translated out of French, and Augmented by more than three hundred Examples*, by Th. Beard. The work has become famous as containing the case of "Marlin", the atheist playwright, and his appropriate death by his own hand which had sinned in writing blasphemies. But leaving the truth of the Marlowe episode aside, the book makes an interesting contribution to

PLATE IV. *La Justice et la Vengeance divine poursuivant le crime,* painted by Prud'hon for the Palais de Justice in 1808.

the common theme of these collections of tragedies. Beard's dedication "To the right Worshipfull, Sir Edward Wingfield, Knight" states the purpose of the book, and we see that the question of the justice with which the mutability of fortune is adjusted is still the central interest: Beard says that men are too prone to think of the mercy of God and to dismiss from their thoughts the justice of God;

and that is the cause why more perish by presumption than despaire: for this cause it seemed to me most necessary to call into mens memories the wonderfull judgements of God, & to set before their eies a view of his justice manifested in the world upon sinners & reprobats, to the end that the drowsie consciences of Gods children might be awakened, and the desperat hearts of the wicked confounded, when they shall see how vengeance pursueth malefactours to their shame and confusion in this life, and to their destruction in the world to come.

In his preface Beard insists that punishment follows sin "as a shadow doth the body". And this lesson he sees inculcated by history:

And in this regard historie is accounted a very necessary and profitable thing, for that in recalling to mind the truth of things past, which otherwise would be buried in silence, it setteth before us such effects (as warnings & admonitions touching good and evill) and laieth vertue and vice so naked before our eyes, with the punishments or rewards inflicted or bestowed upon the followers of each of them, that it may rightly be called, an easie and profitable apprenticeship or schoole for every man to learne to get wisedome at another mans cost. Hence it is, that Historie is tearmed of the ancient Philosophers, *The record and register of Time, the light of Truth, and the mistresse and looking glasse of mans life.* Insomuch as under the person of another man it teacheth and instructeth all those that apply their minds unto it, to governe and carry themselves vertuously and honestly in this life.

Beard denied the element of chance in events, insisting that all is of God,

that nothing in the world commeth to passe by chance or adventure, but onely & alwaies by the prescription of his wil; according to the which he ordereth & disposeth by a straight and direct motion, as well the generall as the particular, and that after a strange and admirable order.

Beard, however, makes it plain that God elevates or debases men as he pleases, intimating that God's pleasure is in accordance with men's deserts, however, and that the punishment of men is "according to their demerits".

Beard says that in using the word *judgements* he is referring to the ordinances and commandments of God, which are forever just, but he is also referring to the punishments inflicted upon men, for they also are just, "proceeding from none other fountaine save the most righteous judgement of God, whereof none can complaine but unjustly". Yet in recounting his "histories", Beard recognizes the fact that there were apparently good men who suffered evil, and he explains:

> For though it may seeme for a time that God sleepeth, and regardeth not the wrongs and oppressions of his servants, yet he never faileth to carry a watchfull eie upon them, and in his fittest time to revenge himself upon their enemies.[1]

Very interestingly, too, Beard attacks the problem of the punishment of those in high places, for they are apt to regard themselves as above or outside human law, "so much the rather God himselfe becommeth executioner of his owne justice upon their pates: and in such sort, that every man may perceive his hand to be upon them".[2]

The record of God's judgments is then carefully analysed on the basis of the sins committed: blasphemy, murder, adultery, etc. But always there is shown the ambition or the lust or the superstition or whatever motive or passion it may be that impels to sin. And here we find listed as instances of God's judgments a record of a great mass of the Elizabethan stories that are familiar in dramatic tragedies. Here are *Richard the Second, Richard the Third, Julius Caesar, Antony and Cleopatra,* the *Duchess of Malfi, Cambyses, Arden of*

[1] Beard, *op. cit.* p. 56.
[2] *Ibid.* p. 7.

Lately Committed at Bury Assize, 1620.

LONDON,

PLATE V. From *The Cry and Revenge of Blood*, by Thomas Cooper, 1620. The method is continuous. The murders are depicted, then the attempt to hide the bodies in a pond, and finally the discovery of the bodies

Feversham, and numbers of such tragedies explained significantly.

Beard's work was issued in new editions in 1612 and 1631. And such works continued to be popular. There was Edmund Rudierd's *The Thunderbolt of Gods Wrath, or an abridgement of Gods fearefull judgements*, published in 1618, as the title indicates, an abridgment of Beard's work. There is no need to give here a complete history of the *Mirrour for Magistrates* and its imitators and successors. My purpose is solely to show how in these non-dramatic tragedies the problem of tragedy was being set.

In 1621 there was published the first volume of another great collection of these tragedies, which it is necessary to consider if we would see the way in which the central problem of tragedy was evolved. This collection by John Reynolds was called *The Triumphs of Gods Revenge, Against the crying, and Execrable Sinne of Murther: or His Miraculous discoveries and severe punishments thereof. In thirty severall Tragicall Histories (digested in sixe Bookes) acted in divers Countries beyond the Seas, and never till now published, or imprinted in any Language. Histories, which containe great variety of memorable accidents, Amorous, Morall and Divine, very necessary to restraine, and deterre us from this bloody Sinne, which, in these our dayes, makes so ample, and so lamentable a progression.*

Reynolds, in his address "To the Reader", divides the temptations of men which lead them on to the sin of murder as temptations of the world, the flesh, and the devil. The world offers men wealth, preferments, pompous apparel, masks and stage plays, etc.; the flesh tempts with youth, beauty, strength, sloth, etc.; the devil uses pride, arrogance, ambition, etc., on the one hand, and sorrow, grief, choler, envy, revenge, etc., on the other. Of his purpose in collecting these "Tragicall Histories", he says that the reader may observe and see "as in a Christall myrrour, the variety of the divels temptations, and the allurements of sinne" to the end

> that the consideration of these bloody and mournefull Tragedies, may by their examples, strike astonishment to our thoughts, and amazment to our sences, that the horrour and terrour thereof may hereafter retaine and keepe us within the lists of Charity towards men, and the bonds of filiall and religious obedience towards God.

But the later note of this collection is struck when Reynolds explains his method of work:

> For mine own parte, I have illustrated and polished these Histories, yet not framed them according to the modell of mine owne fancies, but of their passions, who have represented and personated them.

That Reynolds was interested not only in God's revenge for crime, but also in the passions which led to crime, is further attested in these histories. He begins the first history:

> If our contemplation dive into elder times, and our curiositie turne over the variety of ancient and moderne Histories (as well Divine as Humane) wee shall finde that Ambition, Revenge, and Murther, have ever prooved fatall crimes to their undertakers: for they are vices which so eclipse our judgements, and darken our understandings, as wee shall not onely see with griefe, but finde with repentance, that they will bring us shame for glory, affliction for content, and misery for felicity.

And in the second history he explains again:

> Where Affection hath Reason for guide & Vertue for object, it is approved of Earth, and applauded of Heaven: but where it exceeds the bounds of Charity, and the lists of Religion, Men pitie it, Angels lament it, and God himselfe contemnes it....

Reynolds' method is illustrated significantly in the sixth history, the story of Antonio and Berinthia, where we find lust leading to choler, choler to revenge, revenge to murder.[1]

---

[1] The idea is traditional, as may be seen in the description of the progeny of Sin in Gower's *Mirour de L'omme*. Cf. also *Pericles*, I, i, 137–8.

> "One sin, I know, another doth provoke;
> Murder's as near to lust as flame to smoke."

This collection of histories was augmented[1] and re-published until 1669, when there was added to it a new series, *God's Revenge against the Abominable Sin of Adultery*, and this newly amplified work was republished as late as 1770.

The moral purpose of tragedy was thus continuously stressed in these stories of the fall of princes, from the Middle Ages throughout the Renaissance. Not only the mutability of men's fortunes, but the eternal justice involved in the change of fortune constituted the persistent subject of tragedy. Even so had Aristotle's too-often quoted words explained:

> The change in the hero's fortunes must be...from happiness to misery; and the cause of it must lie not in any depravity, but in some great error on his part.[2]

For the tragic fact is for ever found in the change from happiness to misery; such is the permanent and essential material of tragedy. The inconstant element in tragedy is the way in which the change is accounted for. When Fortune's wheel is turned unaccountably, the fall of princes may make men wonder and distrust all happiness. But when the exigencies of Christian teaching demand that Fortune's wheel be turned at least with the knowledge or permission of God, if not directly by his command, then the moral order of the universe, the eternal justice of God which permits or orders change, is the problem which faces the recorder of tragedies.

It is, then, in the changing explanation of the why of the tragedies recorded that we can see the mediaeval tragedies becoming Renaissance tragedies. Lydgate was typically

---

[1] Vol. I, 1621; vol. II, 1622; vol. III, 1624.

[2] Throughout my work the references are made to the Oxford Aristotle unless I specifically state otherwise. The translation of *De Poetica* is by Professor Ingram Bywater. Cf. 1453ᵃ, 13–16.

mediaeval when he moralized his song and justified the ways of God to men by making his princes "in chaieres hih sittyng", "for vices ther unwar fallyng". For the later writers, of the Renaissance, the problem was more complicated. They came to see in tragedies the records of God's revenge against sin, and they came to trace the cause of sin to the passions which motivated sin. Baldwin was speaking in the language of the Renaissance when he had Jack Cade give the warning:

> And therefore Baldwin warne men folow reason,
> Subdue theyr wylles, and be not Fortunes slaves.[1]

Reynolds was writing in Renaissance terms when he organized his histories about the passions which led to the murders rehearsed. But always there was the attendant problem of why the good as well as the wicked were made to suffer.

If we are to see the full significance of tragedy, we must then turn to philosophy, where in its literature of consolation we find a massive attempt to reconcile the irreconcilables of life.

The Renaissance inherited from the Middle Ages its great document of consolation, Boethius' *De Consolatione Philosophiae*, in which work Boethius explicitly accepted the challenge of tragedy:

> What other thynge bywaylen the cryinges of tragedyes but oonly the dedes of fortune, that with unwar strook overturneth the realmes of greet nobleye?[2]

Recognizing the fact that changes of fortune were often seemingly unrelated to desert, Boethius, as the great harmonizer of Christian and ancient philosophical teaching,

---

[1] Baldwin, *op. cit.* ed. 1559, fol. xlvii.

[2] *The Works of Chaucer*, Globe edition, p. 366. The gloss which Caxton printed added to this passage: "*Glose*. Tragedye is to seyn a dite of a prosperite for a tyme, that endeth in wrecchidnesse".

yet reconciled apparent injustice on the basis of two fundamental assumptions: (1) there is happiness only in virtue,
and therefore the wicked, though they may be prosperous,
are not happy; (2) chance proceeds from the Providence that
knows all and directs all.

This teaching of Boethius was of incalculable importance
in Renaissance thinking, and his book was very popular.
Chaucer's translation printed by Caxton was followed by
other editions and translations, even Queen Elizabeth, like
the early King Alfred, being numbered among the trans-
lators.

Sir Thomas More followed the example set by Boethius
by writing, when he was in prison, *A Dyalogue of Comforte
agaynst Tribulacyon,*[1] a treatise primarily concerned with
the reconciling of God's goodness with the evil that befalls
good men. He is not much concerned with the problem of
sin and punishment, but tries to find his answer as to why
good men must suffer evil in the strengthening and medi-
cining of the soul through evil, and in the possibility of
finding good through evil.

Probably the most popular of these books of consolation
was that known as Cardan's *Comforte*, translated in 1573 by
Thomas Bedingfield, another edition following in 1576. This
is the book that has been traditionally associated with
Hamlet. Here again the solution of the problem of evil is
undertaken, Cardan insisting that "good or evill fortune,
importeth nothing to blessed life",[2] and likewise,

A man is nothinge but his mynde: if the mynde be discontented, the
man is al disquiet though al the reste be wel, and if the minde be contented thoughe all the rest misdoe it forseeth little.[3]

Cardan sums up the evils which men encounter as of
three sorts.

---

[1] The dialogue was written in 1534, and was printed in 1553, 1557
and 1573.

[2] Cardan, *Comforte*, A iii *verso*.   [3] *Ibid.* A viii.

The firste within us and our mindes, with which temperancy do mete.

The second without us, and they by wisedome are prevented. The thirde are those, that al be it they be in deede without us, yet are they unevitable, and against them none other defence we have then fortitude.[1]

And he insists:

Who so doth marke it wel, shall fynde that for the most part we are causes of oure owne evill.[2]

It is in keeping with this reasoning that Cardan justifies the choice of princes' palaces as the background for tragedies:

As fynely the tragicall poetes have fayned the tragedies and furies to be only in kinges courtes, & the comodies & pleasant playes in privat houses. The pallaces of princes are ever open to great evills, neither are these monsters at any time from thence: as envy, hate, grudge, poyson, & persecution. Yea the princes mynde is the seat of al these, wherby it is neither suffered to sleepe quietly by night, nor reste by day. Nowe assayleth him the memorye of wickednes, now the suspition of familiers, now the mystrust of people, now feare of other princes, withe care day and night to prevent their practises. But be it, the prince, be never so just, never so holy? yet feare and suspicion doth never wante, and as the poet fayneth of *Ixion* and *Lapithis*—

Whome over hanges a stone that evermore, doth seme to fall.[3]

The second part of *The French Academie*, translated into English in 1594, gave lengthy consideration to this problem, treating it, however, as a practical problem of ethics. This work contends that there is justice in the world, and warns men against trying by revenge to remedy apparent evil:

Therefore wee may well conclude, that all private Revenge proceeding of envy, or of hatred, or of anger, is vicious and forbidden by God, who commaundeth us to render good for evill, and not evill for evill. For hee hath ordained the meanes, whereby hee will have vengeance executed among men. Therefore hee hath appointed Magistrates to execute it according to his Lawe, and following his ordinaunce, not with any evill affection, but with just indignation proceeding from love, and from true zeale of justice.... Wee must therefore followe his example. For hee suffereth not evill to goe

[1] Cardan, *Comforte*, D vi.   [2] *Ibid*. B i.   [3] *Ibid*. B iii. *verso*.

unpunished, if men avoide not punishment by his grace and mercie, and by those meanes which he hath appointed for the obtaining thereof. Therefore it is often saide of the wicked in the Scripture, that G O D will returne into their bosome the evill which they have done....And as himselfe commeth in judgment to take vengeance, so hee woulde have them that supplie his place among men, unto whome hee hath committed the sworde for the defence of the good and punishment of evill doers, to followe his example. But whether they doe so or no, there is no sinne that can avoide punishment, and that findeth not a Judge even in him that committed it, to take vengeance thereof by meanes of the affections, which God placed in man to that ende. [1]

Repeatedly the author of *The French Academie* insists upon this premise, that there is justice in the world, that God executes this justice directly as his vengeance for sin, or indirectly through his appointed representatives, the magistrates. Repeatedly he insists that even where there is no punishment of the body, yet a man who has sinned is punished in a troubled mind, in such affections as shame and fear. Repeatedly he insists that private revenge, the attempt to take God's vengeance into private hands, springs from passions and must result in disaster.

The same problem and much the same answer are to be

[1] *The French Academie*, Second part, 1594 ed. pp. 326, 327. This is one of the most interesting books of the Renaissance and one which very frequently gives a key to Shakespeare's meaning. It was published in four parts. The title of the first translation read: "*The French Academie, wherin is discoursed the institution of maners, and whatsoever els concerneth the good and happie life of all estates and callings, by precepts of doctrine, and examples of the lives of ancient Sages and famous men.* By Peter de la Primaudaye Esquire...and newly translated into English by T. B(owes). London. 1586". This first part appeared in new editions in 1589, 1594, 1602 and 1611. The second part, "Concerning the Soule and Body of Man", though entered in 1589, was first published in English in 1594, and again in 1605. The third part, "A notable description of the whole World", was published in 1601. Then in 1618 was published the whole of the work, the fourth part, "Christian Philosophie, instructing the true and onely meanes to eternall life", being added to the three parts already published. The 1618 edition, so far as I have been able to compare it with the earlier editions, reprints the earlier parts faithfully and accurately.

found in Sir Richard Barckley's *Discourse of the Felicitie of Man: or his Summum bonum*, published in 1598. Barckley considered the causes of evil and found them in the passions that make men bring down evil on themselves, ambition, lust, etc. He listed the evils of existence as they have been eternally bewailed by philosophers, and he listed even the specific evils which beset certain classes of men. Yet he sums up all:

We must purifie and cleanse our minds from our corrupt and uncleane affections, that we may bee the better able to see and desire those things which bee good indeed, and avoide those thinges that bee good in shew only: wherin morall vertues are verie necessarie: for by them our unruly affections and unprofitable desires are brideled or suppressed, or at least moderated, which are the chiefe cause of an unhappie life. They move mens desires to pleasures, to riches, to honour and glorie, which hath bene shewed before by many examples and sayings of wise men, to bee the cause of infelicitie; they stirre up pride, envy, hatred, malice, desire of revenge, feare, and such like perturbations and unquietnesse of the mind, and will never suffer the soule or mind to be in quiet and rest, which is contrary to felicity and a happy life; which consisteth not in fleshlie pleasures, nor in the abundance of riches or possessions, nor in principalitie or power, but in a contented & quiet mind, voyd of sorrow and feare, which cannot be obtained without Gods speciall grace and gift, and his assistance to our endevours.[1]

Such a statement is a typical statement of the Renaissance answer to the persistent problem of evil.

Yet perhaps the most definite statement of the whole problem was made for the Renaissance in one of the moral essays of Plutarch, the philosopher who was often found, though a pagan, able to guide Christian teaching. The treatise was published in 1603 among the *Morals*[2] translated

[1] Sir Richard Barckley, *op. cit.* p. 472.

[2] "*The Philosophie, commonlie called, The Morals written by the learned Philosopher Plutarch of Chaeronea.* Translated out of Greeke into English, and conferred with the Latin translations and the French, by Philemon Holland of Coventrie, Doctor in Physicke." The first edition is of 1603, though the work was entered for publication in 1600.

by Philemon Holland, and was entitled *How It Commeth that the Divine Justice deferreth other-whiles the punishment of Wicked Persons*. Two of the arguments with which Plutarch answers those who question the divine justice are of particular significance. The first of these answers is that God, in deferring the punishment of the wicked, acts as a pattern which men should follow:

wherefore if we perceive him to proceed slowly, and in tract of time to lay his heavie hand upon the wicked, and to punish them, it is not for any doubt or feare that he should doe amisse, or repent afterward if he chasticed them sooner, but by warning us from all beastly violence, & hastinesse in our punishments, to teach us not immediately to flie upon those who have offended us, at what time as our bloud is most up, and our choler set on a light fire,

> When furious yre in hart so leapes and boiles,
> That wit and reason beare no sway the whiles.

making haste as it were to satisfie some great hunger, or quench exceeding thirst, but (by imitating his clemencie, and his maner of prolonging and making delay) to endevor for to execute justice in all order, at good leisure, and with most carefull regard; taking to counsell Time, which seldome or never is accompanied with repentance: for as Socrates was wont to say: Lesse harme and danger there is, if a man meet with troubled and muddie water, and intemperately take and drinke thereof, than whiles his reason is confounded, corrupt, and full of choler and furious rage, to be set altogether upon revenge, and runne hastily upon the punishment of another bodie, even one who is of his own kinde and nature, before the same reason be settled againe clensed and fully purified.[1]

The second answer is the one which seems to me most clearly to have been accepted by Shakespeare, for it affirms that sin brings inevitably its own punishment to the heart and conscience of the sinner:

but wickednesse ingendering within it selfe (I wot not what) displeasure and punishment, not after a sinfull act is committed, but even at the very instant of committing, it beginneth to suffer the pain due to the offence: neither is there a malefactour, but when he seeth others like himselfe punished in their bodies, beareth forth his own crosse;

[1] Holland's Plutarch, *Morals*, p. 542.

wheras mischievous wickednesse frameth of her selfe, the engines of her owne torment, as being a wonderful artisan of a miserable life, which (together with shame and reproch) hath in it lamentable calamities, many terrible frights, fearfull perturbations and passions of the spirit, remorse of conscience, desperate repentance, and continuall troubles and unquietnesse.[1]

Thus Plutarch stressed the fact that the punishment of evil is not to be reckoned in terms solely of the final end of a man's life. In the reckoning there must be considered also this punishment engendered at the very moment when a sinful act is committed.

It is possible, then, to trace the gradually emerging idea of the significance of tragedy in its answering as well as in its setting of the problem of evil, and it can be seen that the Renaissance idea of tragedy is but a natural development of the mediaeval idea. Tragedy started to picture the fall of princes. It came to seek an explanation that could justify the ways of God to men. It came to seek the justice which must inhere in such falls if there was a God of justice in his heaven. And it found that justice in the error or the folly which caused men to bring down evil on themselves. And gradually it came to find in men's passions the cause of their errors and their folly, and therefore the cause of the evil which they bring upon themselves. Thus fortune is not to be dissociated from cause in the change from happiness to unhappiness. Hamlet tells us that fortune's star is not to be separated from that defect in a man's nature that makes it operative:

> ...these men,
> Carrying, I say, the stamp of one defect,
> Being nature's livery, or fortune's star,—
> His virtues else—be they as pure as grace,
> As infinite as man may undergo—
> Shall in the general censure take corruption
> From that particular fault. The dram of eale
> Doth all the noble substance often dout
> To his own scandal.[2]

[1] Holland's Plutarch, *Morals*, pp. 545, 546.   [2] *Hamlet*, I, iv, 30–8.

But more than this, tragedy, guided by philosophy, came also to show that those who do evil are never unpunished, since an unquiet mind is the inevitable reward of evil doing. Passions create in the heart of a man such turbulence that there is no longer possible to him the quiet mind on which happiness is conditioned. It is thus that the King laments in *Hamlet*:

> My soul is full of discord and dismay.[1]

Likewise Richard the Third cries out on the morn of battle:

> All several sins, all us'd in each degree,
> Throng to the bar, crying all, Guilty! guilty!
> I shall despair.[2]

Lady Macbeth is "troubled with thick-coming fancies", that, the doctor tells us "keep her from her rest". And Macbeth moves from fear to horror until he cries:

> I am sick at heart.

> . . . . . .

> I have liv'd long enough. My way of life
> Is fallen into the sear, the yellow leaf;
> And that which should accompany old age,
> As honour, love, obedience, troops of friends,
> I must not look to have; but, in their stead,
> Curses, not loud but deep, mouth-honour, breath
> Which the poor heart would fain deny, and dare not.[3]

Of Lear, too, Kent must say:

> O, let him pass! He hates him
> That would upon the rack of this tough world
> Stretch him out longer.[4]

Even as tragedy came, then, to prove that justice must prevail, that God did punish evil, it came to stress more and more the teaching of Renaissance philosophy, that the man sins who would undertake to execute privately the justice of God. The great popularity of the so-called revenge tragedies

[1] *Hamlet*, IV, i, 45.   [2] *Richard III*, V, iii, 198–200.
[3] *Macbeth*, V, iii, 19–28.   [4] *King Lear*, V, iii, 313–15.

attests the interest which the Renaissance took in this theme. God will Himself execute justice through calamity visited upon the sinner, or through justice executed by the magistrates as His agents, or through the troubled heart and uneasy conscience which are the penalty of sin. It is the lesson which we hear in the great cry of Clarence in *Richard the Third*:

> If God will be avenged for the deed,
> O, know you yet, He doth it publicly.
> Take not the quarrel from His powerful arm;
> He needs no indirect or lawless course
> To cut off those that have offended Him.[1]

More than all others did the passion of revenge lead to tragedy. And conversely tragedy might become comedy whenever men, like Prospero, could say:

> Though with their high wrongs I am struck to the quick,
> Yet with my nobler reason 'gainst my fury
> Do I take part. The rarer action is
> In virtue than in vengeance.[2]

Thus are tragedies the *exempla* by which men are taught the lessons of moral philosophy, lessons which Lodge summed up in his address "To the Courteous Reader" prefixed to his translation of Seneca:[3]

Learne in these good lessons, and commit them to memory, That to be truly vertuous is to be happy, to subdue passion is to be truely a man, to contemne fortune is to conquer her, to foresee and unmaske miseries in their greatest terrors is to lessen them, to live well is to be vertuous, and to die well is the way to eternitie.

Tragedy teaches negatively, however, and so by tragedy "we are taught, by a Collection of fatal Events, to avoid Ruin and Misery".

[1] *Richard III*, I, iv, 221–5.
[2] *The Tempest*, V, i, 25–8.
[3] *The Workes both Morall and Natural of Lucius Annaeus Seneca.* Translated by T. Lodge, D. of Phis. 1614.

CHAPTER II

The Value of Imitation in Teaching
Drama as Teaching by Imitation

THE theory of the drama in England during the Renaissance was largely the result of the engrafting of the rediscovered classical doctrine of imitation upon this tradition continued from the Middle Ages of teaching by *exempla*. It is my purpose, therefore, to trace the form which this theory gradually assumed as the result of the fusion of the tradition of tragedies as *exempla* and of dramatic poetry as imitation. The resulting theory is that which was concerned with dramatic tragedies, and is therefore the theory which is concerned with justifying, in a commonwealth where Puritan ideas were flourishing, the existence of tragedies and comedies presented as stage plays.

More often than is generally realized the Renaissance discussion of poetry and drama as imitation took its point of departure from the third book of Plato's *Republic*, where there was rather confusingly discussed the question of admitting tragedies and comedies into the ideal state. The one point about which there could be no confusion was that this discussion was concerned with tragedies and comedies as forms of imitation.

Aristotle's treatment of imitation in the *Poetics* also gave texts to the more learned critics. The critics were, of course, concerned with the endlessly quoted definition of tragedy as "an imitation of an action that is complete in itself, as a whole of some magnitude".[1] But they were also concerned with the fact that Aristotle pointed out that "imitation is natural to man from childhood",[2] and, furthermore, that "it

---

[1] *De Poetica*, 1450^b, 25–27.   [2] *Ibid.* 1448^b, 5, 6.

is also natural for all to delight in works of imitation".[1]
Thus it was perceived that since man naturally learns by
imitation and delights in works of imitation, imitation must
be considered not only as the method of tragedy, but also
as the means of instructing delightfully through tragedy.

Horace was instanced to the same effect:

> Poets aim either to benefit, or to amuse, or to utter words at once
> both pleasing and helpful to life.[2]

And further:

> Either an event is acted on the stage, or the action is narrated. Less
> vividly is the mind stirred by what finds entrance through the ears than
> by what is brought before the trusty eyes, and what the spectator can
> see for himself.[3]

Plutarch too was often cited as authority. The works
which were collected under the title of *Morals* in the 1603
translation of Philemon Holland gave numerous texts. In
the treatise *Of the Nouriture and Education of Children* there
was stated the pure doctrine of teaching by *exempla*:

> For the remembrance of matters past, furnisheth men with examples
> sufficient to guide and direct them in their consultations of future
> things.[4]

In *How a Young Man ought to heare Poets: and how he may
profit by reading Poems* there was to be found the moral
justification of poetry as imitation, the favourite comparison
of the Renaissance being also enunciated "that Poesie is a
speaking picture, and picture dumb Poesie". Plutarch said

> that Poesie is the very imitation of maners, conditions and lives,
> yea and of men, such as are not altogither perfect, pure and irrepre-
> hensible, but in whom passions, false opinions and ignorance bear
> some sway.... When a yoong man is thus prepared, and his under-
> standing so framed, that when things are well done and said, his heart

---

[1] *De Poetica*, 1448^b, 8.
[2] *Ars Poetica*, ll. 333, 334. Loeb Classical Library ed.
[3] *Ibid.* ll. 179–82.
[4] Holland's Plutarch, *Morals*, p. 11.

is mooved and affected therwith as by some heavenly instinct: and contrariwise not well pleased with lewd deeds or words, but highly offended therat, certes, such instruction of his judgement will be a meanes that he shal both heare and reade any Poemes without hurt and danger.[1]

On the basis of such authority the new Renaissance doctrine was evolved. Briefly, this doctrine, which motivates the defences of poetry now regarded as the chief documents of early English literary criticism, is a doctrine which holds that poetry is imitation; that dramatic poetry is the most lively and hence the most impressive form of imitation; that men naturally learn by imitation and are pleased by imitation; and therefore that tragedies teach by lively examples a willing and receptive audience.

Ascham's *Scholemaster* devoted a whole section of Book II to the discussion of "Imitatio", which he defined:

Imitation is a facultie to expresse livelie and perfitelie that example which ye go about to folow. And of it selfe it is large and wide: for all the workes of nature in a maner be examples for art to folow.[2]

Of the first of the "three kindes of it in matters of learning", he wrote:

The whole doctrine of Comedies and Tragedies is a perfite *imitation*, or faire livelie painted picture of the life of everie degree of man. Of this *Imitation* writeth *Plato* at large in 3 *de Rep.*, but it doth not moch belong at this time to our purpose.[3]

Lodge's *Defence of Poetry*, framed as an answer to Gosson, specifically discussed the usefulness of plays in a commonwealth:

Men that have knowledge what comedies and tragedis be wil comend them, but it is sufferable in the folish to reprove that they know not....Firste...the reder shal perceive the antiquity of playmaking, the inventors of comedies, and therwithall the use and comoditye of them....For tragedies and comedies, Donate the gramarian sayth,

---

[1] Holland's Plutarch, *Morals*, p. 34.
[2] Roger Ascham, *The Scholemaster*, 1570, ed. by G. Gregory Smith, in *Elizabethan Critical Essays*, Oxford, 1904, vol. I, p. 5.
[3] *Ibid.* p. 7.

they wer invented by lerned fathers of the old time to no other purpose but to yeelde prayse unto God for a happy harvest or plentiful yeere. And that thys is trewe the name of Tragedye doth importe....But to wade farther, thys fourme of invention being found out, as the dayes wherein it was used did decay,...so the witt of the younger sorte became more riper, for they leaving this fourme invented an other,...; for, for sonnets in prayse of the gods, they did set forth the sower fortune of many exiles, the miserable fal of haples princes, the reuinous decay of many countryes; yet not content with this, they presented the lives of Satyers, so that they might wiselye, under the abuse of that name, discover the follies of many theyr folish fellow citesens....As for Commedies, because they bear a more pleasanter vain, I will leave the other to speake of them. Tulley defines them thus: *Comedia* (saith he) is *imitatio vitae, speculum consuetudinis, et imago veritatis.*[1]

Thus, while he recognized some abuses in contemporary customs, Lodge yet says:

But (of truth) I must confes with Aristotle that men are greatly delighted with imitation, and that it were good to bring those things on stage that were altogether tending to vertue:[2]

and he concludes:

But sure it were pittie to abolish that which hath so great vertue in it, because it is abused.[3]

Sidney's *Apologie for Poetrie* gives a more elaborate statement of the same theory on the basis of the same oft-repeated texts:

Poesie therefore is an arte of imitation, for so *Aristotle* termeth it in his word *Mimesis*, that is to say, a representing, counterfetting, or figuring foorth: to speake metaphorically, a speaking picture: with this end, to teach and delight. Of this have beene three severall kindes.[4]

Of the third sort, the "right Poets", he says:

---

[1] Thomas Lodge, *Defence of Poetry, Music, and Stage Plays*, 1579, in Smith, *op. cit.* vol. I, pp. 79–81.

[2] *Ibid.* p. 83.

[3] *Ibid.* p. 84.

[4] Sir Philip Sidney, *An Apologie for Poetrie*, 1595 (written *c.* 1583), in Smith, *op. cit.* vol. I, p. 158.

...these indeede doo meerly make to imitate, and imitate both to delight and teach, and delight to move men to take that goodnes in hande, which without delight they would flye as from a stranger; and teach, to make them know that goodnes whereunto they are mooved, which being the noblest scope to which ever any learning was directed.[1]

His basis for the judging of comparative values in learning is explicitly stated:

so that, the ending end of all earthly learning being vertuous action, those skilles that most serve to bring forth that have a most just title to bee Princes over all the rest.[2]

The historian and the philosopher are the competitors with the poet, but while the historian teaches by example and the philosopher by precept, the poet combines both methods of teaching:

Nowe dooth the peerelesse Poet performe both: for whatsoever the Philosopher sayth shoulde be doone, hee giveth a perfect picture of it in some one, by whom hee presupposeth it was done. So as hee coupleth the generall notion with the particuler example. A perfect picture I say, for hee yeeldeth to the powers of the minde an image of that whereof the Philosopher bestoweth but a woordish description: which dooth neyther strike, pierce, nor possesse the sight of the soule so much as that other dooth.[3]

Thus it is that

the Philosopher with his learned definition, bee it of vertue, vices, matters of publick policie or privat government, replenisheth the memory with many infallible grounds of wisdom, which, notwithstanding, lye darke before the imaginative and judging powre, if they bee not illuminated or figured foorth by the speaking picture of Poesie.[4]

Some of the specific instances offered to illustrate his point are particularly significant:

Anger, the *Stoicks* say, was a short madnes: let but *Sophocles* bring you *Ajax* on a stage, killing and whipping Sheepe and Oxen, thinking them the Army of Greeks, with theyr Chieftaines *Agamemnon*

[1] Sir Philip Sidney, *An Apologie for Poetrie,* 1595 (written *c.* 1583), in Smith, *op. cit.* vol. I, p. 159.
[2] *Ibid.* p. 161.　　　[3] *Ibid.* p. 164.　　　[4] *Ibid.* p. 165.

and *Menelaus*, and tell mee if you have not a more familiar insight into anger then finding in the Schoolemen his *Genus* and difference. See whether wisdome and temperance in *Ulisses* and *Diomedes*, valure in *Achilles*, friendship in *Nisus* and *Eurialus*, even to an ignoraunt man carry not an apparent shyning: and, contrarily, the remorse of conscience in *Oedipus*, the soone repenting pride of *Agamemnon*, the selfe-devouring crueltie in his Father *Atreus*, the violence of ambition in the two *Theban* brothers, the sowre-sweetnes of revenge in *Medea*, and, to fall lower, the *Terentian Gnato* and our *Chaucers Pandar* so exprest that we nowe use their names to signifie their trades: and finally, all vertues, vices, and passions so in their own naturall seates layd to the viewe, that wee seeme not to heare of them, but cleerely to see through them.[1]

Sidney points out that Christ himself taught like a poet, with parables rather than platitudes. And he sums up his contention:

For conclusion, I say the Philosopher teacheth, but he teacheth obscurely, so as the learned onely can understande him, that is to say, he teacheth them that are already taught; but the Poet is indeed the right Popular Philosopher....[2]

Sidney insists upon the fact that it is necessary not only to show men how to do well, as is the way of philosophy, but also to entice them on to do well, as is the way of the poet. And then he discusses each form of poetry to see what men could find in it to object to, and of plays he concludes:

So that the right use of Comedy will (I thinke) by no body be blamed, and much lesse of the high and excellent Tragedy, that openeth the greatest wounds, and sheweth forth the Ulcers that are covered with Tissue: that maketh Kinges feare to be Tyrants, and Tyrants manifest their tirannicall humors; that, with sturring the affects of admiration and commiseration, teacheth the uncertainty of this world, and upon how weake foundations guilden roofes are builded; that maketh us knowe,

> *Qui sceptra saevus duro imperio regit,*
> *Timet timentes, metus in auctorem redit.*

[1] Sir Philip Sidney, *An Apologie for Poetrie*, 1595 (written *c.* 1583), in Smith, *op. cit.* vol. I, pp. 165, 166.
[2] *Ibid.* p. 167.

But how much it can moove, *Plutarch* yeeldeth a notable testimonie of the abhominable Tyrant *Alexander Pheraeus*; from whose eyes a Tragedy, wel made and represented, drewe aboundance of teares, who, without all pitty, had murthered infinite nombers, and some of his own blood. So as he, that was not ashamed to make matters for Tragedies, yet coulde not resist the sweet violence of a Tragedie....

But it is not the Tragedy they doe mislike: for it were too absurd to cast out so excellent a representation of whatsoever is most worthy to be learned.[1]

To recall each instance of this popular defence of poetry as the most effective of moral teachers, and of plays, especially tragedies, as being the most impressive type of poetry would be indeed "a work of supererogation", for it is upon this basis that all the defenders of poetry establish its right to recognition as the "Popular Philosophy". Newton's preface to the 1581 edition of Seneca's tragedies insists that there is no one of the "Heathen wryters" more than Seneca

that with more gravity of Philosophicall sentences, more waightynes of sappy words, or greater authority of sound matter beateth down sinne, loose lyfe, dissolute dealinge, and unbrydled sensuality: or that more sensibly, pithily, and bytingly layeth down the guerdon of filthy lust, cloaked dissimulation & odious treachery: which is the dryft, wherunto he leveleth the whole yssue of ech one of his Tragedies.[2]

Puttenham speaks gravely of "three kinds of poems reprehensive, to wit the *Satyre*, the *Comedie*, and the *Tragedie*",[3] in his discourse *Of Poets and Poesie*, and describes each in its turn, saying of tragedy:

But after that some men among the moe became mighty and famous in the world, soveraignetie and dominion having learned them all maner of lusts and licentiousness of life, by which occasions also their high estates and felicities fell many times into most lowe and lamentable

[1] Sir Philip Sidney, *An Apologie for Poetrie*, 1595 (written *c.* 1583), in Smith, *op. cit.* vol. I, pp. 177, 178.

[2] Thomas Newton, *Seneca His Tenne Tragedies*, 1581. Spenser Society Reprint, 1887.

[3] George Puttenham, *The Arte of English Poesie*, 1589, in Smith, *op. cit.* vol. II, p. 32.

fortunes: whereas before in their great prosperities they were both feared and reverenced in the highest degree, after their deathes, when the posteritie stood no more in dread of them, their infamous life and tyrannies were layd open to all the world, their wickednes reproched, their follies and extreme insolencies derided, and their miserable ends painted out in playes and pageants, to shew the mutabilitie of fortune, and the just punishment of God in revenge of a vicious and evill life.[1]

Similarly Nashe argued in *Pierce Penilesse, his Supplication to the Divell*:

In plays, all coosonages, all cunning drifts overguylded with outward holinesse, all stratagems of warre, all the canker-wormes that breede on the rust of peace, are most lively anatomiz'd: they shewe the ill successe of treason, the fall of hasty climbers, the wretched ende of usurpers, the miserie of civil dissention, and how just God is evermore in punishing of murther...they are sower pills of reprehension, wrapt up in sweete words...for no Play they have, encourageth any man to tumults or rebellion, but layes before such the halter and the gallowes; or prayseth or approoveth pride, lust, whoredome, prodigalitie, or drunkennes, but beates them downe utterly.[2]

Sir John Harrington, in the defence of poetry which he prefixed to his translation of *Orlando Furioso*, used the same arguments, saying particularly of tragedy:

And for Tragedies, to omit other famous Tragedies, this that was played at S. *Johns* in Cambridge, of *Richard the* 3, would move (I thinke) *Phalaris* the tyraunt, and terrifie all tyrannous minded men from following their foolish ambitious humours, seeing how his ambition made him kill his brother, his nephews, his wife, biside infinit others, and, last of all, after a short and troublesome raigne, to end his miserable life, and to have his body harried after his death.[3]

---

[1] George Puttenham, *The Arte of English Poesie*, 1589, in Smith, *op. cit.* vol. II, p. 35.

[2] Thomas Nashe, *Pierce Penilesse, his Supplication to the Divell*, 1592. Reprinted in *The Complete Works of Thomas Nashe*. Ed. by A. B. Grosart for the Huth Library, 1883, 1884, vol. II, pp. 90, 91.

[3] Sir John Harrington, *A Preface, or rather a Briefe Apologie of Poetrie, and of the Author and Translator*, prefixed to the edition of *Orlando Furioso*, 1591, in Smith, *op. cit.* vol. II, p. 210.

However, the most detailed and significant treatment of plays as teachers of morality by means of *exempla* is found in Thomas Heywood's *An Apology for Actors*.[1] Heywood describes himself as falling asleep; at once there appeared in all her ancient dignity Melpomene, who bewailed:

> *Grande sonant tragici, tragicos decet Ira Cothurnos.*
> Am I Melpomene, the buskend Muse,
> That held in awe the tyrants of the world,
> And playde their lives in publicke Theaters,
> Making them feare to sinne, since fearlesse I
> Prepar'd to wryte their lives in Crimson Inke,
> And act their shame in eye of all the world?
> Have not I whipt Vice with a scourge of steele,
> Unmaskt sterne Murther; sham'd lascivious Lust.
> Pluct off the visar from grimme Treasons face,
> And made the Sunne point at their ugly sinnes?
> Hath not this powerful hand tam'd fiery Rage,
> Kild poysonous Envy with her own keene darts,
> Choak't up the Covetous mouth with moulten gold,
> Burst the vast wombe of eating Gluttony,
> And drownd the Drunkards gall in juice of grapes?
> I have showed Pryde his picture on a stage,
> Layde ope the ugly shapes his steele-glasse hid
> And made him passe thence meekly.[2]

Heywood offers evidence as to the effect of such plays on the beholders. Before Hercules his tutor caused to be presented the history of his father, Jupiter, so acted that he was moved to emulation of his father's valour. In like fashion Theseus was moved to imitate Hector, and Achilles, Theseus. Then the great Aristotle caused the destruction of Troy to be acted before his pupil, Alexander, and caused him to be moved to valour by the image of Achilles. Caesar, in turn, was moved to achievement by seeing Alexander represented on the stage.

[1] *An Apology for Actors*, printed in 1612, includes three books or treatises on actors, entitled respectively: *Their Antiquity, Their Ancient Dignity,* and *The True Use of their Quality*.

[2] Heywood, *op. cit.* B 2 *recto*.

Why should not the lives of these worthyes, presented in these our dayes, effect the like wonders in the princes of our times, which can no way bee so exquisitely demonstrated, nor so lively portrayed as by action...

A Description is only a shadow received by the eare but not perceived by the eye: so lively portrature is meerly a forme seene by the eye, but can neither shew action, passion, motion, or any other gesture, to moove the spirits of the beholder to admiration: but to see a souldier shap'd like a souldier, walke, speake, act like a souldier: to see a Hector all besmered in blood, trampling upon the bulkes of Kinges, a Troylus...Oh these were sights to make an *Alexander*.[1]

So could Englishmen be moved to valour by the sight of the older heroes of England on the stage. In fact,

so bewitching a thing is lively and well spirited action, that it hath power to new mold the harts of the spectators and fashion them to the shape of any noble and notable attempt.[2]

In Book III of the *Apology* Heywood gives a résumé of the teaching value of plays, particularly of historical plays. They are, he says, an ornament to the city and admired of strangers; they refine the rude English tongue; they make the ignorant "more apprehensive"; they instruct such as cannot read in the English chronicles, and finally they are justified:

For, or because, Playes are writ with this ayme, and carryed with this methode, to teach the subjects obedience to their King, to shew the people the untimely ends of such as have moved tumults, commotions, and insurrections, to present them with the flourishing estate of such as live in obedience, exhorting them to allegeance, dehorting them from all trayterous and fellonious stratagems.[3]

Then he again discusses tragedy:

Omne genus scripti gravitate Tragedia vincit.

If we present a Tragedy, we include the fatall and abortive ends of such as commit notorious murders, which is aggravated and acted with all the Art that may be, to terrifie men from the like abhorred

---

[1] Heywood, B 3 *verso*.
[2] *Ibid.* B 4.
[3] *Ibid.* F 3.

practises. If wee present a forreigne history, the subject is so intended. that in the lives of *Romans, Grecians,* or others, either the virtues of our Country-men are extolled, or their vices reproved, as thus, by the example of *Caesar* to stir souldiers to valour, & magnanimity; by the fall of Pompey, that no man trust in his owne strength; we present Alexander, killing his friend in his rage, to reprove rashnesse.

Thus tragedy is seen

either animating men to noble attempts, or attaching the consciences of the spectators, finding themselves toucht in presenting the vices of others. If a morall, it is to perswade men to humanity and good life, to instruct them in civility, and good manners, shewing them the fruit of honesty and the end of villainy.[1]

Briefly, there is neither Tragedy, History, Comedy, Morall or Pastorall, from which an infinite use cannot be gathered.[2]

To end in a word, Art thou addicted to prodigallity? envy? cruelty? perjury? flattery? or rage? our Scenes affoord thee store of men to shape your lives by, who be frugall, loving, gentle, trusty, without soothing, and in all things temperate.[3]

Heywood, like his predecessors, gave instances in which unchastity, murder, and other sins have been brought home to men's consciences through the witnessing of plays.

But Shakespeare himself has given us this philosophy of tragedy as the stimulus to conscience, for Hamlet's speech but sums up the tradition:

> I have heard
> That guilty creatures sitting at a play
> Have by the very cunning of the scene
> Been struck so to the soul that presently
> They have proclaim'd their malefactions;
> For murder, though it have no tongue, will speak
> With most miraculous organ. I'll have these players
> Play something like the murder of my father
> Before mine uncle. I'll observe his looks;
> I'll tent him to the quick. If he but blench,
> I know my course....
>   ...The play's the thing
> Wherein I'll catch the conscience of the King.[4]

[1] Heywood, F 3 *verso.*   [2] *Ibid.* F 4 *recto.*   [3] *Ibid.* G 1.
[4] *Hamlet,* ii, ii, 617–34.

The conception of tragedies as moral teaching was, how-ever, as has been pointed out, much more than a conception of plays as mouse-traps for unwary consciences. And, indeed, Shakespeare again stated the basic belief in another famous speech of Hamlet:

> For anything so overdone is from the purpose of playing whose end, both at the first and now, was and is, to hold, as 'twere, the mirror up to nature; to show virtue her own feature, scorn her own image, and the very age and body of the time his form and pressure. [1]

It is, however, in the summing up of moral philosophy which Bacon gave in his *Advancement of Learning* that we see the function of drama perhaps most clearly expressed. It must be remembered that Bacon says that "poetry serveth and conferreth to magnanimity, morality, and to delecta-tion". [2] He also makes three divisions of poetry: "Narrative, Representative, and Allusive", defining the second: "Repre-sentative is as a visible history, and is an image of actions in nature as they are, (that is) past". [3]

In outlining the province of moral philosophy, Bacon also says:

> Another article of this knowledge is the inquiry touching the affections; for as in medicining of the body it is in order first to know the divers complexions and constitutions, secondly the diseases, and lastly the cures; so in medicining of the mind, after knowledge of the divers characters of men's natures, it followeth in order to know the diseases and infirmities of the mind, which are no other than the perturbations and distempers of the affections....And here again I find strange, as before, that Aristotle should have written divers volumes of Ethics, and never handled the affections, which is the principal subject thereof; and yet in his Rhetorics, where they are considered but collaterally and in a second degree (*as they may be moved by speech*), he findeth place for them, and handleth them well for

---

[1] *Hamlet*, III, ii, 22–6.
[2] *The Twoo Bookes of Francis Bacon of the Proficience and Advance-ment of Learning Divine and Human*, 1605. Riverside ed. vol. I, Bk. ii, p. 203.
[3] *Ibid.* p. 204.

the quantity;...But the poets and writers of histories are the best doctors of this knowledge; where we may find painted forth with great life, how affections are kindled and incited; and how pacified and refrained; and how again contained from act and further degree; how they disclose themselves, how they work, how they vary, how they gather and fortify, how they are inwrapped one within another, and how they do fight and encounter one with another, and other the like particularities....[1]

Thus it is seen that the idea of tragedies as presenting the fall of princes continued to dominate the Renaissance. But gradually the interest changed from the mere wonder and bewilderment of witnessing the tragic fall of princes to tracing the cause of the change of fortune. And even as the idea of the fickle goddess Fortune changed to that of a God just and computative in his justice, so the idea of the fall of princes as depending on variable fortune changed to the idea of sin or folly as the cause of the change from happiness to misery;[2] and finally the cause of the sin or folly which led to punishment was found in the passions which moved men to such deeds.

Furthermore, tragedies came to be regarded as indeed mirrors for magistrates and mirrors for all men whereby they might be either called to repentance or warned by the images of their own vices and passions to turn to virtue.

Finally the method by which tragedies were to be used as guides to virtue was the same which had come to be familiar in the mediaeval habit of teaching by *exempla*. But in the Renaissance new reasons were given for following old habits. And particularly in regard to stage plays was the newly discovered classical doctrine of imitation useful in

[1] *The Twoo Bookes of Francis Bacon*, pp. 336, 337.

[2] Bacon's essay *Of Fortune* suggests rather than develops the idea that there are a "number of little and scarce discerned virtues, or rather faculties and customs, that make men fortunate", but he is so far from making fortune reward virtue that he adds his statement that "there be not two more fortunate properties than to have a little of the fool, and not too much of the honesty".

explaining the why and the how of the teaching value of these acted examples. The tendency of men to learn by imitation, the faculty of men for being pleased with imitation, the inevitable idea of plays and acting as perfect types of imitation—these were the bases for proving how useful plays might be in teaching virtue so delightfully and so vividly that men would hold her in their hearts. Imitation was the key to the whole theory. Plays were imitation. Imitation pleased men. Men learned by imitating what they saw.

The definition of "An Excellent Actor" published in the later editions of Sir Thomas Overbury's *Wife* gives the essence of the whole argument:

> By his action hee fortifies morall precepts with examples; for what wee see him personate, we thinke truly done before us.

The fact that the Renaissance conception of poetry was of poetry as philosophy has long been recognized,[1] though inadequately recognized. But that the drama was accepted as having peculiar value as teaching because of its impressiveness as imitation has not been emphasized. The significance that attaches to dramatic tragedies is, however, a double significance. For tragedies teach by *exempla* how to avoid ruin and misery by avoiding the loose and ungoverned passions which lead thereto. And dramatic tragedies teach by their *exempla* so much the more effectively in that they are imitation, and imitation pleases and convinces. Dramatic tragedies are, therefore, the most effective method of teaching by *exempla* the lessons of moral philosophy.

[1] Cf. especially the discussion in J. E. Spingarn, *A History of Literary Criticism in the Renaissance*, 1899, chapters i and ii.

CHAPTER III

Neo-Classical Interpretations of Tragedy

DRYDEN in *The Grounds of Criticism in Tragedy*, which he used as a preface to *Troilus and Cressida*, gave an illuminating summary of the currently accepted idea of the purpose of tragedy:

> To instruct delightfully is the general end of all poetry. Philosophy instructs, but it performs its work by precept; which is not delightful, or not so delightful as example. To purge the passions by example is therefore the particular instruction which belongs to Tragedy. Rapin, a judicious critic, has observed from Aristotle, that pride and want of commiseration are the most predominant vices in mankind; therefore, to cure us of these two, the inventors of Tragedy have chosen to work upon two other passions which are fear and pity.

Here there is evidenced the desire so apparent in most seventeenth-century criticism to blend the teachings of the *Poetics* concerning the katharsis of pity and terror with the more universally recognized doctrine of the function of tragedy as teaching by example. Dryden himself in this same essay crowds rules into a pot-pourri of literary dicta.

> 'Tis the moral that directs the whole action of the play to one centre; and that action or fable is the example built upon the moral, which confirms the truth of it to our experience; when the fable is designed, then, and not before, the persons are to be introduced, with their manners, characters, and passions.
>
> The manners, in a poem, are understood to be those inclinations, whether natural or acquired, which move and carry us to actions, good, bad, or indifferent, in a play; or which incline the persons to such or such actions. . . .
>
> The manners arise from many causes; and are either distinguished by complexion, as choleric and phlegmatic, or by the differences of age or sex, of climates, or quality of the persons, or their present condition. They are likewise to be gathered from the several virtues, vices, or passions, and many other commonplaces, which a poet must be sup-

posed to have learned from Natural Philosophy, Ethics, and History; of all which whosoever is ignorant does not deserve the name of poet.

From the manners, the characters of persons are derived;...A character,...cannot be supposed to consist of one particular virtue, or vice, or passion only; but 'tis a composition of qualities which are not contrary to one another in the same person;...yet it is still to be observed that one virtue, vice, and passion ought to be shown in every man as predominant over all the rest;....

The chief character or hero in a tragedy, as I have already shown, ought in prudence to be such a man who has so much more of virtue in him than of vice, that he may be left amiable to the audience, which otherwise cannot have any concernment for his sufferings; and it is on this one character that the pity and terror must be principally, if not wholly, founded:...

'Tis one of the excellencies of Shakespeare that the manners of his persons are generally apparent, and you see their bent and inclinations....

In later paragraphs in this same important essay Dryden distinguishes these passions which are part of dramatic characters and the pity and fear that tragedy are to produce. Returning to the discussion of manners, he says:

Under this head of manners the passions are naturally included as belonging to the characters. I speak not of pity and of terror, which are to be moved in the audience by the plot; but of anger, hatred, love, ambition, jealousy, revenge, etc., as they are shown in this or that person of the play. To describe these naturally, and to move them artfully, is one of the greatest commendations which can be given to a poet;...A poet must be born with this quality; yet, unless he help himself by an acquired knowledge of the passions, what they are in their own nature, and by what springs they are to be moved, he will be subject either to raise them where they ought not to be raised, or not to raise them by the just degrees of nature...; all which errors proceed from want of judgment in the poet, and from being unskilled in the principles of moral philosophy....

If Shakespeare be allowed, as I think he must, to have made his characters distinct, it will be easily inferred that he understood the nature of the passions....

And in his conclusion he seems to me to be more just than he has been given credit for being, more discriminating than we have been able to understand:

Shakespeare had an universal mind, which comprehended all characters and passions; Fletcher a more confined and limited: for though he treated love in perfection, yet honor, ambition, revenge, and generally all the stronger passions, he either touched not, or not masterly. To conclude all, he was a limb of Shakespeare.[1]

Dryden, indeed, seems to me here to state in general the theory of tragedy as it gradually evolved from the first assumption that it was to teach by example the uncertainty of prosperity; to the second assumption that it was to teach by example the sins that must be avoided if the destruction demanded as God's revenge were to be escaped; to the third assumption that tragedy was to teach by enabling men to see their own vices and passions which moved them to the sins that led to destruction. Here we see that in the plot or fable the destruction is revealed; in the characters we are to see the passions that act as the ultimate causes of sins. The passions are, indeed, if I understand Dryden—and Shakespeare—aright, the passions are the subject of the sentence, the plot acts as the predicate.

Rymer's *Short View of Tragedy* gives in the midst of its curious judgments on *Othello* as evidently undisputed critical premises:

The *Fable* is always accounted the *Soul* of Tragedy. And it is the *Fable* which is properly the *Poets* part. Because the other three parts of Tragedy, to wit, the *Characters* are taken from the Moral Philosopher; the *thoughts*, or sence, from them that teach *Rhetorick*: And the last part, which is the *expression*, we learn from the Grammarians.[2]

Dr Johnson's translation of Brumoy's *Dissertation on Greek Comedy* (published by Mrs Lennox in 1759) accounted for the permanent interest of tragedy over comedy by the fact that

tragedy having the passions for its object, is not wholly exposed to the caprice of our taste, which would make our own manners the

[1] *Dramatic Essays by John Dryden.* Everyman's Library ed. pp. 131–44.
[2] Thomas Rymer, *A Short View of Tragedy*, 1693, in J. E. Spingarn, *Critical Essays of the Seventeenth Century*, 1908, vol. II, pp. 219, 220.

rule of human kind....The passions of *Greece* and *France* do not so much differ by the particular. characters of particular ages, as they agree by the participation of that which belongs to the same passion in all ages.[1]

That the poet was a "popular philosopher", then, in the thought of the Renaissance from the sixteenth century through the eighteenth, seems to me established. The poet was no true and just poet unless he knew the moral philosophy where men's moral natures were described. In all this criticism there is little suggestion that the artist look about him at living men to obtain his material. In fact, the inductive method for artists had not yet been discovered. The artist took his characters from moral philosophy.

Dr Johnson himself said, much in the strain of Dryden, in his preface to his edition of Shakespeare:

His persons act and speak by the influence of those general passions and principles by which all minds are agitated, and the whole system of life is continued in motion.[2]

Upon every other stage the universal agent is love....But love is only one of the many passions, and as it has no great influence upon the sum of life, it has little operation in the dramas of a poet, who caught his ideas from the living world, and exhibited only what he saw before him. He knew, that any other passion, as it was regular or exorbitant, was a cause of happiness or calamity.[3]

This therefore is the praise of Shakespeare, that his drama is the mirror of life;...by scenes from which an hermit may estimate the transactions of the world, and a confessor predict the progress of the passions.[4]

Yet Dr Johnson fell into the error of us all in assuming that Shakespeare's day must not have had the advantages of our own, that Shakespeare's excellence must have

[1] *The Works of Samuel Johnson, LL.D.* Ed. by A. Murphy, Esq., 1806, vol. III, pp. 36, 37.
[2] *The Plays of William Shakespeare.* Johnson-Steevens-Reed ed. 1813, vol. I, p. 249.
[3] *Ibid.* p. 250.
[4] *Ibid.* p. 251.

been in some way a miracle of nature, for of Shakespeare's time, he said:

> Speculation had not yet attempted to analyse the mind, to trace the passions to their sources, to unfold the seminal principles of vice and virtue, or sound the depths of the heart for the motives of action.[1]

To prove how amazingly wrong is this statement is to be the object of the next section of this book.

[1] *The Plays of William Shakespeare.* Johnson-Steevens-Reed ed. vol. I, 1813, p. 281.

SECTION II

Moral Philosophy in Shakespeare's Day

CHAPTER IV

The Uses of Philosophy

THE sentence which opens the chapter in *The Cambridge History of English Literature* on "The Beginnings of Moral Philosophy in England" is significant of the general failure to consider seriously that great body of popular philosophy which made a large part of the published books of the sixteenth century in England. Professor Sorley, in the opening sentence of the chapter cited, says:

> The English language may be said to have become for the first time the vehicle of philosophical literature by the publication of Bacon's *Advancement of Learning*, in 1605.

Yet a survey of the books published in England before 1605 shows a massive array of works in many editions dealing with moral philosophy. It is not my purpose to trace this early history of English moral philosophy, however, for I am not a philosopher. Rather I purpose to trace in the works on moral philosophy published in England during the sixteenth century the main ideas which seem to me to have formed the background of the conception of tragedy which is shown in the tragedies of Shakespeare, ideas which were fundamental ideas held by Shakespeare in common with the best philosophical thinkers of his generation.

That there was little new in these ideas no one can deny, for they represent something like a composite picture of the works of the most revered ancients and the most influential Schoolmen. Hippocrates, Galen, Aristotle, Plato, Plutarch, Cicero, Quintilian, Seneca, Hesiod, Thomas Aquinas, Augustine—these are the names which are mingled with others of less frequent recurrence in the list of authorities for philosophical ideas throughout the century. Furthermore, it must be taken into consideration that Greek was a language in which Englishmen worked without great confidence, so that men like Ascham, Bacon, and Bryskett, spoke despairingly and disparagingly of their countrymen's adventures in translation and interpretation.

Many of the philosophical works were translations, too, from contemporary European treatises—French, Spanish, Italian, as well as Latin. But there were numerous works for which no known foreign original exists, and the whole list of translations, adaptations, original treatises, constitutes an amazing array of books which testify to the tremendous popularity of moral philosophy during this period.

Popular philosophy was represented, of course, in the great collections of aphorisms in which this generation considered there was stored the wisdom of the ancients. And there were numerous collections of philosophical catechisms like T(homas) C(rewe)'s *Nosegay of Morall Philosophie*, the popularity of which collections explains the form of the only catechism most of us have been exposed to. But of these assemblings of concentrated wisdom I do not intend to speak here. From them I do not doubt Shakespeare gathered many of the flowers of Polonius and Cordelia and Portia and those others who have furnished us with so many "quotations". But in the forming of the idea of the purpose and function of tragedy there were concerned the more weightily discussed problems of moral philosophy. And these were current in treatises the number of which gives them their significance.

In any discussion of Renaissance moral philosophy, however, it is well to recall first the zeal which was carried over from the Middle Ages into the Renaissance for assembling and organizing knowledge into logical systems. Knowledge was regarded as an organon, to which fact the work of Bacon offers monumental testimony. The comprehensiveness of Aristotle was enough alone to give him supreme rank. And compendious tomes like that of *Bartholomeus de Proprietatibus Rerum* and *The French Academie* went in many editions to the popularizing of philosophy.

All knowledge was directed, however, to a single end, the fostering of virtue. Just as Lydgate wrote:

> Ther be thre partes, as tresours of gret pris,
> Compiled in bookis & of old provided,
> Into which philosophie is devyded.
>
> The first of them callid is morall,
> Which directeth a man to good thewes;
> And the secounde, callid naturall,
> Tellith the kynde of good men & shrewes;
> And the thridde, raciounal, weel shews
> What men shal voide & what thing undirfonge,
> And to that parti rethorik doth longe,[1]

so William Baldwin in his *A Treatise of Morall Phylosophie*, first published in 1547, wrote in his prefaced explanation:

Philosophie is sorted into .iii. partes, Phisicke, Ethicke, and Dialectyke. The offyce of phisicke is, to discerne and Judge of the worlde, and of such thinges as are therein: It is the parte of Ethicke, to trete of lyfe and maners, and it is the dutie of Dialectike, that is Logicke, to make resons to prove and improve both phisicke and also Ethicke, which is moral Philosophye.[2]

And it is, therefore, in Wilson's *Arte of Rhetorique* that we find one of the most illuminating discussions of virtue in the period.

The means by which virtue might be attained was dependent upon following the great imperative of the Renaissance, *Nosce teipsum*, "Know thyself". To the achieving of this supreme command three methods became popular.

[1] *The Fall of Princes*, Bk. VI, ll. 3288–3297. E.E.T.S. Ex. Ser., vol. CXXIII, p. 763.

[2] In this connection it is interesting to note that Baldwin divides moral philosophy into three kinds of teaching: the first "by councelles, lawes, & preceptes"; the second "by Proverbes & Adages"; the third "by Parables, Examples, and Semblables". Cf. *ante*, Section I, Chapter ii.

The first method was based upon the idea explained in the opening words "To the Christian Reader" of Part II of *The French Academie*:

Seneca the Philosopher reporteth...that the looking glasse was first invented to this end, that man might use it as a meane to know himselfe the better by.

Hence came all the mirrors of which I have spoken in the first chapter. The second method was based upon the idea that man can know himself as a little world, comprising in himself the elements from which the world is fashioned. Hence came the study of microcosmography, as it was called. The third method was pursued in anatomies of the soul, of which Burton's *Anatomy of Melancholy* has continued as the single persistent representative of a multitude. The mirror, the microscosmos, the anatomy came to dominate titles as well as method, so that the most sceptical must be convinced of the pervasiveness of these ideas if he but glance over a list of titles of sixteenth and seventeenth century books in England.

CHAPTER V

This Little World. Man as Microcosmos

B ACON summed up in his *Advancement of Learning* the theory of man as microcosmos:

The ancient opinion that man was Microcosmus, an abstract or model of the world, hath been fantastically strained by Paracelsus and the alchemists, as if there were to be found in man's body certain correspondences and parallels, which should have respect to all varieties of things, as stars, planets, minerals, which are extant in the great world. But thus much is evidently true that of all substances which nature hath produced, man's body is the most extremely compounded. For we see herbs and plants are nourished by earth and water; beasts for the most part by herbs and fruits, man by the flesh of beasts, birds, fishes, herbs, grains, fruits, water, and the manifold alterations, dressings, and preparations of these several bodies, before they come to be his food and aliment. Add hereunto that beasts have a more simple order of life, and less change of affections to work upon their bodies; whereas man in his mansion, sleep, exercise, passions, hath infinite variations; and it cannot be denied but that the Body of man of all other things is of the most compounded mass.[1]

The first translator of Galen into English, John Jones, Physician, published in 1574 *Galens Bookes of Elementes, as they be in the Epitome (whiche may very aptly, in my judgement, be Entituled, for the better understanding of the Readers, the Originall of all thinges naturall in the whole worlde: Confuting, as well the Errours of all them that went before time, as that hath or shal folowe hereafter of the Paracelcians: marveilous pleasaunt, and most acceptable for all sharpe wittes, desirous of wisedome, published foorth of Latine into English.* In his dedication to the Earl of Shrewsbury, Jones wrote:

Hippocrates, thauctor and parent preordinated by Goddes divine providence, for the helthe, welthe, and benifite of all mankynd, whose

[1] Bacon, *op. cit.* Bk. II, pp. 241, 242.

wordes, and aucthorities we admitte, receive, and allowe, together with Galen, as Oracles from Heaven, seemeth unto me, most noble Earle, neither to have written rashely, as divers did of olde, nor yet unprobably, as other have of late,...But rather most divinely, and Philosophically intreating of the Elements of mans life, Fire, Ayre, Water, Earthe, omitting with Hipp. the moste simple,...entreateth here of those simple bodies, the Elementes, receivers of the foure qualities, whiche be the beginners of all thinges under the Moone: whether they be *Inanimata*, without life, and imperfectly mixt, as the Meteors, or perfectly, as the Minerals, or *Animata*, with life, vegetat, sensit, & Rational, growing thinges, as Hearbes, Plantes, and Trees, &c. Living thinges, as Beastes, Foules, and Fishe, and reasonable, as Mankinde, all having their originall of the Elementes....

Jones' translation of Galen is not very clear, but it introduces us to the chief authorities, Hippocrates and Galen, and to the chief antagonists, the Paracelsians. It also brings out one of the most fundamental considerations of this discussion of microcosmography, the question whether man is to be analysed on the basis of the four elements, which determine his temperament; or whether he is to be considered primarily with regard to the humours "which are the proper Elements or beginning of things endowed with blood". The complete analysis of man as microcosmos as Jones conceived it is to be seen in the accompanying tables which he added to his *Bathes of Bathes Ayde* in 1572. And with slight variations these tables represent the theory generally accepted during the Renaissance as to the constitution of man's body.

To summarize very briefly the whole schematic analysis of man as microcosmos: man is thought of as a little world, comprising in himself all the elements that go to the making of the great world. These elements are four: fire, air, water, earth. Four qualities inhere in these elements: hot, cold, moist, dry. Fire is hot and dry, air is hot and moist, water is cold and moist, earth is cold and dry.

In every man there are four humours, all existing in the blood: blood, choler, phlegm, and melancholy. Blood, like

HE TABLE OF THE SEVEN THINGS NATVRAL, OVT OF THE VVHICH THE ACTIONS
according to Nature doe spring, may be perceiued in this Table: howbeit not so often deuided as it might be done: supposing there will serue to giue the wise
and learned patient matter sufficient to consult with the Phisition, wherby that which is according to nature may be preser-
ued and ayded: and those things which be against Nature expelled, the
scope of Phisicke as is shewed.

...rum is a simple and most ... she, and the best parte, of ... erein it is, can not be deui- ... any other kind and of it ... naturall haue their be- ... without al generation or ... ió. Howbeit of Fire made ... ommeth Ayre. Of Aire ... ack commeth water. Of ... made thick, cōmeth Earth. ... there is neither corruptiō ... eration of the whole. For

Elementes foure.	Fyre.	Absolutelie hot, and moderately dry.
	Ayre.	Absolutely moyst, and moderately hot.
	vvater.	Absolutely cold, & moderatly moyst.
	Earth.	Absolutely dry, and moderatly cold.

this is but a mutation of the parts onely. And the consent and agre- ment of them is, the fyre in heate, in drynes with the Earth, in moisture the Aire with the water, & in heate with the fire, in coldnes the water with the earth and in moisture with the ayre, the earth in drynes with the fyre, and in coldnes with the water & as the water to the fyre is extreme con- trary, so is the aire to the earth.

...ramentum, is a tempering ...s qualities of the foure E- ...s in one body.

Temperaments or complections. ix.	Simple	Hot.	Actiues.
		Cold.	
		Moyst.	Passiues.
		Dry.	
	Compound	Hot and moyst.	
		Hot and dry.	
		Cold and moyst.	
		Cold and dry	
	Teperate		Of all alike as it were by waight, the very trew and iust complection: but as hard to be found as Plato his Idea, or Arist summum bonum, or as the prouerbe is, a black Swan. Neuer- theles, he that will iudge trew of complexions must alwayes haue in his imagination, the a- foresayd perfect temperament.

Humors. foure.	Naturall.	Blud.	Temperate, nerishing the body contained in the vains swetish raigning in the spring.
		Flewme	Cold and moyst, suppling the drie and hard parts without proper mocion, tastles, raigning in winter
		Choler.	Hot and drie, clensing and quickning contemed in the gall bitter raigning in sommer.
		Melacholie	Cold and dry, staying and binding, contained in the Splene, sower, raigning in haruest
	Vnnatural (as)	Blud distempered with other humors.	And euen day they are thus moued as the blud betwen the ninth houre at night, and iij. in the morning.
		Flewm, watrie, glasfie, slime, plastone, salt, sower, harsh, rugh (lities, killing.	Choler betwen iij. & ix afore none Melacolie, betwen
		Choler, Citrine, yelkie, like, cankrie.	ix and iij. Flewine betwen iij. & ix. at night.
		Melacholie cōmixed & aduslid with other dangerous qua-	

x(which may be called the ...of Elements) is a part con- ...substisting the bodie.

| | Simple, as | Skin, fatte, flesh, muscles, fillets, guts, veins, artires, Sy- nowes, chords, gristles, bones, tunicles, &c. |

...res, are bodies that are in- ...d of the fyrst communion ...nours.

Members	Spermatike (as)	Braine, synewes.		
		Kells, bones, grisells &c.		
	Sanguine, as	Liuer, hart, kidnes.		
		Milt, fatte flesh. &c.		
	Compound, as	Hed. Armes. Legs.	Principal as	Hart, braine.
				Liuer, stones.
			Officiall. as	Synowes, seruing the brain.
				Artires, seruing the hart.
				Veins, seruing the Liuer.
				Vessels spermatike, seruig the stons
			Instrumē tall, as	Stomake.
				Rayns.
				Bowels.
				Great synewes. &c.

...ewith see that you consider the composition, the complexion, the substance, the quantitie, the number, the figure, the operation, the vse & the disease, in part & in all the mēbres.

	Faculties or power.	Animal.	Ordeneth, discerneth, compofith.
			Mouth by voluntarie will.
			Sentith wherof procedeth the fiue wits.
		Vital.	working, delating and wrayning the artires
			vvrought which is stirred by an exterior cause wherof cōmeth substance & prouideth.
		Natural.	Doth minister. Apetite. Retaineth. Digesteth. Expelleth. Ingendreth.
			Is ministrid. Norisheth. Feedeth.

as, faculte, or power, is the ...f doing that which is don: ...water is the cause of the ...going about.

	Vital.	Mouth mirth, sadnes, hope, trust, feare, dispaire, loue, hatred, mercie, enuie, wrath, wodnes, wildnes, stobernes, humanitie, Empire, glorie, victorie. &c.		
	Natural.	Altereth. Ioineth. Formith.		
	Animal.	Apprehendeth. Fantasieth. Imagineth. Opinioneth. Cōmonsenteth.	In the two former ventricles.	Iudgeth. Estemeth. Thinketh. Disposith.	In the middle vētricle.	Remembrith. Knoweth. calleth to memory in the hinder part

et opus, doing & working, ...which by the power is don: ...wheate conuerted to meale, ...grist of the mill.

	Spirits.	Natural.	From the Liuer taketh his beginning and by the veines which haue no pulse dis- persith in to all the hole bodie.
		Vital.	From the hart procedeth and by the artires or pulses is sent in toall the hole body
		Animal.	From the braine is ingendred, and is sent by the sinewes throughout the body and maketh sence or feeling. &c.

...us, is an ayrie substance, sub- ...ırring the powers of the bo- ...performe their operation : ...as a prince doth his counsel, ...the counsell doth the sub- ...euery one according to his ...ion and to that is limited by ...e, wherin was neuer serue re-

...bellion, but euery inferior redy to serue his superior, a paterne of a heauenly common weale, and for euery reasonable bodie to note & obserue, although he were an E- then ek: how much rather then of Christians, euery faithfull manne knoweth.

Now that you haue here in this Table noted vnto you, the things wherof the Natural bodies is made, with the powers and ac- tions of the same: so likewise foloweth the things not naturall, (so called) by cause they be in parde of the natural body, and yet by the temperance of them, the body being in health so consisteth, and yet by the distemperance of them, sicknes is induced, and the body dissolued

John Iones.

PLATE VI. Table from *Bathes of Bathes Ayde*, by John Jones, 1572.

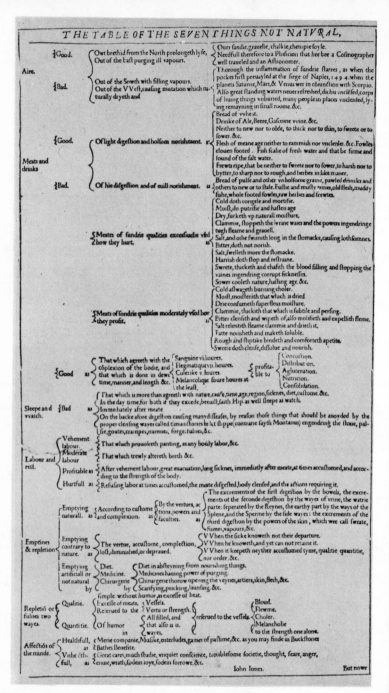

PLATE VII. Table from *Bathes of Bathes Ayde*.

air, is hot and moist; it is also sweet to the taste. Choler, like fire, is hot and dry; it is bitter to the taste. Phlegm, like water, is cold and moist; it is unsavoury and tasteless like water also. Melancholy, like earth, is cold and dry; it is sharp, "eigre", or tart to the taste. Bright's description in *A Treatise of Melancholie* will serve:

The purest part which we call in comparison and in respect of the rest bloud, is temperate in qualitie, and moderate in substance, exceeding all the other parts in quantitie, if the bodie be of equall temper, made for the nourishment of the most temperate parts, and ingendring of spirits. The second is fleume, next to bloud in quantitie, of a waterie nature, cold and moyst, apt to be converted into the substance of purebloud if nature faile not in her workinge ordained for nourishment of moyster partes. The thirde is melancholie, of substance grosse and earthie, cold and drie in regard of the other, in quantity inferiour to fleume, fit nourishment for such partes as are of like temper. The fourth, choler, fierie, hote, and driest of qualitie, thin in substance; least in quantitie, and ordained for such parts as require subtiller nourishment, and are tempered with greater portion of the fierie element.[1]

Or the description in Newton's translation of *The Touch-stone of Complexions* may seem more picturesque:

All these differences of humours, when a veyne is opened (for it is not all pure bloud that gusheth therout) is playnly of all men to be perceyved. First before it be cold it doth shewe and represent to the eye, an ayry & fomy spirite, which by and by vanisheth away: then an exact & pure licour of most perfect & excellente ruddines, the which is pure and right bloude: in which there swymmeth Choler, and sometime tough clammy Phlegme, sometime liquide and thin, according to the nature, condition and state of man.

Last of all, if you tourne up the whole masse or lumpe, you shall finde Melancholy, altogether of colour black.[2]

[1] *A Treatise of Melancholie*, pp. 4, 5. By T. Bright, Doctor of Physicke, 1586. (Printed by Vautrollier.) Timothy Bright (or Timothe Bright) is generally known as the father of modern shorthand. His connection with Shakespeare is traditional, but the tradition seems to be apocryphal. For a list of references in this connection, see William J. Carlton, *Timothe Bright*, 1911, especially pp. 55–7.

[2] Thomas Newton, "*The Touchstone of Complexions*. First written in Latine, by Levine Lemme, and now Englished by Thomas Newton.

All of these humours are "engendered" of food and drink, and hence they are in any case related to the four elements. Thus *The French Academie* records:

> We understand by a *Humor*, a liquide and running body into which the foode is converted in the liver, to this ende that bodies might be nourished and preserved by them. And as there are foure elements of which our bodies are compounded, so there are foure sorts of humors answerable to their natures, being al mingled together with the blood.[1]

The humours have their various special seats, however, to which they are naturally retired from the liver to serve as in some sort reservoirs of superfluous humour. Choler thus retires naturally to the gall; melancholy goes to the spleen; phlegm retires to the kidneys.

But furthermore, *The French Academie* explains:

> besides the distribution of all the humours together with the blood into all parts of the bodie by the veines, and that for the causes before learned, there is yet another meane wherby these humours, especially the flegmaticke humour, which is of the nature of the water, ascend up unto the braine, by reason of vapours arising upward out of the stomacke, like to the vapour of a potte seething on the fire with liquor in it, and like to vapours that ascend up from the earth into the ayre, of which raine is engendred.[2]...

From such unnatural rising up of phlegm to the brain come the discharges known as catarrh, apoplexy, etc. But it is generally recognized that vapours of this sort may rise from any humour. Bright speaks especially of such rising up of melancholy from the spleen to the brain.

Every writer of the day was much concerned with this excess of humour. Newton explains particularly of melan-

---

Nosce teipsum. 1581". Cf. p. 86. There were earlier editions of this work in 1565 and 1576. It is interesting to remember that in 1581 this same Thomas Newton published the ten tragedies attributed to Seneca.

[1] *The French Academie*, 1594 ed. p. 358.
[2] *Ibid.* p. 364.

choly that the melancholy juice goes in part to the veins to help blood, in part to the spleen or mylt, but the spleen being like a sponge, when it is obstructed or falls into weakness, it forces or permits melancholy to get into every other part of the body. If the bladder of the gall does not function properly in receiving choler, Newton explains also, then jaundice results.[1]

Such is the explanation of the natural humours and of the excess of such humours in the body. Of the unnatural humour, which may arise also, I shall speak a little later.

But there are in man beside this vital moisture, also natural heat and spirits. In Newton's words:

> For seeing there bee three especiall thinges, in whose temperature and moderation the health of mans body doth principally consist, viz. vitall moysture, naturall heate, & Spirite, which combineth all thinges, and imparteth his force, vertue & nature, unto them:... Vitall moysture is the nourishment and matter of naturall heate, whereupon it worketh, and by the benefite therof is maintayned and preserved. With this Humour or vitall moysture, is naturall heate fed and cherished, and from the same receyveth continuall mayntenaunce, and from it participateth vitall power, whereby all Creatures do live, are nourished, encreased, preserved & procreated. Spirite is the seate and caryer of Heate, by whose helpe and ministerye, it is conveyed and sente by the conduites and passages of the Arteryes to every severall part of the body.[2]

As is seen from the accompanying tables, Jones described "spirits" in his definition, "Spiritus, is an ayrie substance, subtile stirring the powers of the bodie to performe their operation": and he explained the mission of the natural, vital, and animal spirits as distinct. Natural spirits rise in the liver

[1] Newton, *op. cit.* p. 137. It must be noted that from the theories concerning the disposal of the excess of the humours there came the assumption on the part of some writers that the passions were not all centred in the heart but were centred rather in the appropriate repositories of superfluous humours.

[2] Cf. Newton, *op. cit.* chapter ii, for the full account of this subject, especially p. 7.

from a sort of fume or smoke originating apparently during the conversion of food into blood, and they are conveyed into all the body with the blood in the veins. Thus the description given earlier in Newton's words shows the vein opened to show first "an ayry & fomy spirite". Vital spirits are the result of the transforming of natural spirits in the heart through the effects of heat and of the admixture of air from the lungs; they are sent out through the arteries. Animal spirits rise from the further refining of vital spirits in the brain and are sent out through the body in the sinews, thus becoming the means by which the commands of the brain for moving the body are sent, and also the means by which the messages of the senses are sent to the brain. The animal spirits are, therefore, the connecting link between body and soul.

As to the centres of these things, Donne explained in *The Progress of the Soul*:

> ...and part did become
> A spongy liver, that did richly allow
> Like a free conduit on a high hill's brow,
> Life-keeping moisture unto every part;
> Part hardened itself to a thicker heart,
> Whose busy furnaces life's spirits do impart.
>
> Another part became the well of sense,
> The tender well-arm'd feeling brain, from whence
> Those sinewy strings, which do our bodies tie,
> Are ravelled out, and fast there by one end,
> Did this soul limbs, these limbs a soul attend.[1]

The healthy body maintains an appropriate equilibrium between the four humours in the blood; it also maintains in proper relationship and proportion vital moisture, natural heat, and spirits.

Different temperaments were recognized as existent, however, and as I have said, the chief conflict of opinion in the whole matter seems to have been as to whether temperaments must be regarded as determined by humours or by

[1] Stanzas 50, 51.

qualities inherent in the elements; that is to say, whether men must be classed as of hot, cold, moist, and dry temperaments or as of sanguine, choleric, phlegmatic, and melancholy humours. Newton's *The Touchstone of Complexions* argues for the first method, but compromises by calling the types simple and compound, giving the simple complexions as hot, cold, moist and dry; and the compound complexions as hot and moist (sanguine), hot and dry (choleric), cold and moist (phlegmatic), and cold and dry (melancholic). Both divisions were pretty generally recognized.

The temperaments of men of different complexions seem in the reading to be inferred from the qualities predominant in them. Thus, men of hot complexions are in colour red, brown, or tawny, are nimble and active, are for the most part "of strength and courage invincible", yet are often carried by wilful affection and unruliness of mind to do things neither allowable nor honest.

The cold complexion is furthest removed from perfection, some heat being absolutely necessary to life. Cold men are light in their colouring in both skin and hair. They are slothful, sluggish, and inactive generally.

The dry complexion resembles the cold. Its possessors tend to be thin and shrunken, to have poor memories, to doubt and waver.

The moist complexion is in youth not of the best, but is better as age and heat are added. Its possessors have white, bright, yellow, or red hair, and grey eyes, and are short and stout. They are not quick in mind or speech.

Men may be judged by their complexions, and hence come the old adages quoted by Wright in *The Passions of the Minde*:

> To a red man, reade thy reed:
> With a brown man breake thy bread:
> At a pale man draw thy knife:
> From a black man keepe thy wife.

The redde is wise,
The brown trustie,
The pale peevish,
The blacke lustie. [1]

Similarly men may be described by the dominance of humours. Newton explains:

For sythens (as Galene saith) sharpnes & finenes of wit commeth of Choler, Constancy and stedfastnes of Melancholy, & Phlegme to the framyng and disposing of the maners, helpeth nothynge neyther standeth in any steede: it remayneth that simplicity and foolishness proceedeth of bloud. [2]

Yet the sanguine man is considered the nearest perfection, Newton calling blood that "pure, cleare, delecate, lovely, and amyable Juyce" and commenting:

For such is the force & power of bloud in mans body, specially when through accesse of age, it groweth to heate, & daily more and more increaseth in vitall spirite, that it causeth a promptnes of mynde, quicknesse in devyse, and sharpnes in practise, which by dayly use & exercise atteineth in thende to wisedome, knowledge & experience of many things. And thus by the benefyte of nature and good bringing up, it is brought to passe that they be garnished with many excellent gifts of the mynd, and through a readye utterance in the discourse of matters, be to theire Countrey a great stay and ornament. [3]

Distinguishing the choleric from the sanguine the same author continues:

And althoughe hoate and dry natured men (which are the Cholerique) be right well furnished and skilful in perfecte utterance, vehemence of speach, and readines of toungue; yet is there not in them such

[1] Thomas Wright, *The Passions of the minde in generall*, 2nd ed. 1604. Cf. pp. 42, 43, for these and similar sayings. The first edition of this work was published in 1601 without the author's supervision. The second edition is dedicated to Henry Wriothesley, the Earl of Southampton, and the author says the work was written seven years earlier (1597) and was printed in the first edition from an imperfect copy. The second edition, however, follows the first closely except that it makes certain additions, of which these adages are part.

[2] Newton, *op. cit.* p. 96.

[3] *Ibid.* p. 99.

waighte of wordes and pithinesse of Sentences, neyther can they so well rule theyr own affections, because in their reasonings and discourses they be very earnest and hastye....

This difference also is betweene them, that the Cholerike are bitter taunters, dry bobbers nypping gybers, and skornefull mockers of others, but the Sanguine nothing given that way, medle not at all with such dogge eloquence...: but they bee pleasaunte and curteous natured, wythout scurrility, and civill without filthy rybauldry...delightfull and welcome to all.[1]

The phlegmatic persons lack quickness of wit, are apt to be lethargic in tendency, but have a good memory. And though Newton speaks of phlegm as "grosse and clammy glewish flegme", he still says it may become more like blood through the effects of heat. All the writers find it hard apparently to describe the effects of phlegm for the reason that they insist upon its essential likeness to colourless, tasteless water.

Most interest in the sixteenth and seventeenth century writers centred about the melancholy man. But the melancholy man may be a man in whom there predominates a natural melancholy humour or the man in whom unnatural melancholy humour (melancholy adust) has been unnaturally created. It is of this first type of melancholy persons that I am speaking here. The melancholy juice is "the settling and refuse of Bloude". The melancholy man is sorrowful, lumpish, sour, and dark. But I shall speak much more of this much misunderstood humour a little later.

It was acknowledged that men might be characterized by a still further combination of dominant humours, but these further complexities were not definitely worked out.

The humours were considered specially active in those periods which were characterized by the same qualities. Thus, blood is most active in the spring, choler in summer, melancholy in autumn, phlegm in winter. Further, blood was most active between nine at night, and three in the

[1] Newton, *op. cit.* pp. 99, 100.

morning, choler between three and nine in the morning, melancholy between nine in the morning and three in the afternoon, phlegm between three in the afternoon and nine at night. Even in the ages of man these humours were dominant in turn; blood in youth, then choler, then melancholy, and finally phlegm in old age (as was most evident in the white hair and watery eyes, etc., of old men).

Man's body is thus compounded of humours which are engendered of food and drink. However, Hippocrates pointed out in his *Airs, Waters, Places* the importance of these geographical elements also in determining the nature of a people, and the Renaissance writers saw not only the overcoming of nature as the cause of this influence in determining racial and individual characteristics. They saw man quite literally drinking the waters and feeding on things grown in the soil and breathing the air of different places— water, earth, air differing in qualities, especially in heat. Thus Newton says that Indians, Aethiopians, Moors, Spaniards, Frenchmen, Dutchmen, etc.,

are of sundry and different Complexions, & every one in his kinde hath of heate, severall and sundry differences.

He continues:

So likewyse in every mans body according to the nature of the place, and order of life and diet, this heate is encreased or diminished....

And specifically he says that

Curled and crooked hayres proceede of a drynesse of Complexion, caused through immoderate heate;

and that all in hot and dry regions thus have black and "small growing" hair, etc.[1]

The most curious statement of this theory of the effect of climate on temperaments is to be found in the *Microcosmos* of John Davies of Hereford, published in 1603:

[1] Newton, *op. cit.* p. 39.

From *Regions*, *Winds*, & *standing* of the *place*
Where we abide, come the *Aires* qualities;
Under the *Poles* (the *Sun* nere showing *face*
But as a *stranger*) the *Aire* so doth freeze
That whosoever breathes it, starving dies:
And in the Torrid *Zone* it is so hott
That *flesh* and *Bloud* (like flaming *fire*) it fries,
And with a *Cole*-blacke beautie it doth blott,
Curling the *Haires* upon a *wyry* knott.[1]

The way in which air affects men was explained by Davies also, so that it becomes apparent that not only climate but also weather may affect men's temperaments and passions:

The *winds*, though *Aire*, yet *Aire* do turne & wind:
Which Passions of the *Aire*, our sp'rits affect;
These by the *Nose* and *Mouth* a waie doe finde
To *Braines*, and *Hart*, and there their *kindes* effect,
And as they are, make them, in some respect:
For, where the *Windes* be cold and violent,
(*As* where rough *Boreas* doth his *Throne* erect)
There are the *People* stronge, and turbulent,
Rending the *Sterne* of *civill government*.

The situation of the *place* likewise
The *Aire* therein doth wel or ill dispose;
If, to the *Sea*, or Southerne winde it lies,
It's humid, putrifactive, & too close:

.   .   .   .

Thus *Place* with *Aire* doth chang our quality.[2]

Again, in a summary of the determining factors in the body's temperature Davies reiterates the same ideas:

Five waies the *Bodies* temperature is knowne,
By *Constitution, Operation, Clime,*
Coulor, and *Age,* by these the same is showne,
As *Dials* by an *Index* shew the time.
The *Body* fat is *cold*, for fat doth clime
By cold degrees; and that, full-flesht is hot,
For *heate* proceedes from *bloud*, as doth my *rime*
From *braines*; where no *heate* were, if *bloud* were not,
And bee'ing too cold they would my *sense* besot.

[1] Davies, *op. cit.* p. 67.   [2] *Ibid.* p. 67.

By *Operation* too, the *temper's* found,
For when a *creature*, (*Man, Beast, Hearbe*, or *Plant*)
Doth that which they by right of *kinde* are bound,
Then no good temperature those *bodies* want:
The *Clyme* in shewing this is nothing skant;
For South-ward, Men are cruell, moody, madd,
Hot, blacke, leane, leapers, lustfull, usd to vant,
Yet wise in action, sober, fearfull, sad,
If good, most good, if bad exceeding bad.

The Northern *Nations* are more moist, and cold,
Lesse wicked and deceiptfull, faithfull, just,
More ample, strong, couragious, martiall, bold,
And, for their bloud is colder, lesse they lust:
Then cold *bloud* being thicke, it follow must
They are lesse witty, and more barberous;
And for they inwardly are more adust,
They *meate* and *drinke* devoure as ravenous,
The *paunch* and *pot* esteeming precious.[1]

Man's body is thus a little world indeed, made up of those elements which go to the forming of the greater world and curiously compounded. Of the almost innumerable variations that are possible from the various compoundings of hot and cold, and moist and dry it is not necessary to speak further. If the premises are accepted, the system is easily comprehended.

[1] Davies, *op. cit.* pp. 62, 63.

PLATE VIII. Frontispiece of the 1734 edition of the English translation of Le Brun, *A Method to learn to Design the Passions*.

CHAPTER VI

The Anatomy of the Soul. The Anatomy of the Passions

THE popularity of literary anatomies during the late sixteenth as well as the seventeenth century is well attested by existing titles. And the habit of anatomizing all things was very evidently applied to the soul and particularly to the passions of the soul. Since it is to the philosophy of the passions that tragedy is related, I propose briefly to sketch the background of moral philosophy in which these anatomies of the passions rested. And in spite of the conflicts of thought concerning the nature and the substance of the soul, concerning the immortality of the soul, and concerning other questions which involved defending or attacking certain theological premises, it is quite possible to find much fundamental agreement in regard to the anatomy of the soul, between Stoics and Peripatetics, Platonists and Aristotelians, followers respectively of St Thomas Aquinas and of St Augustine, Catholics and Protestants. For there was a common agreement among all these authorities in regard to much that we should to-day class as psychology. The *De Proprietatibus Rerum* of Bartholomew said:

Yf we take hede to the soule in comparyson to his werkyng, we fynde thre maner vertues, Vegetabilis, that gevethe lyfe Sensibilis, that geveth felynge, Racionalis, that geveth reason.[1]

[1] *Bartholomeus de Proprietatibus Rerum* was one of the best known of Renaissance books. The tale of Caxton's learning the printer's art in setting up this work has familiarized modern readers with its name, but its importance is better attested by its persistence. Supposedly written about 1360, it was first published in England in 1495, then in this edition of 1535. The original text with comments added by Batman was published in 1582 and is generally referred to as *Batman uppon Bartholome*. The text remained unmodified in any appreciable way save in spelling and punctuation and was authoritative throughout the century. Cf. p. xii, 1582 ed. p. 14.

In this work too is given the old doctrine current in Elizabethan England that the vegetable soul is like a triangle with
its three virtues of engendering, nourishing, and waxing
and growing. The sensible soul is like a quadrangle, a line
drawn from corner to corner of which may make two
triangles, for the vegetable soul must exist where the sensible
soul exists. The sensible soul is concerned with apprehending
and with moving. Apprehending comes through common
or "innerwytte" in relation to imagination, judgment, and
memory, and through particular or outer "wytte". Its
moving powers are concerned with moving the humours in
the liver, the spirits in the heart, and the limbs. The rational
soul is like a circle and is concerned with *intellectus specu-
lativus* and *intellectus practicus*.

Further, this work notes that imagination is located in the
foremost womb of the brain, reason in the middle and highest
womb, recordation (memory) in the hindermost womb.[1]

Only slightly different is the division of the soul given
in Wylkinson's 1547 translation of Aristotle's *Ethics*:

> The Solle of Man hath thre powers, one is called the lyfe vegitable:
> in the whiche man is partener with tres & with plantes; The second
> power, is the life sensible in the whiche a man is partener with beastes,
> for why al beastes have lifes sensible. The third, is called solle reason-
> able, by the whiche a man differeth from all other thinges, for there is
> none reasonable but man, And this power reasonable is sometyme in
> acte, and sometime in power, from whence the Beatitude is when it
> is in acte and not whan it is in power.[2]

Whether there were said to be three souls in man or three
powers of the soul, the practical result for moral philosophy
was the same; it was only when metaphysics and theology
were in question that the difference became important, and

---

[1] *De Proprietatibus Rerum.* Cf. Bk. III.

[2] John Wylkinson, *The Ethiques of Aristotle, that is to saye, preceptes of good behavoure and perfighte honestie*, now newly translated
into English, 1547. Cf. chapter iv.

with metaphysical and theological considerations I do not propose to deal here.

According to much of the thinking of the time, however, there were two rather than three souls or parts of the soul or powers of the soul. Wylkinson's translation of Aristotle was rather confusing on this point in its comment on the powers of the soul as rational and irrational, with the concupiscible (or appetitive) as being called reasonable when it obeyed reason. Plato's confused authority was sometimes influential, and the effect of Christian teaching in opposing divine and human was often apparent. But perhaps Plutarch is here, as in so many other matters, the safest guide to this modified teaching. Plutarch in his essay *Of Moral Vertue* said that each of us is "double and compound". Not only are we body and soul, but also the soul is in itself twofold:

but one part thereof is more spirituall, intelligible and reasonable, which ought of right and according to nature have the soveraigntie and command in man: the other is brutish, sensuall, erronius, and disorderly of it selfe, requiring the direction and guidance of another.

But Plutarch would subdivide this other part into two again; the corporal or vegetative, and the "Thymoeides", irascible and concupiscible. He explained:

Now the difference between the one and the other, may be knowen principally by the fight and resistance that often times is betweene understanding and reason on the one side, and the concupiscence and wrathfull part on the other; which sheweth that these other faculties are often disobedient and repugnant to the best part.[1]

Obviously, then, according to the majority opinion there were three souls or three powers of the soul or three parts of the soul, whether the primary division be into three parts or entities or into two which are in turn subdivided. The vegetative soul is possessed by man in common with plants and animals; the sensible soul is possessed by man in common with the animals; the rational soul is possessed by man alone.

[1] Holland's Plutarch, *Morals*, pp. 65, 66.

The vegetative soul is concerned with "engendering, nourishing, waxing and growing".

The sensible soul both knows and desires, knowing and desiring being necessary to the attainment of the ends prescribed by nature. The knowing part of the sensible soul has both exterior and interior parts. The exterior part is the five senses that send messages to the brain by the sinews. The interior parts are the common sense, the imagination, and the memory, having their seats, the common sense in the foremost hollow of the brain, the imagination in the middle, and the memory in the rear. The common sense is "the Center, to which doe flow the formes which are sent unto it from the other sences". The imagination (sometimes considered as two things—imagination and fantasy) is that "wherein are graven the form of things which are offered unto it by the Common sence to the end knowledge may remaine after they are vanished away".[1] Memory (or recordation) is the storehouse and treasure which yet can represent unto the common sense the forms which are consigned to her. Memory is the recorder, the amanuensis, and at the same time the storehouse of the soul.

The desiring part of the sensible soul, the appetitive part, has two parts or faculties: the concupiscible or desiring power; and the irascible power, which inflames the blood, excites choler, etc., to make its possessor surmount difficulties encountered in getting what he wants. The sensible soul, then, knowing and desiring, is also generally regarded as the soul that has the moving power which resides in the sinews, muscles, ligaments, etc., by which power the soul effects its purposes. The animal spirits are the carriers of such commands, I have already pointed out, and the animal spirits flow through the sinews from the fourth lobe of the brain.

The rational soul has two great powers: the understanding or knowing or judging power; and the will or desiring

---

[1] The description is from Coeffeteau. See below, p. 67 and note.

power—the intellectual appetite. It knows what 'twere good to do and has the power of desiring to do that which it judges good to do.

A quotation from Coeffeteau's *A Table of Humane Passions* as it was translated into English in 1621 gives a view of the working of the mind or soul as it was conceived in Shakespeare's day:

As soone as the Exterior sences, busied about the Objects which are proper for them, have gathered the formes of things which come from without, they carry them to the common sence, the which receives them, judgeth of them, and distinguisheth them; and then to preserve them in the absence of their objects, presents them to the Imagination, which having gathered them together, to the end she may represent them whensoever need shall require, she delivers them to the custody of the Memory; from whence retiring them when occasion requires, she propounds them unto the Appetite, under the apparance of things that are pleasing or troublesome, that is to say, under the forme of Good and Evill; and at the same instant the same formes enlightned with the Light of the understanding, and purged from the sensible and singular conditions, which they retaine in the Imagination, and instead of that which they represented of particular things, representing them generall, they become capable to be imbraced by the Understanding; the which under the apparance of things which are profitable or hurtfull, that is to say, under the forme of Good or Evill, represents them unto the Will: the which being blind referres it selfe to that which the understanding proposeth unto it: And than as Queene of the powers of the soule she ordaines what they shall embrace, & what they shal fly as it pleseth her; whereunto the Sensitive Appetite yeelding a prompt obedience to execute her command, from the which it never straies, so long as it containes it selfe within the bounds and order prescrib'd by Nature, quickneth all the powers and passions over which shee commands, and sets to work those which are necessary to that action, and by their meanes commands the moving power, dispersed over all the members, to follow or fly, to approch or to recoyle, or to do any other motion which it requireth.[1]

[1] "*A Table of Humane Passions. With their Causes and Effects.* Written by the Reverend Father in God F. N. Coeffeteau....Translated into English by Edw. Grimeston...London, 1621." With this passage should be compared the following passage from Wright, *op. cit.* pp. 45, 46 in the 1604 ed.; pp. 83, 84 in the 1601 ed.: "First

teau points out that if because of bad education,
unsound organs, bad inclination of the will, etc.
ppetite is not subjected to reason, if appetite is not
subjected to understanding, then the passions of the sensitive
appetite divert a man from following the laws of reason.

If the soul is considered under two rather than three
divisions, it is apparent that the same fundamental distinctions hold, for if the soul is twofold, the part opposed to
the rational is subdivided into the corporal or vegetative
and the appetitive, and the appetitive is that which should
be subject to the rational part but which may not be so
subject. In any case the appetitive part of the soul, the part
of the sensitive soul which desires or avoids, is considered
as the great opponent of reason for supremacy in man. And
it is in this appetitive part of the sensible soul, or at any rate
according to any possible division of the soul, it is in this
appetitive part of the soul that the passions reside. Hence the
fundamental moral concern of the period is with the passions
and the reason.

then, to our imagination commeth, by sense or memorie, some object
to be knowne, convenient, or disconvenient to Nature, the which
beeing knowne (for *Ignoti nulla cupido*) in the imagination which
resideth in the former parte of the braine,...presently the purer spirites
flocke from the brayne, by certayne secret channels to the heart, where
they pitch at the doore, signifying what an object was presented,
convenient or disconvenient for it. The heart immediately bendeth,
either to prosecute it, or to eschewe it: and the better to effect that
affection, draweth other humours to help him, and so in pleasure
concurre great store of pure spirites; in payne and sadnesse, much
melancholy blood, in ire, blood and choler; and not onely (as I sayde)
the heate residing in other partes, sendeth the humours unto the heart,
to performe their service in such a woorthie place: In like maner as
when we feele hunger (caused by the sucking of the liver and defect of
nourishment in the stomacke) the same soule which informeth the
stomacke, resideth in the hand, eyes, and mouth; and in case of hunger,
subordinateth them all to serve the stomacke, and satisfie the appetite
thereof: Even so, in the hunger of the heart, the splene, the liver, the
blood spirites, choller, and melancholy, attend and serve it most
diligently".

PLATE IX. Title-page from Coeffeteau, *A Table of Humane Passions*, 1621, showing the primary passions.

Thomas Rogers writing *A Philosophicall Discourse, Entituled, The Anatomie of the minde*, in 1576, divided his work into two parts: one of "Perturbations (and discourseth of that parte of the minde of man which is voide of reson)"; and the second of "Morall vertues (so called because it is of that parte of the minde which is endued with reason)". And in this division he expressed the current notion of moral virtue as having to do with the conflict between reason and unreason, the irrational being represented by the passions. The passions were variously spoken of on older authority during the Renaissance as perturbations, affections, and passions. When they were spoken of as passions, it was obviously because they were regarded as opposed to actions, for in actions man acted upon external things: in passions man was acted upon by external things.

Of the number and variety of the passions as thought of during the Renaissance it is not possible to make dogmatic statements. Aristotle said that there were many passions without names, and yet he finally tended to reduce all passions to an ultimate division based on pleasure and pain, the desire to obtain pleasure and the desire to avoid pain being regarded as the primary movers to passions. Practically all authorities accepted during the Renaissance the concupiscible and irascible faculties of the appetitive part of the sensible soul, and hence the division of the passions accepted by St Thomas Aquinas continued to be generally popular:

Concupiscible	*Irascible*
Love and Hatred	Hope and Despair
Desire and Aversion	Courage and Fear
Joy (or Pleasure) and Sadness (or Grief)	Anger

Though these eleven passions were then usually accepted as basic passions,[1] innumerable subdivisions were referred to,

---

[1] A complete discussion of such divisions is given by Burton in the *Anatomy of Melancholy*, Part I, Sect. II, Mem. III, Subs. III.

the differences arising from the consideration of whether the object causing the passion was present or to come, and from the consideration of the nature of the object of the passion. Thus love relates to that which is present, hope to that which is in the future. Also desire of money is called covetousness, desire of food gluttony, desire of flesh lust, etc. There must, furthermore, be reckoned with, the compounded passions, derived by combination of the simple passions in various groupings; such a passion is jealousy. And it must be remembered also that there are passions which have a natural affinity, so that they are regularly found together or coming in sure succession. Such are pride, anger, and revenge.

The fundamental difference in the treatment of the passions in the Renaissance was a difference inherited from the conflicting attitudes of Stoics and Peripatetics in regard to the passions. The Stoics considered all passions as evil in themselves. The Peripatetics taught that passions were evil if they were not governed by reason. Some passions were, according to Aristotle, named because they were excesses; some because they were defects. Virtue is, he said, to be found in the temperate mean between the passions of excess and the passions of defect, as for example:

Irascibility	Lack of feeling	Gentleness
Audacity	Cowardice	Bravery

The Stoic attitude toward passion, that of complete rejection, met an objection in Christian teaching; it was pointed out that the passions could not be evil in themselves, since the Scriptures attributed certain passions to Christ and to God himself. If God loved or was angry or was jealous, then it was impossible that love and anger and jealousy were evil in themselves. Thus the Peripatetic doctrine was generally upheld by Christian authority, and tables were drawn up showing that good and evil depended upon the temperate control of passion by reason, or upon the occasion upon which the passion was roused, or upon the object of the passion.

Another question which arose as the result of Protestant and Catholic differences of opinion was as to the origin and cause of this war between the passions and the reason, which was the general concern of moral philosophers. The best summary of this difference is probably that found in Bishop Reynolds' *Treatise of The Passions and Faculties of the Soule of Man*, published in 1640, but reviewing doctrinal differences of the preceding generation:

...we are first to remember, that there is in every man a native and originall strugling betweene Appetite and Reason; which yet proceedeth from Corruption, and the Fall of Man, not from Nature entire, as the *Papists* contend; who affirme, That the strife and reluctance betwene Sense and Understanding, ariseth from Physicall and created constitution; and that therefore, that sweet harmonie which was betweene all the Faculties of Man, Animall and Rationall, in his Creation, proceeded from the government of a super-naturall Grace added thereunto :...

An argument as weake, as the Opinion which it defends, is dangerous and prejudiciall to the honor of Mans Creation; as tending to prove, that the first risings and rebellions of Appetite against Reason, and all inordinate desires of inferior Faculties, till they taint the Will, are not formally sinnes, as having been naturall to *Adam* himselfe in Innocencie, though by infused and supernaturall Grace bridled and suspended. An Opinion, which retaineth that odious scandall which they fasten upon us, more justly and truly on their owne heads, touching making God the Author of Sinne:...

And for the Argument which they bring, we answer, That naturally, and from the Law of Creation, there was no formall opposition, but a subordination betweene Spirit and Sense. And therefore, notwithstanding the operations of Appetite are common unto Men and Beasts; yet we may not grant, that they have the same manner of being educed and governed in both these. For, as the operations of the vegetative Soule, though common to Beasts, Men, and Plants, are yet in either of these severally so restrained, as that they are truly sayd to be the proper and peculiar workes of that specificall forme, unto which they are annexed: So likewise, the sensitive Appetite, though generally

it be common to Men and Beasts; yet in Men, it was ordained to proceed naturally from the government of Reason, and therefore may
properly be called a humane Appetite, as being determined, restrained,
and made conformable unto Mans Nature: so that as long as Man
continued entire and incorrupt, there was a sweet harmonie betweene
all his Faculties, and such an happie subordination of them each to other,
as that every motion of the inferior powers was directed and governed,
and therefore might truly and properly be attributed to the superior;
but when once Man had tasted of that murthering Fruit, which
poysoned him and all his posteritie,...whence Passions are become
now, in the state of corruption, beastly and sensuall, which were
before, by Creation, reasonable and humane....

...And though the Light of our Reason be by Mans Fall much
dimmed and decayed, yet the remainders thereof are so adverse to our
unruly Appetite, as that it laboureth against us...to deprive us of those
Reliques of Sight, which we yet retaine.[1]

Bishop Reynolds pointed out also that the reason may be
evil, it may be ignorant, or it may be confounded. But in all
cases repentance and the putting away of lusts are the only
effective preparation for true understanding.

[1] Reynolds, *op. cit.* pp. 61–4.

CHAPTER VII

The Anatomy of Melancholy

JUST as the relation of mind and body is acknowledged to be very close, so is the relation between the passions and the humours. Wright says of his work in its opening chapter:

As this Treatise affordeth great riches to the Physitian of the soule, so it importeth much the Physitian of the bodie, for that there is no Passion very vehement, but that it alters extreamely some of the four humors of the bodie; and all Physitians commonly agree, that among diverse other extrinsecall causes of diseases, one, and not the least, is, the excesse of some inordinate Passion.[1]

How this happens he finds it difficult to explain, but he concludes

that the spirites and humors wait upon the Passions, as their Lords and Maisters.[2]

Remembering that in general the liver was the instrument of nourishment for the body, the heart the seat of the spirits and hence of passions and affections, the brain the instrument of sense and motion, it will be seen that there are two ways in which the passions could be and were considered as affecting body and mind. In the first place, those who thought of the elements as the ultimate basis of all things chose to regard the passions as in themselves having affinity with the elements. Thus the author of *The French Academie* writes:

We see also by experience, that there is great agreement betweene the qualities and temperature of the body, and the affections of the soule: insomuch that as the bodies of men are compounded of the qualities of heate, colde, moisture, and drienesse, so among the affections some are hote, others colde; some moist, others dry, &

[1] Wright, *op. cit.* 1604 ed. p. 4. Also in 1601 ed.
[2] *Ibid.* p. 4.

some mingled of these divers qualities. So that every one is most subject to those affections that come neerest to the nature, temperature, and complexion of his body....And as the affections followe the temperature and complexion of the body, so they for their parts have great vertue and power over the body.[1]

Thus we see that according to this writer joy, being hot and moist, is natural in those of the sanguine temperament, in children and young persons, and in healthy persons; sorrow, being cold and dry, is natural to those of melancholic temperament, and in thôse growing old. And contrariwise, grief or sorrow engenders melancholy.

It is because the passions have their seat in the heart and affect the spirits which are there refined, and because the spirits are the natural conveyers of heat, maintaining the humours at their proper balance by maintaining the proper heat in the blood, that we find, then, the passions having a direct effect on the humours. And it is also through this same channel of the spirits that the humours move the passions directly.

But it is further to be considered how the excess of an humour not contained in its proper "sink" may affect the passions. Bright says of melancholy that is not retained in the spleen that it causes a "splentick fogge" to rise to the brain and destroy discretion, so that the brain passes on goblins to the heart, which acts in passion. This fog may work in various ways: it may cause apparitions to be wrought by apprehension of the common sense, or it may cause fancy to forge disguised shapes, or it may cause memory to neglect other records and regard only the dark and sympathetic ones.

In the same way excessive choler causes the choleric man to feed his passion with ridiculous causes of displeasure.

But besides this natural affinity of humours and passions, besides this effect of humours on passions where an excess of humour of some sort causes in the brain false images

[1] *The French Academie*, 1594 ed. pp. 230, 231.

which rouse the passions appropriate to the humour, there is a third and much more important state in which passions and humours are related, but in order to understand this relation, it is necessary to go back to the thread of the exposition where it was left in the discussion of the humours. There it was seen that there were both natural and unnatural humours to be considered.

Just as the healthy body and the healthy mind are dependent upon the maintenance of the proper equilibrium between the humours, so they are also dependent upon the maintenance of the proper relation between the spirits, the natural heat, and the vital moisture (the humours). Now if for some reason the humours are subjected to excessive heat, there results an unnatural humour that is to be distinguished from the natural humours and from the unnatural excess of a natural humour. This unnatural humour is generally referred to as melancholy adust. Melancholy adust, then, was the unnatural humour that resulted from any one of the humours putrifying or being burnt through excessive heat. And the importance of distinguishing between the natural melancholy humour and the melancholy adust cannot be overstated. It is the melancholy adust with which such writers as Bright and Burton were primarily concerned, and it is the failure of modern students to recognize the distinction that has made all recent discussion of melancholy seem so confusing. But to let the Renaissance writers speak for themselves in the matter, Sir Thomas Elyot said in his *Castel of Health*:

Melancoly is of two sortes, the one is called naturalle, whiche is onely colde and drye, the other is called adust or bourned. . . . Melancolye adust is in foure kindes [burned from the four humours]. . . . But of all other, that melancoly is warste, whiche is ingendred of choler, finally all aduste melancolye annoyeth the witte and jugemente of man. For when that humour is hette, it maketh men madde, and when it is extincte, it maketh men fooles, forgetfulle, and dulle.[1]

[1] Elyot, *op. cit.* 1547 ed. p. 66.

Bright says in *A Treatise of Melancholie*:

Besides the former kindes, there are sortes of unnaturall melancholie:... these are of another nature farre disagreeing from the other,
& by an unproper speech called melancholy. They rise of the naturall
humors, or their excrements by excessive distemper of heate, burned
as it were into ashes in comparison of humour, by which the humour
of like nature being mixed, turneth it into a sharp lye: sanguine,
cholericke, or melancholicke, according to the humour thus burned,
which we call by name of melancholie. This sort raiseth the greatest
tempest of perturbations and most of all destroyeth the braine with all
his faculties, and disposition of action, and maketh both it, & the
hart cheere more uncomfortably: and if it rise of the naturall melancholy, beyond all likelihood of truth, frame monstrous terrors of
feare and heavinesse without cause. If it rise of choler, then rage
playeth her part, and furie joyned with madnesse, putteth all out of
frame. If bloud minister matter to this fire, every serious thing for a
time, is turned into a jest, & tragedies into comedies, and lamentation
into gigges and dances.[1]

The translation from the Spanish of Huarte into English
by way of the Italian in 1594 under the title of *The Examination of Mens Wits* gave perhaps the most interesting
description, however:

there are two spices of melancholy: one naturall, which is the drosse
of the blood, whose temperature is cold and drie, accompanied with
a substance very grosse, this serves not of any value for the wit, but
maketh men blockish, sluggards, and grynnars, because they want
imagination. There is another sort which is called *choler ad-ust*, or
atra bile, of which *Aristotle* sayd, That it made men exceeding wise:
whose temperature is divers, as that of vinegre. Sometimes it per-
formeth the effects of heat, lightning the earth; and sometimes it
cooleth, but alwaies it is drie and of a very delicat substance. *Cicero*
confesseth that he was slow witted, because he was not melancholike
adust, and he sayd true, for if he had bene such, he should not have
possessed so rare a gift of eloquence. For the melancholicke adust
want memorie, to which appertaineth the speaking with great preparation. It hath another qualitie which much aideth the understanding,
namely, that it is cleere like the Agat stone, with which cleerenesse
it giveth light within to the braine, and maketh the same to discerne

[1] Bright, *op. cit.* pp. 110, 111.

well the figures. And of this opinion was *Heraclitus*, when he sayd, *A drie cleerenesse maketh a most wise mind,* with which cleerenesse, natural melancholy is not endowed, but his blacke is deadly: and that the reasonable soule there within the braine, standeth in need of light to the figures and the shapes, we will proove hereafter.[1]

It was a point for discussion whether there were four or only three kinds of melancholy adust, since it was disputed whether or not phlegm might be so changed. The important fact is, however, not affected by this discussion; the inescapable fact is that melancholy humour of the natural sort is very different from melancholy adust. Of most concern were the sorts of melancholy adust that came from the adustion of the melancholic and the choleric humours. And it is significant that these are the two humours that are also represented as passions (for choler and anger seem to be used as synonyms). It therefore behoves all who would understand the writers of the sixteenth and seventeenth centuries to tread warily.

It is apparent that in the thinking of the Renaissance, humours might move passions, and passions might cause the distemperature of the humours. The effect of the passions on the spirits was all-important, because the spirits were the medium or go-between between body and soul. Newton wrote:

So likewyse, if the Spirites be disquieted & out of frame, they ingender and procure divers sortes of affections in the minde, & carye the same (mauger all reason) like a shyppe wythout guide and Rother, uppon the rockes of sundry inconveniences.[2]

Wright summed up the whole matter by saying that there

---

[1] *Examen de Ingenios. The Examination of mens Wits. In whicch, by discovering the varietie of natures, is shewed for what profession each one is apt, and how far he shall profit therein.* By John Huarte. Translated out of the Spanish Tongue by M. Camillo Camilli. Englished out of his Italian by R. C(arew), 1594, pp. 84, 85.

[2] Newton, *op. cit.* chapter II, discusses the whole question of the relation of the spirits to health. Cf. *ante*, p. 55.

are four effects of inordinate passions: (1) blindness of understanding, (2) perversion of the will, (3) alteration of humours, and (4) maladies and diseases together with troublesomeness or disquietness of the soul.[1] Of the first, the blinding of understanding, he said that passion is like a pair of green glasses to the soul. Of the second, he said that passion seduces the will. But it will be easily seen that both the excess of humours (which may be caused by contributory passion) and the unnatural humour, melancholy adust (which may be caused by the heat of passion) are directly responsible for affections of the mind. Whether, then, the passions be regarded as perverting the workings of the mind in the brain, or whether they be regarded as impelling to action the end of which is unjudged, the result is the same: the passions are the potential enemy of the rational soul.

[1] Wright, *op. cit.* 1604 ed. p. 48. The corresponding passage in the 1601 ed. p. 86 reads: "There be three properties consequent to inordinate passions; blindnesse of understanding, perversion of will, alteration of humours; and by them, maladies and diseases".

CHAPTER VIII

Diseases of the Soul. Drunkenness. Fevers.
Melancholy. Frenzy. Madness

T HE moral philosophy of the Renaissance was thus built upon a definite and detailed physiological explanation, and no modern psychologist has more strenuously insisted upon the fundamental relationship between body and mind or body and soul than did these writers of the sixteenth and seventeenth centuries in England. That to a great extent this moral philosophy came to centre about the struggle between the sensitive appetite and the reason meant that to the moral philosopher as well as to the physician the abnormal or diseased conditions of mind and body, where the connection of mind and body was most apparent, were of absorbing interest. And the Renaissance philosophers found these conditions in drunkenness, melancholy, fever, madness, frenzy, etc. That they studied these manifestations as states which had in common the predominance of passion over reason is evident to all readers of Burton. The foundation of such thinking is to be found in Aristotle, perhaps most clearly in the *Magna Moralia*. Aristotle explains that those who have knowledge may still err.

For it is so in the case of persons who are drunk. For those who are drunk, when the intoxication has passed off, are themselves again. Reason was not expelled from them, nor was knowledge, but it was overcome by the intoxication....So, then, it is with the incontinent. His passion gains the mastery and brings his reasoning to a standstill. But when the passion, like the intoxication, has been got rid of, he is himself again.[1]

[1] Aristotle, *Magna Moralia*, trans. by St George Stock, 1202ᵃ, 1–8. That this conception was current on classical authority in Chaucer's day is attested by his Pardoner:

> "Seneca seith a good word, doutelees;
> He seith he kan no difference fynde

And because Hobbes, though writing in 1650, gives such a simple and clear statement of the belief which characterized the thinking of his day in common with that of an earlier generation, I quote his statement here also:

> Again, that madness is nothing else, but too much appearing passion, may be gathered out of the effects of wine, which are the same with those of the evil disposition of the organs. For the variety of behaviour in men that have drunk too much, is the same with that of madmen: some of them raging, others loving, others laughing, all extravagantly, but according to their several domineering passions: for the effect of the wine, does but remove dissimulation, and take from them the sight of the deformity of their passions…passions unguided, are for the most part mere madness.[1]

But the Elizabethan conception of drunkenness is often embodied in language which is the result of two legendary associations of drink. The familiar tale which caused drink to be associated with Circe's cup accounted in one way for the animal natures brought out by drink. But another legend explained by John Day in his *Peregrinatio Scholasticae: or Learning's Pilgrimage* gave other ground for familiar phrases. According to this legend vines watered by the blood of animals became fruitful and the blood living in the wine made from the fruit of the vines sought its like in those who drank it. When the wine is drunk, the lion's blood ministers to the one with furious disposition and produces rage. Thus we speak of one as lion-drunk who rages in his cups; of one as goat-drunk who lusts when he is drunk, etc.[2] Thomas Nashe carefully describes in his *Pierce*

> Bitwix a man that is out of his mynde
> And a man which that is dronkelewe,
> But that woodnesse, fallen in a shrewe,
> Persevereth lenger than dooth dronkenesse".

[1] "Of Man", Part I of *Leviathan*, in *The English Works of Thomas Hobbes*. Ed. by Sir William Molesworth, 1839, vol. III, p. 64.

[2] *The Works of John Day*. Ed. by A. H. Bullen, 1881, p. 52.

Penilesse the eight sorts of drunkenness thus named according to the likeness of the animal in which the dominating passion is one held in common with men.[1] It is important to note this belief in the power of drink to make reason inoperative and hence let passion rule, if we are to understand Shakespeare.

Of fever the ever helpful *De Proprietatibus Rerum* says that it "cometh of distemperaunce of the herte", and comments as to causes:

And sometyme it cometh by reason of another disease: and cometh sometyme of to hotte meate and drinke, and sometyme of greate traveylle and besynes, as of great studiynge or of wakynge/and of other suche that heateth the spirit of felynge.[2]

And again if we are to understand Shakespeare we must see fever as caused by the distemperature of the heart and hence as being both the potential cause and the possible result of passion.

From the *De Proprietatibus Rerum* I quote further an interesting statement concerning madness and its signs and causes:

Amentia and madnes is al one, as Plato sayeth/Madnes is infection of the foremeste celle of the heed, with privacion of imaginacion, lyke as melancolie is the infection of the myddell celle of the heed, with privation of reason/as Constantyn saith in libro de Melancholia. Melancolia (saith he) is an infection that hath maystry of the soule, the whiche cometh of drede & of sorowe. And these passions ben divers after the diversitie of the hurt of theyr workinges: for by madnesse that hyghte Mania principally the imaginacion is hurte. And in the other reason is hurted. And these passions com somtime of melancoly meates & some time of drynke of stronge wine, that brenneth the humours & tornith them into ashes/sometyme of passyons of the soule, as of besines & greate thoughtes/of sorowe & of to grate studie/& of drede....[3]

---

[1] "Pierce Penilesse", in Nashe, *op. cit.* vol. II, pp. 81–2.
[2] *De Proprietatibus Rerum*, 1535 ed. LXXXXVI. 1582 ed. p. 99.
[3] *Ibid.* LXXXVII. 1582 ed. p. 89.

Sir Thomas Elyot explained of anger or ire:

Of this affection commeth sometyme fevers, sometyme apoplexies, or privation of sences, tremblynge, palseys, madnesse, fransies, deformytie of vysage: and that wars is, outragious swearynge, blasphemye desyre of vengeance.... [1]

Newton wrote of choler adust (and hence choler become melancholy adust):

If it bee immoderately and too much enflamed, it bryngeth the mynde into furious fits, phreneticke rages, and braynesicke madnesse: [2]

Bright wrote of unnatural melancholy or melancholy adust:

This excrement, if it keepeth the bounds of his owne nature, breedeth lesse perturbance either to bodie or minde: if it corrupt and degenerate farther from it selfe and the qualitie of the bodie; then are all passions more vehement, & so outragiously oppresse and trouble the quiet seate of the minde, that all organicall actions therof are mixed with melancholie madnesse; and reason turned to a vaine feare, or plaine desperation, the braine being altered in his complexion, and as it were transported into an instrument of an other make then it was first ordained: [3]

Likewise the later Burton gave a section to the discussion of the relation of passions and melancholy, a chapter to a passion, passion by passion.

It is evident that Shakespeare was speaking by the book when he had Aemilia say in *The Comedy of Errors*:

> And what's a fever but a fit of madness? [4]

and also when he had the Messenger announce the coming of the players to Sly in *The Taming of the Shrew*:

> For so your doctors hold it very meet,
> Seeing too much sadness hath congeal'd your blood,
> And melancholy is the nurse of frenzy. [5]

---

[1] Elyot, *Castel of Helth*, 1547 ed. p. 64 *verso*.
[2] Newton, *op. cit.* p. 147.
[3] Bright, *op. cit.* p. 2.   [4] v, i, 76.
[5] Ind. ii, 133–5. Cf. also Sonnet 147.

I shall treat of the relation of passion to these various states more in detail in connection with the several places in which they appear in Shakespeare's tragedies, but it must be stated again and again with all possible emphasis that it was upon the basis of this inter-relation between soul and body that the study of the devastating effect of passion was based during the Renaissance. And it was, I hope to prove, because passion wrought and was wrought upon in these states of unreason that a tragedy of passion is necessarily a tragedy in which drunkenness, fevers, melancholy, and madness appear in turn upon the stage as they do in the great tragedies of Shakespeare.

CHAPTER IX

Those who see Spirits

THE part of the whole subject which attracted most attention just at the time Shakespeare was at the height of his career was, however, the relation between melancholy (with incidentally other forms of madness) and various supernatural appearances. Primarily this discussion was concerned with setting forth the rival positions of those who considered ghosts and dreams and witchcraft to be traceable to the effects of melancholy, and those who considered them as direct manifestations of the supernatural. The full story of this conflict would have to be told in history, in philosophy, in literature, and the full story I make no attempt to tell here. But the signs of the conflict are so deeply imprinted in all the literature of melancholy as well as of demonology in the immediate period under consideration that to the student of Shakespearean tragedy they transcend in interest all else in that literature. When witches were burned, when the whole nation was stirred over the authenticity of witchcraft, it was inevitable that those who wrote on the subject should write vividly and earnestly.

Briefly, the physicians and the realists insisted that the supernatural manifestations variously reported were most often, if not the result of actual fraud, the result of the effect of melancholic humours, apparently either the excess of the natural melancholy humour unduly increased by disease or sympathetic passions, or the melancholy adust burned from one of the natural humours through the influence of a hot passion like anger; the advocates of the supernatural insisted either that ghosts were spirits released temporarily from purgatory, or that ghosts and all the subtleties of witchcraft were manifestations of God and the good angels or Satan and the evil angels. And it must not be forgotten that no less a person than King James entered the lists on the side of the angels.

The whole case was very well set out in *The French Academie*:

But nowe that we are in hand with frenetike persons, and have saide before, that good and ill spirites have great meanes, and such as wee cannot comprehend, whereby they moove the imagination and fantasie of men; it shall not be altogether fruitlesse, if we speake somewhat of them that are possessed with spirites. For there are some who thinke not, that the Devilles in their very substance enter into the bodies or soules, heartes or mindes of men. I speake not heere of such as thinke there is neither God, nor Angelles, nor Devilles, but even of them that beleeve all these things: who neverthelesse thinke, that evill spirites trouble the heartes and mindes of men onely by provocations, temptations, and illusions. Others there are, that referre all the madnesse of Lunatike folkes to naturall causes, as if they proceeded either from melancholike or cholerike humours, or some such like causes, as frensinesse, madnesse, and furie, or some such diseases whereby men are carried beside themselves. True it is, and cannot bee denied, that many are thought to be possessed with Devilles, when in deede they are nothing so. For there are some counterfeit crankes, as many have beene taken with the maner, who upon some occasion have by meere knavery fained themselves such. And some also there are that bee but melancholy madde, and carried away by some disease of the braine: but because their melancholy and furie is very violent and strange, ignorant people suppose they are possessed with some spirite. Notwithstanding wee may not doubt, but that evil spirits desirous to hurt men both in their goodes, bodies, and soules, use all the means and occasions they can possibly invent and finde out, to execute their malices when it pleaseth God to give them leave.[1]

The work of Lavater translated into English in 1572 by "R. H." under the title *Of Ghostes and Spirites Walking by Nyght*[2] presented the argument of the believers in natural

---

[1] *The French Academie*, 1594 ed. pp. 167, 168.

[2] The full title reads: *Of ghostes and spirites walking by nyght, and of strange noyses, crackes, and sundry forewarnynges, whiche commonly happen before the death of menne, great slaughters, & alterations of kyngdomes.* One Booke. Written by Lewes Lavaterus of Tigurine. And translated into English, by R. H. London, 1572.

causes of supernatural events, and argued also the case against the Papists who believed that the spirits of the dead were released temporarily to return to earth. Lavater's work said:

True it is, that many men doo falsly persuade themselves that they see or heare ghostes: for that which they imagin they see or heare, proceedeth eyther of melancholie, madnesse, weaknesse of the senses, feare, or of some other perturbation: or else when they see or heare beastes, vapors, or some other naturall things, then they vaynly suppose they have seene sightes I wote not what.... [1]

And fyrste it cannot be denyed, but that some menne whiche eyther by dispositions of nature, or for that they have susteyned greate miserie, are nowe become heavie and full of melancholie, imagine many tymes with them selves being alone, miraculous and straunge things. [2]

That whiche we have hytherto spoken concerning melancholicke men, and men out of their witts, may also be understood of timorous and fearefull men. For if any man be timourous by nature, or subject to feare through great daungers, or by some other wayes, he also imagineth straunge things which in deede are not so, especially if he have in him any store of melancholie. [3]

In this connection Lavater instanced the tale of Bessus from Plutarch's work on the deferring of divine justice, which work I have already referred to as influencing the theory of tragedy. Bessus murdered his father and escaped justice, but on the occasion of going to supper among strangers one evening, he spied a swallow's nest and thrust it down with his spear. When the supper guests questioned him as to his unnecessary killing of the swallows, he cried out that they were accusing him of the death of his father. Thus was he finally apprehended through the effect of his own fear. Also Lavater tells the tale from Procopius of Theodoricus, who having put to death Boethius and Symmachus, became terrified as he sat at meat, thinking that in a fish's head he saw

[1] Lavater, *op. cit.* pp. 9, 10.
[2] *Ibid.* p. 10.   [3] *Ibid.* p. 14.

the countenance of Symmachus threatening him. And he thereupon fell into a grievous sickness whereof he died.[1]

The Catholic position in regard to the appearance of spirits from the realms of the dead is so convincingly set forth by Lavater that his own contention that dead men's souls do not walk is almost forgotten. This particular problem I intend to treat more fully in my discussion of *Hamlet*, and I note it here only as part of the general argument.

The work of Reginald Scot in 1584 argued the question of the nature and substance of spirits and devils chiefly on the basis that body and spirit are opposites and that devils are spirits and not bodies; as to witchcraft Scot contended that melancholy old women were self-deceived, filled with marvellous imaginations, so that even their confessions were useless.

This work was one of those vigorously attacked in the treatise much more important to the main problem of Shakespearean tragedy, the *Daemonology* of King James, published in Edinburgh in 1597. The first book discussed magic; the second sorcery and witchcraft. All are the work of the Devil, according to James, and at the very outset he asked how the Devil allures persons to these snares. His answer is:

Even by these three passiones that are within our selves: Curiositie in great ingines: thrist of revenge, for some tortes deeply apprehended: or greedie appetite of geare, caused through great poverty. As to the first of these, Curiosity, it is onelie the inticement of *Magiciens*, or *Necromanciers*: and the other two are the allureres of the *Sorcerers*, or *Witches*, for that olde and craftie Serpent, being a spirite, hee easily spyes our affections, and so conformes himselfe thereto, to deceave us to our wracke.[2]

Specifically he advances to attack the advocates of melancholy as the basis for accounting for strange appearances:

As to your second reason grounded upon Physick, in attributing their confessiones or apprehensiones, to a naturall melancholicque

[1] Lavater, *op. cit.* p. 15. Cf. *ante*, pp. 20–22.
[2] King James, *Daemonology*, p. 8.

humour: Anie that pleases Physicallie to consider upon the naturall humour of melancholie, according to all the Physicians, that ever writ thereupon, they sall finde that that will be over short a cloak to cover their knavery with: For as the humor of Melancholie in the selfe is blacke, heavie and terrene, so are the symptomes thereof, in any persones that are subject therunto, leannes, palenes, desire of solitude: and if they come to the highest degre therof, mere folie and *Manie*: where as by the contrarie, a great nomber of them that ever have bene convict or confessors of Witchcraft, as may be presently seene by manie that have at this time confessed: they are by the contrarie, I say, some of them rich and worldly-wise, some of them fatte or corpulent in their bodies, and most part of them altogether given over to the pleasures of the flesh, continual haunting of companie, and all kind of merrines, both lawfull and unlawfull, which are thinges directly contrary to the symptomes of Melancholie, whereof I spake, and further experience daylie proves how loath they are to confesse without torture, which witnesseth their guiltines, where by the contrary, the Melancholicques never spares to bewray themselves, by their continual discourses, feeding therby their humor in that which they thinke no crime.[1]

That witchcraft is the work of the Devil James has no doubt, but that passions play their part in making men susceptible to the wiles of the Devil he likewise accepts as true:

These two degrees now of persones, that practises this craft, answers to the passions in them, which (I told you before) the Devil used as meanes to intyse them to his service, for such of them as are in great miserie and povertie, he allures to follow him, by promising unto them greate riches, and worldlie commoditie. Such as though riche, yet burnes in a desperat desire of revenge, hee allures them by promises, to get their turne satisfied to their hartes contentment. It is to be noted nowe, that that olde and craftie enemie of ours, assailes none, though touched with any of these two extremeties, except he first finde an entresse reddy for him, either by the great ignorance of the person he deales with, joyned with an evill life, or else by their carelesnes and contempt of God: And finding them in an utter despair, for one of these two former causes that I have spoken of; he prepares the way by feeding them craftely in their humour, and filling them further and

[1] King James, *op. cit.* pp. 29, 30.

further with despaire, while he finde the time proper to discover himself unto them. At which time, either upon their walking solitarie in the fieldes, or else lying pansing in their bed; but alwaies without the company of any other, he either by a voyce, or in likenesse of a man inquires of them, what troubles them: and promiseth them, a suddaine and certaine waie of remedie, upon condition on the other parte, that they follow his advise; and do such thinges as he will require of them.[1]

Of the second and third meetings which bind the victim to the Devil James gives also detailed accounts. And it is interesting to note that ambition and revenge are the two passions which give entry to the wiles of the Devil. However, there are three sorts of people tempted: the wicked who are to be punished; the good who are asleep in sin or weakness; the good who are to be tried.

It is interesting to note too that James wrote:

For if the devil may forme what kinde of impressiones he pleases in the aire, as I have said before, speaking of *Magie*, why may he not far easilier thicken & obscure so the air, that is next about them by contracting it strait together, that the beames of any other mans eyes, cannot pearce thorow the same, to see them?[2]

In his third book, which is given over to the description of troublesome spirits, James mentions four sorts of spirits: spirits that trouble houses or solitary places; spirits that follow certain persons and trouble them; spirits that enter into men and possess them; and fairies. Concerning the appearing in the likeness of defunct friends, James reasons:

For if they have assumed a deade bodie, whereinto they lodge themselves, they can easely inough open without dinne anie Door or Window, and enter in thereat. And if they enter as a spirite onelie, anie place where the aire may come in at, is large inough an entrie for them: For as I said before, a spirite can occupie no quantitie.[3]

Another aspect of the question is brought out in one of the most fascinating books of the period, Thomas Nashe's *The Terrors of the Night, or A Discourse of Apparitions*,

[1] King James, *op. cit.* pp. 32, 33.
[2] *Ibid.* p. 39.
[3] *Ibid.* p. 59.

published in 1594. Nashe was particularly interested in the subject of dreams, though the other manifestations are also discussed. And it will be observed in the passages selected for quotation that he goes back to the microcosmography theory in accounting for the terrors of the night:

None of these spirits of the ayre or fire have so much predominance in the night as the spirits of the earth and the water; for they feeding on foggie-braind melancholly, engender thereof many uncouth terrible monsters. Thus much observe by the way, that the grossest part of our blood is the melancholy humor, which in the spleene congealed whose office it is to disperse it, with his thicke steaming fennie vapours causeth a mist over the spirit, and cleane bemasketh the phantasie.

And even as slime and durt in a standing puddle, engender toads and frogs, and many other unsightly creatures, so this slimie melancholly humor still still [sic] thickning as it stands still, engendreth many mishapen objects in our imaginations...so from the fuming melancholly of our spleene mounteth that hot matter into the higher Region of the braine, whereof manie fearfull visions are framed. Our reason even like drunken fumes it displaceth and intoxicates, & yeeldes up our intellective apprehension, to be mocked and troden under foote, by everie false object or counterfet noyse that comes neere it. Herein specially consisteth our senses defect and abuse, that those organicall parts which to the minde are ordained embassadours, doo not their message as they ought, but by some misdiet or misgovernment being distempered, faile in their report, and deliver up nothing but lyes and fables.[1]

More definitely he affirms:

When all is said, melancholy is the mother of dreames, and of all the terrours of the night whatsoever.

Let it but affirme it hath seene a spirit (though it be but the moonshine on the wall) the best reason wee have cannot infringe it.[2]

That dreams but echo the memories of the day Nashe says in various impressive figures:

Of those things which are most knowne to us some of us that have moyst braynes make to our-selves images of memorie: on those images

[1] Nashe, *op. cit.* vol. III, pp. 232, 233.
[2] *Ibid.* pp. 237, 238.

of memorie whereon we buyld in the daye, comes some superfluous humour of ours, like a Jacke-anapes in the night, and erects a puppet stage, or some such ridiculous idle childish invention.[1]

Especially are the guilty the sufferers from dreams:

Dreames to none are so fearefull, as to those whose accusing private guilt expects mischiefe every hower for their merit. Wonderfull superstitious are such persons in observing everie accident that befalls them; and that their superstition is as good as an hundred furies to torment them. Never in the world shall he enjoy one quiet day, that once hath given himselve over to be her slave....[2]

But Nashe accepted also the trafficking of the Devil for men's souls:

so the Divell when with any other sickenes or malladie the faculties of our reason are enfeebled and distemperd, will be most busie to disturbe us and torment us.[3]

Therefore

Children, fooles, sicke-men, or mad-men hee is most familiar with (for he still delights to worke upon the advantage) and to them he boldly revealeth, the whole astonishing treasurie of his wonders.[4]

It is interesting to note that Nashe says also:

Neither in his owne nature dare he come nere us, but in the name of sin, and as Gods executioner. Those that catch birdes imitate their voyces, so will hee imitate the voyces of Gods vengeance, to bring us like birds into the net of eternall damnation.[5]

And more explicitly he brings the discussion into the realm of Shakespearean tragedy when he adds:

It will bee demaunded why in the likenes of ones father or mother, or kinsfolks, he oftentime presents himselfe unto us?

No other reason can bee given of it but this, that in those shapes which hee supposeth most familliar unto us, and that wee are inclined to with a naturall kind of love, we will sooner harken to him than otherwise.

Should he not disguise himselfe in such subtil forms of affection, we should flie from him as a serpent, and eschew him with that hatred he ought to be eschewed.[6]

[1] Nashe, *op. cit.* p. 236. [2] *Ibid.* p. 239. [3] *Ibid.* p. 223.
[4] *Ibid.* p. 224. [5] *Ibid.* p. 224. [6] *Ibid.* p. 224.

As terrors of the night Nashe lists the "scritch-owle" "for her lavish babbling of forbidden secrets"; the nightingale that "puts us in minde of the end and punishment of lust and ravishment"; and the croaking frogs that remind us "we are but slime and mud".[1]

Such quotations might be multiplied almost indefinitely, but the main lines of argument remain the same. Either the strange appearances which come as ghosts to men are the spirits of the dead released to return temporarily to earth, or they are the feigned appearances used by the devil and his angels, or they are the fantastic forgeries of men's minds induced by melancholy or by passion. But it was of witches that King James wrote more especially. And the definition of a witch which was given by Gyffard in *A Discourse of the Subtill Practises of Devilles by Witches and Sorcerers* seems to fulfill the notions of the witch-hunters:

A Witch is one that woorketh by the Devill, or by some develish or curious art, either hurting or healing, revealing thinges secrete, or foretelling thinges to come, which the devil hath devised to entangle and snare mens soules withal unto damnation.[2]

And opposed to this notion of witchcraft was the contention that witches too were merely melancholy persons, for the most part melancholy old women, self-deceived by their own melancholic imaginations.

But it must be remembered that even the Devil's advocates thought that passions and melancholic humours paved the way for the visits of the Devil in disguise, and that the advocates of natural causes saw in these supernatural visitations the evidences of a mind diseased, generally through the ravages of passion. It will thus become apparent why in any English Renaissance tragedy of passion it was appropriate that ghosts and witches should appear.

[1] Nashe, *op. cit.* p. 282.
[2] "*A Discourse of the Subtill Practises of Devilles by Witches and Sorcerers.* By G. Gyfford. 1587". Cf. chapter ii for the discussion of witches.

CHAPTER X

Virtues and Vices.   Mortal and Venial Sin.
Happiness and Misery

THE curious result of mingling the teaching of Plato and Aristotle and Christ with the teaching of all their derivatives, of attempting to psychologize the teachings of all these alike on the basis of Hippocrates and Galen and their derivatives again is nowhere more clearly evident than in the treatment of virtue and happiness.[1] The clear-cut thinking of Thomas Aquinas was gone, but the effect of his intricate analysis of the relation of the passions to sin was apparent in most of the Renaissance discussions of virtue. The whole treatment of virtue was chaotic, mere echoes of earlier and often discordant thinking. But there was always an insistent moral note in the discussion of passion and a determined habit of applying moral judgment to all matters.

The fundamental division of virtue in the sixteenth century seems to have been persistently Aristotelian, virtue being both intellectual and moral, or as the facts were stated in *The French Academie*:

[There is] a double discourse of reason in man: whereof the one is *Theoricall* and *Speculative*, which hath *Trueth* for his ende, and having found it goeth no farther. The other is *Practicall*, having *Good* for his end, which being found it stayeth not there, but passeth forward to the *Will*, which God hath joyned unto it, to the end it should love, desire and follow after the *Good*, and contrariwise hate eschew and turne away from evill.[2]

[1] A very interesting study of a related subject is to be found in an article by Professor L. I. Bredvold, "The Religious Thought of Donne in Relation to Mediaeval and Later Traditions", published in *Studies in Shakespeare, Milton, and Donne*, which constitutes vol. I of the *University of Michigan Publications in Language and Literature.* Cf. pp. 191 *sqq.*
[2] *The French Academie*, 1594 ed. p. 171.

The realm of moral virtue was defined in the accepted words of Plutarch:

> My purpose is to treate of that vertue, which is both called and also reputed Morall, and namely wherein it differeth especially from vertue contemplative: as having for the subject matter thereof, the passions of the minde, and for the forme, Reason.[1]

The explanation of this definition can be understood from Thomas Aquinas:

> The sensitive appetite is related to the will, which is the rational appetite, through being moved by it. And therefore the act of the appetitive power is consummated in the sensitive appetite: and for this reason the sensitive appetite is the subject of virtue.[2]

Aristotle had pointed out that intellectual virtue came largely through teaching, moral virtue through habit. Aquinas said that

> the virtue which is in the irascible and concupiscible powers, is nothing else but a certain habitual conformity of these powers to reason.[3]

The Renaissance was inclined, it would seem, to discuss the question whether virtue is in man by nature or by habit, for Bacon lists this question among the profitless discussions of philosophy.

To quote Wylkinson's Aristotle:

> In the solle of man are three thynges habite power, and passions. Passions be these, Joye, desire, love, envy, and hate: the powers be natural by the whyche we may do the foresaidthinges. Habyte is where a man is praised or dispraysed, then I say that vertue is no power nor passyon but habite.[4]

At times it would seem that the idea of virtue becomes in this confusion of teaching not merely virtue as habit but habitual virtue.

---

[1] "Of Moral Vertue", in Holland's Plutarch, *Morals*, p. 64.

[2] *The "Summa Theologica" of St Thomas Aquinas.* Literally translated by Fathers of the English Dominican Province, vol. VII, p. 82.

[3] *Ibid.* vol. VII, p. 79.

[4] Chapter xii.

The most often reiterated definition of virtue throughout the sixteenth century was that of temperance and moderation. Sir Thomas Elyot said:

The last of thynges called not naturall, is not the leaste parte to be considered, the whyche is of affects and passions of the mynde. For if they be immoderate, they do not onely anoy the body and shorten the lyfe, but also they doo appayre, and sometyme lose utterlye a mans estymation. And that moche more is, they brynge a man from the use of reason, and some tyme in the dyspleasure of almighty god.[1]

Wylkinson translated Aristotle:

Vertues be founde in thynges that have a meane betwene extremeties, which are ether to muche or to little.[2]

Wilson's *Arte of Rhetorique* explained:

Temperance, is a measuring of affections according to the will of reason, and a subduing of lust unto the Square of honestie. Yea, and what one thing doth soone mitigate the immoderate passions of our nature, then the perfect knowledge of right & wrong, & the just execution appointed by a law, for asswaging the wilfull? Of this vertue are three partes.

Sobrietie　　　　Gentlenesse　　　　Modestie[3]

The Holland translation of Plutarch discussed the nature of the mean:

But now, forasmuch as this terme of Meane or Mediocritie may be understoode diverse waies, we are to set downe what kind of meane this Morall vertue is.[4]

Very clearly it is not a mixture of two vices, as some have misunderstood it to be.

Even so, morall vertue being a motion and facultie about the unreasonable part of the soule, tempereth the remission and intention; and in one word taketh away the excesse and defect of the passions, reducing ech of them to a certaine Mediocritie and moderation that falleth not on any side.[5]

[1] Sir Thomas Elyot, *op. cit.* p. 64.
[2] Wylkinson, *op. cit.* chapter xiii.
[3] Sir Thomas Wilson, *The Arte of Rhetorique*. Reprint, Tudor and Stuart Library, 1919, p. 35.
[4] "Of Moral Vertue", in Holland's Plutarch, *Morals*, p. 68.
[5] *Ibid.* p. 69.

Sir William Cornwallis in his *Discourses upon Seneca the Tragedian* wrote, commenting upon the phrase which begins the quotation:

> *Miserrimum est timere, cum speres nihil.*

It is an observation worthy of regard to contemplate how the bodie of man is equally poysed with affections; he hath hope and feare, love and hate, and so the rest, every contrary hath his contrary, but in such an equallitie, as hee goeth right up in these extremities; and the minde doth well amongst these, as the bodies constitution consisting of dissenting elements, so long hath health, as these parts of his are without an extraordinary preeminence: but when any affection in the minde, or any humour in the body, usurps an over-swaying authoritie, the body languisheth, and the minde thinks it selfe miserable.[1]

To multiply quotations is useless, however, for this aspect of virtue as the golden mean is most frequently the one which is emphasized to the point of ignoring all other considerations.

Yet another important aspect of virtue lay in the consideration of the ends to be served. Thomas Rogers wrote:

And therefore, to be angrie, to covet, to lust, is no offence, but to be an angrie, a covetous, and a lecherous man, deserveth great reproche. For he which is an angrye man, is moved, when he should not: and he which is covetous, desyreth which he ought not: and the lecherous hunteth after that which is unlawfull.[2]

Stressing again this matter of the necessity of passions if we are to have virtue at all, he continued:

And therefore as that water which is alwayes standing, and never runneth, must needs bee noysome and infectious: so that man, which is never moved in mind, can never be eyther good to himselfe, or profitable to others. But have them we must, and use them we maye (and that aboundantly) in honest wyse. And therefore the ende of our affections, make them eyther good, and so to be commended: or bad, & therefore to be dispraised.[3]

[1] These discourses are bound with *A Second Part of Essayes*, 1601. Cf. A 7 *verso*.

[2] *A Philosophicall Discourse, Entituled, The Anatomie of the Minde.* Newlie made and set forth by T(homas) R(ogers). B ii, *verso*.

[3] *Ibid.* B iii.

And indeed something of this definition of virtue is implied in all considerations of the control of the passions by reason, since reason judges the ends to be served in reasonable and hence virtuous action. Rogers further defines reason, then, instancing Cicero as authority, to be "an order to do all things, by the consideration of things to come".

The summarizing statement of Aquinas was, indeed, generally accepted:

> The passions of the soul, in so far as they are contrary to the order of reason, incline us to sin: but in so far as they are controlled by reason, they pertain to virtue.[1]

However, the consideration of virtue was during the sixteenth century, as before and since, often converted into a consideration of the virtues. The Platonic virtues vied in popularity with the seven cardinal virtues opposed to the seven deadly sins.

Thomas Aquinas had given the Platonic virtues as prudence, pertaining to reason; justice pertaining to the will; fortitude and temperance to the irascible and concupiscible parts of the sensitive appetite respectively; but this distinction was not, as far as I have been able to observe, much considered during the Renaissance. Prudence was, of course, necessarily a virtue which had to do with the decisions of the reasonable soul. Fortitude was often confused with courage and was itself considered more often as a passion than as a virtue. Justice and to an even greater degree temperance were the chief concern of the moral philosophers. Thus on the one hand Bryskett wrote of:

> Thus holding under reasons awe the disordinate appetites of his mind, with the direct rule of justice, (under which, *Plato* saith, all virtues are contained, because it is grounded upon truth)....[2]

[1] *Summa Theologica*, vol. VI, p. 296.
[2] Lodovico Bryskett, *A Discourse of Civill Life. Containing the Ethicke part of Morall Philosophie*, 1606. Cf. p. 86. The whole treatise is, of course, most important, but I have quoted from it sparingly because it comes late in Shakespeare's life and is confessedly a rehearsal of Italian treatises rather than the traditional English philosophy.

And also he said that the man of fortitude could only be esteemed such if he could "hold a meane betweene furie and feare", thus making fortitude also become the ability to temper passion. This preoccupation with temperance is one of the most interesting characteristics of the time.

The next consideration in regard to virtue was that of decorum, and that decorum was in drama not a law of aesthetic theory but a law of moral philosophy has not generally been recognized. Yet if we understand decorum as the Renaissance understood it, we will see it as a matter of great moral significance, treated in practically every work on moral philosophy. The secret seems to lie in the much reverenced and frequently cited passage in Cicero's *De Officiis*, in which he treated the subject of decorum, asserting definitely that "it is inseparable from moral goodness; for what is proper is morally right, and what is morally right is proper". After discussing the general propriety to be found in moral goodness as a whole and the propriety which is related to each of the cardinal virtues in particular, Cicero's treatise discussed propriety not only as it was concerned with man as man but also as it was involved in the discussion of duty and the individual. It is here that we find his discussion of the duties of men in relation to their different temperaments, their time of life, their environment by Nature and Fortune.[1]

Thus there arise in these works of moral philosophy discussions not only of the races of men and the estates of men but also prolonged considerations of the different ages of man—four, five, six, or seven—in their relation to passions and to virtuous action.

Virtue was thought, then, to be habit; virtue was thought to be the mean between extremes; virtue was thought to be conduct determined by the obedience of the passions to

[1] Cicero, *De Officiis*. Transl. by Professor Walter Miller for the Loeb Classical Library. Cf. Bk. I, xxvii ff.

reason; virtue was thought of as virtues; virtue was thought of as propriety.

But there was always the complementary consideration of vice and sin. And here it is necessary to recognize the older Catholic teaching in regard to venial and mortal sins in their relation to the passions, as well as to recognize the teaching of the pagan philosophers in regard to the rational and the sensible souls. For both considerations entered into the thinking of the Renaissance.

It will be recalled that the will was thought to reside in the rational soul, to be, in fact, the rational appetite, while the passions reside in the sensible soul and are the sensible appetite. The passions, then, make, so to speak, representations to the understanding, which when judged, are referred to the will for action, and are by the will passed on again to the passions. The will may be misdirected through ignorance or through error. And as I have already said, the passions may, according to the Renaissance authorities, blind the understanding or pervert the will as well as cause alteration of humours and bring about maladies and diseases. Sin, therefore, as the result of passion may arise through either cause, blindness of understanding, or perversion of the will. And the Church was interested in the difference in the nature of sin.

Thomas Aquinas defined the difference between venial and mortal sin:

Now the difference between venial and mortal sin is consequent to the diversity of that inordinateness which constitutes the notion of sin. For inordinateness is two-fold, one that destroys the principle of order, and another which, without destroying the principle of order, implies inordinateness in the things which follow the principle:

Such is the difference between death and disease in animals.

Therefore when the soul is so disordered by sin as to turn away from its last end, viz. God, to Whom it is united by charity, there is mortal sin; but when it is disordered without turning away from God, there is venial sin.[1]

Aquinas pointed out repeatedly that mortal sin is imputed to the reason only, not to sensuality, but he made it clear that not only the will but all those powers which can be moved to their acts or restrained from their acts by the will are to be judged morally. Reason sins in not knowing truth, and it also sins in commanding inordinate movements of passion or in failing to check them. When passion is very intense, the use of reason may be lost altogether, and then reason may judge in the particular case against the knowledge which it has in general. But in spite of the fact that Aquinas discussed in detail all the problems of the relation of passion to venial and mortal sin, the distinction was not always made explicit. However, Chaucer wrote in his *Parson's Tale* of anger:

Now understondeth that wikked ire is in two maneres, that is to seyn, sodeyn ire or hastif ire withouten avisement and consentynge of resoun. The menyng and the sens of this is, that the resoun of man ne consente nat to thilke sodeyn ire; and thanne it is venial. Another ire is ful wikked, that comth of felonie of herte, avysed and cast biforn with wikked wil to do vengeance, and therto his resoun consenteth; and soothly this is deedly synne.

The contemporaries of Shakespeare had been brought up on this doctrine of venial and mortal sin, or at least their religious teachers had been brought up on it in the Catholic Church, and no matter how much the Protestant fashion might change the terminology of its expression, the doctrine was persistently influential, for it was deeply imbedded in the thinking of the men who did think. And the distinction expressed by Chaucer's parson indicates the line of cleavage generally assumed.

Thus it was that passion was conceived as clouding the understanding so that judgment could not be well made,

[1] *Summa Theologica*, vol. VII, p. 285.

or as swaying the will by impetuous summons, and thus leading to sin that brought evil upon innocent and guilty alike. But this sin is still a sin that is presented sympathetically.

Further, passion might be so excessive that reason would be through the effect of passion on the humours altogether lost. Then no moral judgment could be given. But that is not to say that the effect of passion in bringing on these abnormal states of unreason was not bringing about its own punishment.

Finally, however, passion might pervert the will, so that it maliciously willed that which it willed. Reason was itself perverted in such a case, and since the "inordinateness" thus destroyed the very principle of order, the sin was mortal.

This distinction it is absolutely necessary to make if we are to see the difference between the villain and the tragic hero in Shakespeare. The tragic hero sins under the influence of passion, his reason failing to check his passion. His passion may lead him to madness, but as long as his passion is in conflict with reason, he has not committed mortal sin. When, however, passion has taken possession of his will, has perverted his will, when in perfect accord with passion his reason directs evil through the will, then we have a villain, one who is dyed in sin, and one whose sin is mortal.

In any case, whatever the vagaries of fortune, happiness is conditioned upon virtue. In the passage already quoted from Plutarch, the truth of the matter is seen:

but wickednesse ingendering within it selfe...displeasure and punishment, not after a sinfull act is committed, but even at the very instant of committing, it beginneth to suffer the pain due to the offence.... [1]

Elsewhere Plutarch said:

But in the soule it is not possible that there should bee engendred anie mirth, joy and contentment, unlesse the first foundation be laied

[1] Cf. Section I, chapter i, *ante.*

in peace of conscience, and tranquillitie of spirit, void of feare, and enjoying a setled calme in all assurance and confidence, without any shew of tempest toward.[1]

Newton in *The Touchstone of Complexions* wrote (or translated):

The mynd therefore must be reined by reason, and curbed by temperaunce, that it yelde not to affections, but procure to it selfe quietnes & tranquility, which (as Tullie witnesseth) is the chiefest poynt that helpeth us in this life to live wel and happely.[2]

Thomas Wright wrote:

Hereby wee may conclude, that Passions well used, may consist with wisdom against the Stoickes; and if they be moderated, to be very serviceable to vertue; if they be abused, and overruled by sinne, to be the nurcerie of vices, and pathway to all wickednesse.[3]

Sir William Cornwallis summed up the whole in less academic language in his essay "Of Affection" printed in *A second part of Essayes* in 1601; for he proclaimed the fact that reason is given to man to purchase virtue with. And he added:

All that I have heard, all that I have read, all that by any meanes hath come to my knowledge performed well, hath beene where Reason hath made Affection his servant: contrariwise, destructions, dishonours, dangers, have beene inforced by the tyrannie of Pride, Disdaine, Hate, Selfe-love, or some other of those Affections unrestrained: so can I fetch Calamitie frome none other originall but this; nor happinesse but from the deprivation of this frailtie.[4]

[1] "Of Vertue and Vice", in Holland's Plutarch, *Morals*. Cf. p. 80.
[2] Newton, *op. cit.* p. 60.
[3] Wright, *op. cit.* chapter iv. 1604 ed. pp. 18, 19. 1601 ed. pp. 33, 34.
[4] Cornwallis, *A second part of Essayes*, "Of Affection"; Essay 26.

CHAPTER XI

Nosce Teipsum. *How to know Men*

THE absorbing problem of the Renaissance, knowledge of one's self, led men into the attempt to know man and to know men. And how to know men became an all-embracing question, the answer to which involved a vast and comprehensive knowledge. Aristotle's *Physiognomonica* was basic in this knowledge, and this work was posited upon the assumption that mental character and bodily condition were mutually sympathetic and influential. We have already seen that this assumption was one acceptable to Renaissance writers. Aristotle proposed, then, that the study of men be made first on the basis of their resemblance to different beasts, since the characteristics of different beasts can be posited. The second method which he proposed was the study of racial characteristics and the study of individuals as they resemble in their characteristics certain defined race types. The third method which he suggested was the study of men to see how they bear permanently those marks which have come to be recognized as distinguishing men under the influence of clearly defined passions. Furthermore, Aristotle suggested that we may consider those character-istics or passions which are usually found together, and that we may hence infer the presence of unknown factors from those that are known. We may also infer much as to the male and the female natures from the assumption that men as compared with women are hot and dry; that women as compared with men are cold and moist, and also from the assumption that the lion typifies the masculine nature and the panther the feminine.

In the *Rhetoric* Aristotle also pointed out that it is neces-sary to study passions and moral qualities of men in relation to their ages and their fortunes. That Cicero and Horace were likewise used as authority to attest the importance of such study we have already seen.

To know men, then, in the Renaissance was to study both morals and manners according to something like the following scheme:

The likeness of men and animals: this study was the basis of the study of physiognomy during the Renaissance. It was the basis upon which the art of mimetic representation was built up in the art of acting, as I hope to show in another work.

The differences between men and women: this study was built up on the assumptions just mentioned and was very important in the general consideration of decorum.

The temperaments or complexions of men: this study concerned, as has been pointed out, the study of the hot and cold and moist and dry types; and the compound types, the sanguine, phlegmatic, choleric, and melancholy. It also included the study of racial types.

The different ages of man: the number of periods into which the life of man is divided were variously judged on the basis of ancient authority as three, four, five, six, and seven. Jaques, and therefore presumably Shakespeare, accepted seven. The important fact is that certain qualities, certain humours, certain passions are proper for each of the ages, and decorum demands that this propriety be observed. As the famous passage of Whetstone's dedication to *Promos and Cassandra* explained:

> For to worke a Commedie kindly, grave old men, should instruct: yonge men, should showe the imperfections of youth: Strumpets should be lascivious: Boyes unhappy: and Clownes, should speake disorderlye:

The varying gifts of fortune: these gifts Aristotle listed under the headings of *birth*, *wealth*, and *power*, and these were recognized as the general basis of classification.

The passions of men: the passions of men must then be

Tranquilla frons.

QVI *serenam, & exporrectam habent frontem, assentatores, ab effectu huiusmodi reddere consueto. Hoc signum in canibus manifestum est, quod assentantes frontem exporrigant. Aristoteles in Physiognomonicis. Intelligendo de domesticis canibus. Albertus ab eo. Qui laxam, & tanquam ridentem habent frontis cutem, blandi quidem, sed non innoxij, sunt enim palam blandientes, clam detractores.*

Tauri, & leonis nubilam frontem hac figura pinximus cum humana, cuiusmodi irati efformare solent ne quid indiligentia, & obseruationis contra nos criminatum sit.

H   *A*   Nebu-

PLATE X. A page from the *De Humana Physiognomonia* of Giovanni Baptista Porta, 1586.

considered not only in themselves but also in their relation to men of different races, complexions, humours, qualities, sexes, ages, fortunes.

The great Thomas Betterton is said to have written in a tract on *The Duty of a Player*, which was found among his papers, the following:

But the Action of a Player is, what is agreeable to Personation or the Subject he represents. Now what he represents is Man in his various Characters, Manners, and Passions, and to these Heads he must adjust every Action; he must perfectly express the Quality and Manners of the Man whose Person he assumes, that is, he must know how his Manners are compounded, and from thence know the several Features, as I may call them, of his Passions. A Patriot, a Prince, a Beggar, a Clown, &c. must each have their Propriety, and Distinction in Action as well as Words and Language.... Sometimes he is to be a Lover, and know not only all the soft and tender Addresses of one, but what are proper to the Character of Him who is in Love, whether he be a Prince or a Peasant, a hot or fiery Man, or of more moderate and flegmatic Constitution, and even the Degrees of the Passion he is possessed with.[1]

But to know the different Compositions of the Manners and the Passions springing from those Manners, he ought to have an Insight into Moral Philosophy.... [2]

This treatise then suggested as models the works of history painters, Le Brun in particular:

Jordan of Antwerp, in a Piece of our Saviour's being taken from the Cross, which is now in his Grace the Duke of Marlborough's Hands, the Passion of Grief is expressed with a wonderful Variety; the Grief of the Virgin-Mother is in all the Extremity of Agony, that is consistent with life; nay, indeed, that scarce leaves any Signs of remaining Life to her; that of St. Mary Magdalen is an extreme Grief, but mingled with Love and Tenderness, which she always expressed, after her Conversion, for our blessed Lord; then the grief of St. John the

[1] *The History of the English Stage. From the Restauration to the Present Time.* By Mr Thomas Betterton. Printed for E. Curll, 1741. Cf. pp. 47, 48.

[2] *Ibid.* p. 49.

Evangelist is strong but manly and mixed with the Tenderness of perfect Friendship; and, that of Joseph of Arimathea, suitable to his Years and Love for Christ, more solemn, more contracted in himself, yet forcing an Apeearance in his Looks.[1]

That Betterton here explained not only the ideal method for the actor but also the actual method used to present men in the plays of the greatest dramatist of all time I am fully convinced. It is to the proof of this theory that I turn in my next section, a study of Shakespeare's four great tragedies.

[1] Betterton, *op. cit.* pp. 49, 50.

SECTION III

Mirrors of Passion

CHAPTER XII

Hamlet: *A Tragedy of Grief*

HAMLET has suffered from an exegesis so minute and so diffuse and varied that essential facts have become commonplaces of criticism without their full significance ever being recognized. And indeed it is almost as hard to read *Hamlet* freshly as to read the Sermon on the Mount as though it were a document and not a collection of texts for sermons. Yet I believe that if *Hamlet* is read against a background of contemporary philosophy, it will come to life as a study in passion, rather obviously constructed to show the profound truth of its dominant idea:

> What to ourselves in passion we propose,
> The passion ending, doth the purpose lose,
> The violence of either grief or joy
> Their own enactures with themselves destroy.
> Where joy most revels, grief doth most lament;
> Grief joys, joy grieves, on slender accident.[1]

But the method which Shakespeare has pursued in his study of passion is here the same as in his other tragedies, a method described in the words of Betterton quoted earlier;[2] persons of different temperaments are shown under the influence of the same passion, so that we may see the passion variously manifested. And as everyone is fully aware, the play of Hamlet is concerned with the story of three young men—Hamlet, Fortinbras, and Laertes—each called upon to mourn the death of a father, each feeling himself summoned to revenge wrongs suffered by his father. Grief in each for the loss of his father is succeeded by the desire for revenge. But each must act according to the dictates of his own temperament and his own humour.

[1] III, ii. 204–9.   [2] Cf. Section II, chapter xi.

The fundamental problem that Shakespeare undertook to answer in *Hamlet*, then, is the problem of the way men accept sorrow when it comes to them. And it is evident throughout the play that the grief of Fortinbras is being presented as a grief dominated by reason, while it is equally evident that the grief of Hamlet and Laertes is excessive grief leading to destruction. That Hamlet himself saw in these two other young men his own image, is of course, evident. Of the resolute Fortinbras he exclaims in self-reproach:

> How all occasions do inform against me,
> And spur my dull revenge!...
>   Examples gross as earth exhort me;
> Witness this army of such mass and charge
> Led by a delicate and tender prince,
> Whose spirit with divine ambition puff'd
> Makes mouths at the invisible event,
> Exposing what is mortal and unsure
> To all that fortune, death, and danger dare,
> Even for an egg-shell. Rightly to be great
> Is not to stir without great argument,
> But greatly to find quarrel in a straw
> When honour's at the stake.[1]

And of Laertes he says regretfully:

> For, by the image of my cause, I see
> The portraiture of his.[2]

That these three young men were of different temperaments is at once apparent. Young Fortinbras is of a northern race, of phlegmatic or possibly of sanguine humour, young, acting steadfastly in pursuance of a plan, regaining lands and honour lost by his father, unmoved by danger, moved by divine ambition and honour.

In many respects and by nature Hamlet is like Fortinbras, but he has been changed by grief into something different. And since Hamlet has of late so often been assumed to be of

[1] IV, iv, 32–56.   [2] V, ii, 77, 78.

PLATE XI. Illustration from the title-page of *The Mirror of Man's Life*, 1576.

the melancholy humour,[1] it is perhaps well to question this assumption somewhat at length. He is a young prince of Denmark, and that Shakespeare accepted the traditional characteristics of the northern peoples and of the Danes especially seems to be indicated in Hamlet's speech concerning the drunkenness of his people. In the northern nations the cold and moist humours must prevail, either phlegm or blood. Furthermore Hamlet is of "too, too solid flesh", and even after the time of his deep grief, the Queen still says of him, "He's fat, and scant of breath". He has been in attendance at the University of Wittenberg, but there is no indication that he has been considered a pale and melancholy student; rather he has been on good terms with the players, he has been friendly with his fellows. Of late, so he explains to Rosencrantz, he has lost all mirth, forgone all custom of exercise, failed to find delight in nature or in man. But these are changes noteworthy because they are changes. And similarly Ophelia's lament must be considered:

> O, what a noble mind is here o'erthrown!
> The courtier's, soldier's, scholar's, eye, tongue, sword;
> The expectancy and rose of the fair state,
> The glass of fashion and the mould of form,
> The observ'd of all observers, quite, quite down![2]

Finally he himself says in his challenging cry to Laertes:

> For, though I am not splenitive and rash,
> Yet have I something in me dangerous,
> Which let thy wiseness fear.[3]

---

[1] The latest summary is that by Mary I. O'Sullivan, *Hamlet and Dr Timothy Bright*, P.M.L.A. vol. XLI, pp. 667–9. Miss O'Sullivan seems, however, not to have realized that Bright made fundamental distinctions between melancholy and melancholy adust. Cf. Section II, chapter vii, *ante*.

[2] III, i, 158–62.

[3] V, i, 284–6.

And if he were melancholy, he must be splenitive. Unless I am greatly mistaken, Shakespeare never trifled with his audience in this fashion; instead, every character in a Shakespearean play is engaged in saying exactly what Shakespeare wanted the audience to know and in saying it over and over again. If a man is a villain, he says so, and everyone else says so. It is quite safe to trust the characters to tell the truth about themselves. Our problem is to read the words as they spoke them and not as we would speak them to-day with different meaning. But in the language of Shakespeare's day it seems certain that Hamlet was not a man of natural melancholy humour.

Instead Hamlet seems quite clearly to be of the sanguine humour, which was characteristically described in *The Optick Glasse of Humors* in 1607:

> They that are of this complection are very affable in speech, and have a gracious faculty in their delivery, much addicted to witty conceits, to a scholerlike εὐτραπελία, being *facetosi*, not *acetosi*: quipping without bitter taunting: hardly taking anything in dogeon, except they be greatly moved, with disgrace especially: wisely seeming eyther to take a thing sometimes more offensively, or lesse greivously then they do, cloaking their true passion: they bee liberally minded; they carry a constant loving affection to them chiefly unto whom they be endeared, and with whom they are intimate, and chained in the links of true amitie, never giving over till death such a converst friend, except on a capitall discontent....
>
> Their weakness is in being somewhat given to "venery"; otherwise the man of sanguine humour
>
> is never lightly variable: but beeing proudly harnest with a steely hart, he will run upon the push of great danger, yea, hazard his life against all the affronts of death itselfe: if it stand ether with the honour of his soveraigne, the welfare and quiet of his own country, the after fame and renowne of himselfe: else is he chary and wary to lay himselfe open to any daunger, if the final end of his endeavour and toile bee not plausible in his demurring judgement.[1]

[1] Thomas Walkington, *The Optick Glasse of Humors*, pp. 59, 60.

The picture of a man of sanguine humour seems to me to be applicable to Hamlet in all essential details. Indeed, I have read no analysis of Hamlet's character which seems so consistently to sum up his character as do these typical descriptions of the man of sanguine humour. Furthermore, blood makes a man of too, too solid flesh,[1] and no melancholy man was ever fat, as King James rightly argued.

But at the beginning of the play Hamlet is changed from his natural humour through excessive grief. The King tells Rosencrantz:

> ...not the exterior nor the inward man
> Resembles that it was.[2]

He is become melancholy, but his is the unnatural melancholy induced by passion, and his melancholy is inevitably the sanguine adust, the characteristics of which we have already seen.

Laertes, unlike Hamlet, is a man of hot complexion. He has been in France rather than in Wittenberg. He is of the choleric humour.[3]

It is characteristic of Shakespeare that he treats the passion of grief in all its possibilities, that he embodies in different characters the different phases of the passion that he wishes to present, and that he discusses the physiological and psychological aspects of the passion, together with the particular moral problems which interested his period, and which were most closely related to the passion anatomized in this particular work. With the passion of grief as the passion to be studied, it was almost inevitable that there should first arise, then, the practical problem of moral philosophy which we have already seen was of persistent interest to the Renaissance, the problem of consolation in grief, the problem of consolation for evil.[4]

Of the fundamental differences in the way in which the

---

[1] Cf. p. 57, *ante.*   [2] II, ii, 6, 7.
[3] Cf. pp. 58, 61, *ante.*   [4] Cf. Section I, chapter i.

passion of grief affects men, much was written, but the words of Sir Thomas More in *A Dyalogue of Comforte agaynst Tribulacyon* explain the essential difference between the grief of two sorts of men, and the sin inherent in each sort of excessive grief:

And here shall I note you two kyndes of folke that are in tribulacion and heavines. One sorte that will seeke for no coumforte, another sorte that will. And yet of those that will not, are there also two sortes. For first one sorte there are, that are so drowned in sorowe, that they falle into a carelesse deaddelye dulnesse, regarding nothing, thinking almost of nothing, no more then if they laye in a letarge, with whiche it may so falle, that witte and remembrance wil weare awaye, and falle even fayre from them. And this comfortles kind of heavinesse in tribulacion, is the highest kind of the deadly sinne of slouth. Another sorte are there, that will seeke for no coumforte, nor yet none receive, but are in their tribulacion (be it losse or sickenes) so testie, so fumythe, and so farre oute of all pacience, that it booteth no man to speake to them, and these are in a maner with impacience, as furious as though they wer in halfe a frenesye, and may with a custome of such fashioned behaveour, falle in therto full and whole. And this kynd of heavinesse in tribulacyon, is even a mischievous hygh braunche of the mortall sinne of yre. [1]

The grief that seeks for consolation is thus put on the one side; on the other is the grief that does not seek for consolation; and this latter inconsolable grief may result either in dullness and loss of memory and in the sin of sloth, or in hasty anger and rashness, and in the sin of ire. That Shakespeare recognized this same essential difference in the possible effects of inconsolable grief is evident in such advice as Malcolm gives to Macduff in *Macbeth*:

> ...let grief
> Convert to anger; blunt not the heart, enrage it. [2]

And that he embodied these possibilities in the three young men represented in this tragedy seems certain. Fortinbras is

[1] Bk. I, chapter iii. Bound with the *Utopia* in Everyman's Library ed. Cf. p. 134.

[2] *Macbeth*, IV, iii, 228, 229.

guided by reason; he is not the victim of his grief. Hamlet is inconsolable, and his grief is of the sort that renders him dull, that effaces memory, that makes him guilty of the sin of sloth. Laertes is neither to be consoled nor to be appeased. His grief converts to anger. He enrages his heart.

Since this tragedy is, then, a study in grief, it was inevitable that Shakespeare begin the study with the emphasis on the pair of passions traditionally yoked as opposites, joy and grief. Just as in *Romeo and Juliet* he opened with variations on the love-hate theme, so here the King's first speech presents the joy-grief theme for which the funeral baked-meats that set out the marriage feast have given just occasion:

> Though yet of Hamlet our dear brother's death
> The memory be green, and that it us befitted
> To bear our hearts in *grief*, and our whole kingdom
> To be contracted in one *brow of woe*,
> Yet so far hath discretion fought with nature
> That we with *wisest sorrow* think on him
> Together with remembrance of ourselves.
> Therefore our sometime sister, now our queen,
> The imperial jointress of this warlike state,
> Have we, as 'twere with a *defeated joy*,—
> With *one auspicious* and *one dropping eye*,
> With *mirth in funeral* and with *dirge in marriage*,
> In equal scale weighing *delight and dole*,—
> Taken to wife.[1]

It would seem that the wisdom here exalted by the King has consisted in trying to find the mean between the extremes by mixing them, and as Plutarch said, virtue is not to be considered as the mixture of two vices. At any rate, the joy-grief theme is sounded clearly.

But as Hamlet comes to his first interview with the King, we sense the real significance of the play in the challenge of philosophy to passion, of consolation to grief. Both King and Queen remonstrate with the too much grieving son of a

[1] *Hamlet*, I, ii, 1–14.

father dead and a mother already married. Even as Seneca
wrote to Polybius:

> It is therefore a great comfort for a man to bethinke himselfe that
> the same hath hapned unto him, which all others have suffered before
> him, and all that follow him must endure,[1]

so the Queen proffers Hamlet this consolation of philosophy:

> Thou know'st 't is common; all that lives must die,
> Passing through nature to eternity.[2]

And Hamlet accepts the consolation offered, "Ay, madam,
it is common". But yet he fails to be comforted, and his
next speech is a cry of passion, of grief that will not be consoled:

> 'T is not alone my inky cloak, good mother,
> Nor customary suits of solemn black,
> Nor windy suspiration of forc'd breath,
> No, nor the fruitful river in the eye,
> Nor the dejected haviour of the visage,
> Together with all forms, moods, shows of grief,
> That can denote me truly. These indeed seem,
> For they are actions that a man might play;
> But I have that within which passeth show,
> These but the trappings and the suits of woe.[3]

The King therefore takes up the burden of the philosophic
discourse, a discourse for which he had excellent authority.
Wise Seneca said to Marcia:

> But yet there is a natural inclination in us to bewaile those whom
> wee love, who denies it as long as it is moderate?[4]

And he further remonstrated:

> Whence grow wee therefore so obstinate in our complaints, if
> this that is done, bee not by the commandement of nature.[5]

[1] "Of Comfort. Addressed by Lucius Annaeus Seneca to Polybius", in Lodge, transl. of Seneca, p. 692.
[2] I, ii, 72, 73.   [3] I, ii, 77–86.
[4] "Of Consolation. Written by Lucius Annaeus Seneca to Marcia",
in Lodge, transl. of Seneca, p. 714.
[5] *Ibid.* p. 715.

PLATE XII. Illustration from Lydgate, *The daunce of Machabree wherin is lively expressed and shewed the state of manne, and howe he is called at uncertayne tymes by death, and when he thinketh least theron.* (Printed with *The Falles of Princes*, 1554.)

Plutarch, too, when he offered consolation to Apollonius for the death of his son reasoned well that we must accept our fortune, for loss is the common experience of men, and he counselled temperance in grief:

Now to sorow and be touched to the quicke for the losse of a sonne, is a passion that ariseth from a naturall cause, and it is not in our power to avoid;...Yet do I not allow that a man should suffer himselfe to be transported and caried away beyond all compasse & measure, making no end of sorow; for even that also is likewise unnaturall, and proceedeth from a corrupt and erronious opinion that we have: and therefore, as we ought to abandon this excesse as simply naught, hurtfull, and not beseeming vertuous and honest minded men;...reason would therefore, that wise men in these and such like crosses, cary themselves, neither void of affections altogether, nor yet out of measure passionate;...[1]

In such fashion the King comforts Hamlet:

> 'T is sweet and commendable in your nature, Hamlet,
> To give these mourning duties to your father.
> But, you must know, your father lost a father;
> That father lost, lost his; and the survivor bound
> In filial obligation for some term
> To do obsequious sorrow. But to persever
> In obstinate condolement is a course
> Of impious stubbornness; 't is unmanly grief;
> It shows a will most incorrect to heaven,
> A heart unfortified, a mind impatient,
> An understanding simple and unschool'd;
> For what we know must be, and is as common
> As any the most vulgar thing to sense,
> Why should we in our peevish opposition
> Take it to heart? Fie! 't is a fault to heaven,
> A fault against the dead, a fault to nature,
> To reason most absurd, whose common theme
> Is death of fathers, and who still hath cried,
> From the first corse till he that died to-day,
> "This must be so".[2]

[1] "A Consolatorie oration sent to Apollonius", in Holland's Plutarch, *Morals*, p. 510.
[2] I, ii, 87–106.

The translator of Plutarch[1] in his preface to his letter to Apollonius was careful to note that the consolation offered was "not sufficient to set the minde and spirit of man in true repose", and his opinion is confirmed by Hamlet's reaction to the King's speech, reflected in the following soliloquy, for this soliloquy is again a cry of passion disregarding the message of consolation offered by philosophy through the King.

But in order to see the significance of this soliloquy in its presentation of passion, it must be remembered that, as has already been said, the play opens when Hamlet has already become the victim of his passion, and we now see the results of passion which *The French Academie* described, recording of the heart in grief:

> Therefore it trembleth and languisheth, as a sicke body, who drying up with griefe by little and little, in the end dieth, except hee have some remedy against his sickenesse. For the like happeneth to the heart of man through griefe as long as it is within it, insomuch that it never forsaketh it, until it hath quite dried up and consumed the same. And therefore as there is pleasure and rest in joy, so in sorrow there is dolour and torment. For it ingendreth melancholy, and melancholy ingendreth it, and increaseth it more.... Moreover, this blacke melancholy humour is of this nature that it will make the spirit & mind darkish, whereby it groweth to be blockish, & the heart looseth al his cheerefulnes. And because the braine is cooled therby, it waxeth very heavy & drowsie. Now when griefe is in great measure, it bringeth withal a kind of loathing & tediousnes, which causeth a man to hate & to be weary of all things, even of the light and of a mans selfe, so that he shal take pleasure in nothing but in his melancholy, in feeding himselfe therwithall, in plunging himselfe deeper into it, & refusing all joy and consolation. To conclude, some grow so farre as to hate themselves, and so fall to despaire, yea many kill and destroy themselves.[2]

Hamlet, then, as the King leads off the Queen, is speaking by the book:

[1] Philemon Holland.
[2] *The French Academie*, 1594 ed. pp. 253, 254.

> O, that this too too solid flesh would melt,
> Thaw, and resolve itself into a dew!
> Or that the Everlasting had not fix'd
> His canon 'gainst self-slaughter! O God! God!
> How weary, stale, flat, and unprofitable,
> Seems to me all the uses of this world!
> Fie on't! oh fie, fie! 'T is an unweeded garden
> That grows to seed; things rank and gross in nature
> Possess it merely.[1]

And in the rest of the soliloquy Hamlet does indeed feed his melancholy with his thoughts of his mother's frailty, thus following the accepted formula of being brought to a loathing of the world, to a condition where he takes delight only in increasing his melancholy, and to a desire to kill himself to escape such a world.

This soliloquy is followed by the entrance of Horatio with the news of the appearance of the ghost. Hamlet's acceptance of the news is the fitting one for his melancholy, but it is also the one which must always be at the basis of any philosophy of tragedy:

> My father's spirit in arms! All is not well;
> I doubt some foul play....
> ...Foul deeds will rise,
> Though all the earth o'erwhelm them, to men's eyes.[2]

The next scene introduces the family of Polonius characteristically advising each other by means of the very best aphorisms known to philosophy. Laertes advises Ophelia as to the virtue of prudence in her dealings with Hamlet, and is in turn counselled sweetly by Ophelia and most thoroughly by Polonius as to what he himself should do. Polonius then, having some few precepts still unspent, proceeds to pour them upon the bewildered Ophelia, who is reduced to promising obedience to his final:

[1] I, ii, 129–37.
[2] I, ii, 255–8.

> I would not, in plain terms, from this time forth,
> Have you so slander any moment leisure
> As to give words or talk with the Lord Hamlet.[1]

The next two scenes are taken up with the appearance of the ghost to Hamlet and the watchers, but before the ghost appears, Hamlet has time to moralize the reputation which his countrymen have for being drunkards into the statement of the theory that is, I believe, at the basis of Shakespearean tragedy:

> So, oft it chances in particular men,
> That for some vicious mole of nature in them,
> As, in their birth—wherein they are not guilty,
> Since nature cannot choose his origin—
> By their o'ergrowth of some complexion
> Oft breaking down the pales and forts of reason,
> Or by some habit that too much o'er-leavens
> The form of plausive manners, that these men,
> Carrying, I say, the stamp of one defect,
> Being nature's livery, or fortune's star,—
> His virtues else—be they as pure as grace,
> As infinite as man may undergo—
> Shall in the general censure take corruption
> From that particular fault.[2]

Here in a "dram of eale" is figured the whole theory of venial and mortal sin, of the sin that though not mortal sin yet brings the whole man into corruption.

And then as the ghost appears to tell his story, to demand revenge, to decree that that revenge shall not touch the Queen, we have the tragedy really beginning with the speech of Hamlet which closes the first act:

> The time is out of joint;—O cursed spite,
> That ever I was born to set it right![3]

But it is time to turn to the ghost, for it will be seen from

---

[1] I, iii, 132-4.   [2] I, iv, 23-36.
[3] I, v, 189, 190.

the earlier discussion of the interest which centred in the philosophical consideration of daemonology[1] that much of the final interpretation of *Hamlet* must depend upon whether Hamlet and Shakespeare accepted the ghost's commands as valid and binding commands. It will be remembered that there were three possible beliefs at this time which were the subject of infinite concern: According to the "Papists" ghosts might be accepted as spirits of the dead permitted to return at times to earth while they were enduring purifying fires of purgatory. Or, according to King James and his fellow-believers, ghosts might be the feignings of the Devil (or even of the good angels), appearing especially to those already prepared in their souls by their desire for revenge or the fulfilment of ambition, in which case the Devil would most frequently choose the likeness of friends who had been dearest in order the more surely to entice his victims to their destruction. Or, according to the third group, of physicians and seekers for natural causes of supernatural appearances, the cause of such ghostly appearances could be traced to the melancholy that was akin to madness.

Lavater sums up the position of the Catholics which he opposes so interestingly in this connection that I shall quote from him the relevant passages:

The Papists in former times have publikely both taught & written, that those spirits which men sometime see and hear, be either good or bad angels, or els the soules of those which either live in everlasting blisse, or in Purgatorie, or in the place of damned persons. And that divers of them are those soules that crave ayde and deliveraunce of men.[2]

Of the four places which receive souls, hell receives those

[1] Cf. Section II, chapter ix.
[2] Lavater, *Of Ghostes and Spirites Walking by Nyght*, transl. R. H., p. 102.

who have been guilty of deadly sin without repentance, and hell is located under the earth. Purgatory receives those who have not committed deadly sin, or else have repented and made satisfaction for their sins; souls that "went hence only stayned with venial sinne".[1] And according to some, Purgatory is also under the earth. Some even say that Purgatory and Hell are the same, but that certain souls stay forever, while others are purged of sin and released. About these matters there is disagreement, however. Then the writer explains in detail:

Farther they teach, that by Gods licence & dispensation, certaine, yea before the day of Judgement, are permitted to come out of hell, and that not for ever, but only for a season, for the instructing and terrifying of the lyving....Moreover that God dothe licence soules to returne from those two places, partely for the comfort and warning of the living, and partly to pray aide of them.[2]

And whersoever these spirits be, they say, that they endure punishment. Besides that soules do not appeare, nor answeare unto every mans interrogatories, but that of a great number they scantlie appeare unto one. And therefore they teache. Whensoever suche visions of spirits are shewed, men should use fasting and prayer or ever they demaund any question of them:[3]

Furthermore it is necessary to wait until the sign has been repeated three times to be sure that the devil does not delude us. The witness may choose various ceremonies by which to fortify himself.

Yet do they teache, that a man may choose to use this or some other forme of prayer, and ceremonies: bicause that without these, spirites have often appeared, & shewed what they required. This doon, we shold (as they teach) fall to questioning with them, and say: Thou spirite, we beseech thee by Christ Jesus, tell us what thou art, and if there be any amongst us, to whom thou wouldest gladly make

---

[1] Lavater, *op. cit.* p. 103.
[2] *Ibid.* pp. 104, 105.
[3] *Ibid.* pp. 105, 106.

answere, name him, or by some signe declare so much. After this, the question is to be moved, eche man there presente being recited whether he wold aunswere unto this or that man. And if at the name of any, hee speake, or make a noyse, al other demaundes remayning, should be made unto him: As these and suche lyke; What mans soule he is? for what cause he is come, and what he doth desire? Whether he require any ayde by prayers and suffrages? Whether by Massing, or almes giving he may be released?...

Furthermore, by what signe it may be perfectly known that he is released, and for what cause he was first shut up in Purgatorie. And yet they hold, that no curious, unprofitable, or superstitious questions shold be demaunded of the spirit except he wold of his own accord revele & open them. And that it wer best, that sober persons shold thus question with him, on som holyday before diner, or in the night seson, as is commonly accustomed. And if the spirite will shewe no signe at that tyme, the matter should be deferred unto some other season, untill the spirite woulde shewe hymselfe agayne:...for that by the secret judgement of God, it was ordeyned, that they shold appeare at certeine houres, and to certeine persons, and not unto all men. And farther they say that we neede not to feare, that the spirit would do any bodily hurte unto that persone, unto whome it doth appeare. For if such a spirit would hurte any, he might justlie be suspected that he were no good spirit.[1]

There are four ways in which, the "Papists" teach, good spirits may be distinguished from bad: the good spirit at the beginning terrifies men but soon revives and comforts them; his outward appearance will indicate his nature, for the evil spirit is apt to come as a lion, bear, or black ghost, and moreover we must listen "whether the voice whiche we heare be sweete, lowly, sober, sorowfull, or otherwise terrible and full of reproch"; his teachings must be judged as to whether they conform to those of the apostles and the church; and

Fourthly we must take diligent heede whether in hys words, deeds, and gestures, he do shew forth any humilitie acknowledging or confessing of his sinnes & punishments, or whether we heare of him any

[1] Lavater, *op. cit.* pp. 107, 108.

groning, weeping, complaint, boasting, threatning, slaunder or blasphemie. For as the begger doth reherse his owne miserie, so likewyse doo good spirits that desire any helpe or deliverance.[1]

After discussing the means of succour through sacrifice, alms, prayer, and fasting, Lavater shows that the Papists teach that it is a man's duty to give whatever aid the ghost seeks, and

On the other side, they teach that it is an horrible and heynous offence, if a man give no succoure to suche as seeke it at his hands, especially if it be the soule of his parents, brethren and sisters.[2]

Certainly the ghost of the elder Hamlet answers all the tests here made. It appears on three successive nights to the watchmen, passing before them three times each evening in its stately march. Horatio's questioning is of the proper nature:

> If thou hast any sound, or use of voice,
> Speak to me;
> If there be any good thing to be done
> That may to thee do ease and grace to me,
> Speak to me;
> If thou art privy to thy country's fate,
> Which, happily, foreknowing may avoid,
> O speak!
> Or if thou hast uphoarded in thy life
> Extorted treasure in the womb of earth,
> For which, they say, you spirits oft walk in death,
> Speak of it; stay, and speak![3]

Likewise his decision as the ghost vanishes at the crowing of the cock without having divulged his secret is consistent with this acceptance of the ghostly appearance:

> Let us impart what we have seen to-night
> Unto young Hamlet; for, upon my life,
> This spirit, dumb to us, will speak to him.[4]

---

[1] Lavater, *op. cit.* pp. 108, 109.   [2] *Ibid.* p. 109.
[3] i, i, 128–39.   [4] i, i, 169–71.

The cry of Hamlet to the ghost also follows the prescribed outline:

> Angels and ministers of grace defend us!
>
> .   .   .   .
> .   .   .   . O, answer me!
> .   .   .   .
> Why .   .   .   .   .   .
> .   .   .   . why.   .   .
> .   .   .   .
> .   .   .   . What may this mean
> .   .   .   .
> Say, why is this? Wherefore? What should we do?[1]

And also the reply which Hamlet makes when Horatio would stay him from following the ghost, refusing to be afraid that the ghost will do him harm, is in this tradition.

As for the tests, we are told of the frightening power of the ghost, but whether he later comforts to the same degree is less certain. The second test is answered by Horatio's description of "A countenance more in sorrow than in anger".[2] The third test is not clearly answered, but of the fourth there can be no doubt. The ghost says plainly:

> I am thy father's spirit,
> Doom'd for a certain term to walk the night,
> And for the day confin'd to fast in fires,
> Till the foul crimes done in my days of nature
> Are burnt and purg'd away. But that I am forbid
> To tell the secrets of my prison-house,
> I could a tale unfold whose lightest word
> Would harrow up thy soul, freeze thy young blood,
> Make thy two eyes, like stars, start from their spheres,
> Thy knotty and combined locks to part.... [3]

To such a rehearsing of his misery, Hamlet cannot but reply:

> Haste me to know 't, that I, with wings as swift
> As meditation or the thoughts of love,
> May sweep to my revenge.[4]

[1] I, iv, 39–57.   [2] I, ii, 232.   [3] I, v, 9–18.   [4] I, v, 29–31.

And to the tale which the ghost unfolds, his promise to
erase all else from the table of his memory is followed by his
sending his companions to their various businesses, while
he will go to pray. His demand that they swear secrecy in
the matter is echoed by the ghost under the earth, where
Hell and Purgatory were supposed to be. Then he can cry,

> Rest, rest, perturbed spirit!

even as he decides:

> The time is out of joint;—O cursed spite,
> That ever I was born to set it right![1]

In all these matters Shakespeare has pictured a ghost from
Purgatory according to all the tests possible; a ghost which,
especially since it appeared in the form and likeness of a
parent, Hamlet must obey, failure in obedience being well
reckoned as guilt. But that is not the whole story. King
James, it will be remembered, pictured the Devil as leading
his victim on to guilt through desire of revenge, as appearing
in the likeness of one dear to the victim in order to secure his
attention, as taking advantage of his victim's despair to
entice him to his own destruction. And it will be remembered
that Hamlet's first cry to the ghost is one in which determination conquers doubt:

> Angels and ministers of grace defend us!
> Be thou a spirit of health or goblin damn'd,
> Bring with thee airs from heaven or blasts from hell,
> Be thy intents wicked or charitable,
> Thou com'st in such a questionable shape
> That I will speak to thee.[2]

Also he assures Horatio:

> There are more things in heaven and earth, Horatio,
> Than are dreamt of in our philosophy.[3]

Yet at the end of the second act, even as he chides himself for

[1] I, v, 189–91.   [2] I, iv, 39–44.   [3] I, v, 166, 167.

his failure to find revenge, he reasons in the manner of
King James:

> The spirit that I have seen
> May be the devil; and the devil hath power
> To assume a pleasing shape; yea, and perhaps
> Out of my weakness and my melancholy,
> As he is very potent with such spirits,
> Abuses me to damn me.[1]

Also it must be remembered that in the third act when
Hamlet speaks daggers to his mother in her closet, his cry
at the appearance of the ghost is:

> Save me, and hover o'er me with your wings,
> You heavenly guards![2]

And while the Queen can see nothing, Hamlet speaks to the
ghost. Now James had said that the Devil could so thicken
the air about a ghost that no other save the one person might
see it. And James had also said that the Devil appeared a
second time to the victim to whet his purpose.

All this proves to me that Shakespeare was presenting the
problem exactly as it was presented to the thinking men of
his day. But he did not neglect the third alternative. Hamlet
is preyed upon by grief until we see him, when the play
opens, the victim of unnatural melancholy. And we have
seen that unnatural melancholy was the cause of false shapes
being presented unto the fantasy. There never seems to be
forgotten this possibility in *Hamlet*. Horatio has first
refused to believe in the ghost, telling Bernardo and Marcel-
lus that the ghost exists but in their fantasy. Yet he is in
his turn convinced. Hamlet himself fears his own melancholy
as having been responsible for his acceptance of the ghost,
as is seen in the passage quoted above, when he determines
to use the players to test the King's conscience. Furthermore,
in the Queen's closet, the ghost does not appear to anyone

---

[1] II, ii, 627–32. [2] III, iv, 103, 104.

else, the Queen takes the ghost to be the coinage of Hamlet's brain, and he himself cries out that it is not his madness that has spoken, fearing that his mother will take all that he has said as but of a piece with his invisible vision.

The whole picture is skilfully wrought to show the reality viewed so contradictorily from many angles. And I truly believe that if a Papist and King James and Timothy Bright had seen the play, as they all probably did, each would have gone home confirmed in his own opinion about ghosts. The important thing is, however, that the study could not have been made in Shakespeare's day with any but a central figure who had been made melancholy by passion, and one who could be led fittingly to a desire for revenge.

The second act of *Hamlet* presents a curious conflict of opinion among the other characters in the play as to the nature of the passion which has brought on Hamlet's madness, for that which was seen in the first act as the melancholy of excessive grief is now regularly referred to by all the characters as simply madness.

We are soon aware that the prophecy of Hamlet's closing speech to his friends in the first act is being fulfilled:

> As I perchance hereafter shall think meet
> To put an antic disposition on... [1]

For Ophelia describes to her father the appearance of Hamlet as the melancholy lover:

> Lord Hamlet, with his doublet all unbrac'd,
> No hat upon his head, his stockings foul'd,
> Ungart'red, and down-gyved to his ankle,
> Pale as his shirt, his knees knocking each other,
> And with a look so piteous in purport
> As if he had been loosed out of hell
> To speak of horrors.... [2]

And every reader of Shakespeare will recognize the symp-

[1] I, v, 171, 172.   [2] II, i, 78–84.

toms as those described as traditional by the taunting Rosalind:

> Then your hose should be ungarter'd, your bonnet unbanded, your sleeve unbutton'd, your shoe unti'd, and everything about you demonstrating a careless desolation.[1]

Certainly Polonius needs no further evidence. He reaches his conclusion at once:

> This is the very ecstacy of love,
> Whose violent property fordoes itself
> And leads the will to desperate undertakings
> As oft as any passion under heaven
> That does afflict our natures.[2]

Meanwhile the King is discussing Hamlet's case with Rosencrantz and Guildenstern:

> Something you have heard
> Of Hamlet's transformation; so I call it,
> Since not the exterior nor the inward man
> Resembles that it was. What it should be,
> More than his father's death, that thus hath put him
> So much from the understanding of himself,
> I cannot dream of.[3]

But even as Rosencrantz and Guildenstern depart from the royal presence, Polonius enters to proclaim his discovery that he has found "The very cause of Hamlet's lunacy". And after the interrupting visit of the ambassadors from Norway, he resumes the recital of his good news. Finishing a lengthy panegyric on brevity, he seems to be starting an equally lengthy exposition of madness when the Queen interrupts him with her,

> More matter, with less art;[4]

[1] *As You Like It*, III, ii, 397–400.
[2] *Hamlet*, II, i, 102–6.
[3] II, ii, 4–10.
[4] II, ii, 95.

so that he is finally forced to arrive at the worthy conclusion:

> Mad let us grant him then; and now remains
> That we find out the cause of this effect,
> Or rather say, the cause of this defect,
> For this effect defective comes by cause. [1]

To find the cause of this effect defective Polonius, being always the philosopher, merely follows the traditional history of those afflicted with love melancholy. Out of no more information than Ophelia's poor words of Hamlet's visit, he is able to create the history of the disease:

> And he, repulsed—a short tale to make—
> Fell into a sadness, then into a fast,
> Thence to a watch, thence into a weakness,
> Thence to a lightness, and, by this declension,
> Into the madness whereon now he raves,
> And all we wail for. [2]

After the brilliant demonstration that Hamlet gives of madness in what follows, Polonius is a little less dogmatic, however. Hamlet first takes him for a fishmonger. Finally he gives a clever extract from the moral philosophies of the day, laying down in firm fashion the decorum for old men, who (being dominated by phlegm) should have grey beards, wrinkled faces, eyes purging dregs of this humour, slow wits, and weak bodies.[3] And at this recognized wisdom, Polonius is moved to his famous utterance:

> Though this be madness, yet there is method in 't. [4]

And I take it that this is just what Shakespeare wanted the audience to understand.

To Rosencrantz and Guildenstern, Hamlet is melancholy rather than mad at first. He talks of Fortune, of his prison Denmark, of dreams, and then recites all the symptoms of the man made melancholy by grief:

[1] II, ii, 100–3.   [2] II, ii, 146–51.
[3] Cf. *ante*, pp. 53, 54, 59.   [4] II, ii, 207, 208.

I have of late—but wherefore I know not—lost all my mirth, foregone all custom of exercise; and indeed it goes so heavily with my disposition that this goodly frame, this earth, seems to me a sterile promontory, this most excellent canopy, the air, look you, this brave o'erhanging firmament, this majestical roof fretted with golden fire, why, it appears no other thing to me than a foul and pestilent congregation of vapours. What a piece of work is a man!...And yet, to me, what is this quintessence of dust? Man delights not me,—no, nor woman neither, though by your smiling you seem to say so.[1]

Here are all the symptoms of melancholy rehearsed once more; the audience cannot be misled if they listen. But still he adds to his friends his confidential

I am but mad north-north-west. When the wind is southerly I know a hawk from a handsaw.

Hamlet's ingenious planning with the players, his calling for the old speech, Aeneas's tale to Dido, his impatient hurrying on to the account of Hecuba, even while he plays his own part with them before Polonius to that wise man's utter confusion is followed by the important soliloquy on the players. This soliloquy has two separate themes. The first is that of the mock passion of the players as they described Hecuba. Now the key to the significance of this introduction of Hecuba so insistently made in this parley with the players and in the soliloquy is to be found in a passage in *Titus Andronicus*, where young Lucius says:

> For I have heard my grandsire say full oft
> Extremity of griefs would make men mad,
> And I have read that Hecuba of Troy
> Ran mad for sorrow.[2]

And that this stock instance of the grief that would make men mad should be introduced here is typical of the thoroughness with which Shakespeare presented each passion that he studied. Hecuba was the traditional figure to associate with inconsolable grief, and the mock passion now presented by

[1] II, ii, 306–23.   [2] *Titus Andronicus*, IV, i, 18–21.

the players serves as reproof to Hamlet for his slothfulness. But the grief that leads to the deadly sin of sloth was one of the regularly recognized types of that wicked grief which refuses to be consoled, as we have seen in the passage quoted from Sir Thomas More. That such grief results in melancholy, a melancholy which so dries and cools the brain that the images of memory cannot clearly be retained and a man's mind becomes dark and sluggish, we have also seen in the accounts quoted from the authorities on the passions. To the philosophers of Hamlet's day the picture, then, of one moved to revenge by heaven and hell and yet stayed by excess of grief from action, of one impelled by passion to revenge and yet through excess of passion having the cause of his passion blurred in his memory, would not have seemed to call for poetic exposition. Hamlet's type of grief was one generally accepted in his day.

The second theme of the soliloquy is concerned with the play as a device to catch the conscience of the King, a device which we have already seen was recognized as traditional in the literary criticism of the day.[1]

After all the searching for the cause of Hamlet's madness where they would most like to find it, the King in grief, Polonius in love, the third act of *Hamlet* opens with the search still going on. The King is again questioning Rosencrantz and Guildenstern, apparently with some impatience, as to why Hamlet "*puts on* this confusion". But Rosencrantz is forced to confess that Hamlet will not speak of causes, and Guildenstern to acknowledge that "with a *crafty madness*" Hamlet refuses to confide in them. Then as the King and Polonius go off to their eavesdropping to test the love theory, Hamlet takes up in his "To be or not to be" soliloquy the analysis of his grief just where he left it off in the first act. The letter of consolation from Plutarch to Apollonius stated the theme thus:

[1] Cf. Section I, chapter ii, especially p. 35.

Consider now the troubles and sorrowes of this life; how many cares and crosses it is subject unto: certes, if wee went about to reckon and number them, wee would condemne it as most unhappie.... Wise *Socrates* said, that death resembled for all the world, either a most deepe and sound sleepe, or a voiage farre remote into foraine parts, in which a man is long absent from his native country; or else thirdly, an utter abolition and finall dissolution both of soule and bodie;... [1]

In no case, then, can death be thought to be evil; it is life that is evil:

For what else bringeth upon us warres, seditions, battels, and fights, but the bodie and the greedie appetites and lusts proceeding from it.... [2]

The well-known Cardan's *Comforte* stated the same theme with only slight variations:

Alas what evyll can it be to want honger, thyrst, gryefe, labor, sadnesse, feare, and fynallye the whoole heape of evylles, whych the soule beynge parted from the bodye we must of necessity want....

Therefore *Socrates* was wont to say, that death might be resembled eyther to sound sleape, a longe jorney, or destruction, as is the death of bruit beastes: If the soule doth lyve and after death feeleth nothinge, then is it lyke unto a sound sleape, because therein we rest without eyther felinge or understanding, and after a whyle return to the same exercyses. Mooste assured it is that such sleapes are most sweete as be most sound. For those are the best where in lyke unto dead men we dreame nothinge. The broken sleapes, the slomber, and dreames ful of visions, are commonly in them that have weake and sickly bodies.... But quiet and sound slepes and such as weary men commonly have, are accompted sweetest. [3]

---

[1] Holland's Plutarch, *Morals*, p. 516.   [2] *Ibid.* p. 517.

[3] Cardan's *Comforte*, D ii. The Sidney Lee *Catalogue of Shakepeareana* printed for presentation only at the Chiswick Press in 1899 listed this work as No. 136, quoting from Hunter's *New Illustrations of Shakespeare*, "it seems to be the book which Shakespeare placed in the hands of Hamlet". Douce's *Illustrations of Shakespeare* (1839 ed. p. 461) comments on the "To die,—to sleep,—" portion of Hamlet's soliloquy: "There is a good deal on the subject in Cardanus's *Comforte*, 1576, 4to, a book which Shakespeare had certainly read. In fol. 30, it is said, 'In the holy scripture, death is not accompted other than sleap, and to die is said to sleape'". Douce comments on "The

But if thou compare death to long travayl and that the soule beinge let lose from prison of the bodye seeth al thinges and walketh everye where....[1]

For there is nothing that doth better or moore truely prophecy the ende of lyfe, then when a man dreameth, that he doth travayle and wander into farre countries, and chiefly, if he imagineth hym selfe to ryde uppon a whyte horse, that is swifte, and that *he travalyeth in countries unknowen wythout hope of retourne*, in such sort naturallye devyninge of that shortlye wyll come to passe in dede.[2]

If death is destruction, there cannot be fear of what is not, Cardan says, and he concludes:

Death dooth take away more evylles, then it bringeth, and those more certeyn.[3]

It is thus in the accepted tradition that Hamlet argues in the best known of all his soliloquies the problem of whether life or death must be reckoned as the greater evil. And that these three possibilities of death as a sleep, as a journey, or as total destruction are the same accepted alternatives to the evils of life is at once evident:

> To be, or not to be: that is the question.
> Whether 't is nobler in the mind to suffer
> The slings and arrows of outrageous fortune,
> Or to take arms against a sea of troubles,
> And by opposing end them. To die; to sleep;
> No more; and by a sleep to say we end
> The heart-ache and the thousand natural shocks
> That flesh is heir to. 'T is a consummation
> Devoutly to be wish'd. To die; to sleep;—
> To sleep? Perchance to dream! Ay, there's the rub;

undiscovered country, from whose bourn No traveller returns", however, as very like the passage instanced from Catullus by Steevens, adding that there was no translation of Catullus into English. It is easily seen that this book of Cardan has long been associated with *Hamlet*. I should like to believe that Hamlet was actually reading it or pretending to read it as he carried on his baiting of Polonius.

[1] Cardan's *Comforte*, D iii.   [2] *Ibid.* D iii. *verso.*
[3] *Ibid.* D iii *verso.*

> For in that sleep of death what dreams may come,
> When we have shuffl'd off this mortal coil,
> Must give us pause. There's the respect
> That makes calamity of so long life.[1]

And then after the enumeration of the evils of life, he returns to the other alternative:

> Who would fardels bear,
> To grunt and sweat under a weary life,
> But that the dread of something after death,
> The undiscovered country from whose bourn
> No traveller returns, puzzles the will
> And makes us rather bear those ills we have,
> Than fly to others that we know not of?

But here Hamlet turns from the thought of death and life to the related thought of his own indecision:

> Thus conscience does make cowards of us all;
> And thus the native hue of resolution
> Is sicklied o'er with the pale cast of thought,
> And enterprises of great pith and moment
> With this regard their currents turn awry,
> And lose the name of action.[2]

From this soliloquy he turns to play his rôle with Ophelia before the listening King and Polonius. His condemnation of women and their wantonness, his exclamation that it has made him mad, his final passionate "To a nunnery, go", furnish the subject of the next puzzled discussion between the eavesdroppers, even while Ophelia grieves over the overthrow of a noble mind. The King is still unconvinced that Polonius has found the cause of Hamlet's malady:

> Love! his affections do not that way tend;
> Nor what he spake, though it lack'd form a little,
> Was not like madness. There's something in his soul
> O'er which his melancholy sits on brood,[3]

[1] *Hamlet*, III, i, 56–69.   [2] III, i, 76–88
[3] III, i, 170–3.

and "in quick determination" he plans to send Hamlet to England in an attempt to dispel

> This something-settled matter in his heart,
> Whereon his brains still beating puts him thus
> From fashion of himself.[1]

But Polonius still clings to his belief that

> The origin and commencement of this grief
> Sprung from neglected love.[2]

And the King accedes to the plan for further eavesdropping, since

> Madness in great ones must not unwatch'd go.

Before the play within the play, Hamlet talks to Horatio of his friendship for him, and incidentally gives definite utterance to that conception of the relation of tragic guilt to reward and punishment which lies at the heart of all Shakespeare's tragedy:

> ...for thou hast been,
> For one, in suffering all, that suffers nothing,
> A man that Fortune's buffets and rewards
> Hath ta'en with equal thanks; and blest are those
> Whose blood and judgement are so well commingled,
> That they are not a pipe for Fortune's finger
> To sound what stop she please. Give me that man
> That is not passion's slave, and I will wear him
> In my heart's core, ay in my heart of heart,
> As I do thee....[3]

In the play within the play which follows, the theme of the play proper is announced, as it should be. Not only is the central plot of *Hamlet* mirrored in the *Mouse-trap*, but there also is found the most condensed expression of the meaning of the whole in the speech of the Player King:

[1] III, i, 181–3. [2] III, i, 185, 186.
[3] Note the reference to Fortune's slaves in the *Mirror for Magistrates* quoted on p. 16, *ante*.

> But what we do determine oft we break.
> Purpose is but the slave to memory,
> Of violent birth, but poor validity;[1]

and more definitely still,

> What to ourselves in passion we propose,
> The passion ending, doth the purpose lose.
> The violence of either grief or joy
> Their own enactures with themselves destroy.
> Where joy most revels, grief doth most lament;
> Grief joys, joy grieves, on slender accident;[2]

and finally:

> Our wills and fates do so contrary run
> That our devices still are overthrown;
> Our thoughts are ours, their ends none of our own.[3]

The play is ended precipitately, the King is reported drunk with choler, Hamlet affirms of himself with apparent sincerity that his wit is diseased, and in the midst of it all he goes to his interview with his mother. But as he goes to his mother, he passes the King at prayer, the King who cannot pray because of his own guilt.[4] Hamlet pauses to contemplate his opportunity for revenge, but he will not kill the King while he is in the very act of purging his soul, for Hamlet thinks of his own father sent to eternity "With all his crimes broad blown".

Hamlet's interview with his mother is no more than begun when Polonius's untimely response to the Queen's fearful cry for help gives occasion for a passionate outbreak on Hamlet's part and a thrust at the concealing curtain, a thrust fatal to the guiltless Polonius. Hamlet's thought is that he has killed the King, but finding his victim to be Polonius, he proceeds to the business of wringing his mother's

---

[1] III, ii, 197–9.   [2] III, ii, 204–9.
[3] III, ii, 221–3.
[4] The fact that mortal sin alienates the soul from God is here stressed, of course. Cf. Section II, chapter X, pp. 99–101.

heart until the appearance of the ghost, and then again we hear Hamlet's self-chiding:

> Do you not come your tardy son to chide,
> That, laps'd in time and passion, lets go by
> The important acting of your dread command?[1]

In the same strain is his repentance for his rash killing of Polonius:

> For this same lord,
> I do repent; but Heaven hath pleas'd it so,
> To punish me with this and this with me,
> That I must be their scourge and minister.[2]

That he knows the King suspects his madness is clear in what follows, and that he in turn trusts neither the King nor his King-chosen companions for his journey to England is also clear.

The fourth act begins with the picturing of the consternation of the King and the Queen over the killing of Polonius, and with the harsh mirth of Hamlet. The King must not seem to countenance the deed. His soul is, indeed, "full of discord and dismay". He hastens to send Hamlet on his way, but Hamlet has still time to anatomize his soul once more in another soliloquy occasioned by his seeing young Fortinbras on his journey to conquer valueless soil in Poland. The interesting thing about this soliloquy is that Hamlet here lists his reasons for revenge:

> Sith I have *cause* and *will* and *strength* and *means*
> To do 't.[3]

Thus he sees himself pausing while he recognizes

> Excitements of my *reason* and my *blood*;[4]

which is to say that both reason and passion should move him to his deed. His is not a case where reason stays passion, but where momentary passion absorbs him to the exclusion

---

[1] III, iv, 106–8.
[3] IV, iv, 45, 46.
[2] III, iv, 172–5.
[4] IV, iv, 58.

of all else. He acts quickly at the command of passion or not at all. The one command which he seems to have accepted as reasonable and right, he has not acted upon. But he has been brutal with Ophelia and cruel with his mother, and he has killed Polonius under the stress of passion.

The scene which follows reveals the pitiful Ophelia in her gentle madness, madness which is the result of intemperate grief. The King says it is grief for her father, but he thinks of his own sorrows rather than hers when he says:

> When sorrows come, they come not single spies,
> But in battalions. [1]

And it must be recalled that Cardan's *Comforte* listed "private calamities manifold" as one of the three divisions of evil, saying:

Private calamities manifold we accompt those when a man by many mishaps at one instant is molested. [2]

But the entry of Laertes demanding vengeance for his father tends to increase the sorrows of the already beset King.

Laertes, as I have already said, is a complete foil for Hamlet in all his actions. His cry is an absolute contrast to Hamlet's timorous testing of the ghost's truthfulness:

> I dare damnation. To this point I stand,
> That both the worlds I give to negligence,
> Let come what comes; only I'll be reveng'd
> Most thoroughly for my father. [3]

And as Ophelia appears again, taking the office of the ghost in stimulating Laertes to revenge, he cries again,

> Hadst thou thy wits and didst persuade revenge,
> It could not move thus. [4]

We hear of Hamlet's escape and his imminent return, but before the King hears of it, we find him placating Laertes,

[1] IV, v, 78, 79. [2] Cardan's *Comforte*, A iii.
[3] IV, v, 133–6. [4] IV, v, 168, 169.

explaining why he has not avenged the death of Polonius, and then as the news arrives, we see him moving to enlist Laertes to take action against the returning Hamlet. And with bitter irony he repeats the theme which the player king announced:

> That we would do,
> We should do when we would; for this "would" changes,
> And hath abatements and delays as many
> As there are tongues, are hands, are accidents;
> And then this "should" is like a spendthrift sigh,
> That hurts by easing.[1]

To emphasize the irony, too, Laertes says that to take vengeance for his father he would undertake to cut Hamlet's throat in the church.

And with the same ironical effect Shakespeare makes the King say:

> No place, indeed, should murder sanctuarize;
> Revenge should have no bounds.[2]

Because he knows Hamlet to be "generous and free from all contriving", the King then plans with Laertes the business of the poisoned foils[3] and the poisoned cup, taking advantage of Hamlet's simplicity.

When, then, the Queen comes to tell of the drowning of Ophelia (in one of the worst speeches in all Shakespeare), Laertes emphasizes his own subjecting of grief to revenge in contrast to Hamlet's subjecting of revenge to grief:

---

[1] IV, vii, 119–24.
[2] IV, vii, 128, 129.
[3] A curious possible connotation of the poisoned foils is found in Holland's Plutarch, "Of Meeknes, or How a man should refraine choler", in *Morals*, p. 125: "And verily, some barbarous nations there are who use to poison their swords, & other weapons of iron; but valour hath no need at all of the venim of choler, for dipped it is in reason & judgement; whereas whatsoever is corrupted with ire and furie is brittle, rotten, & easie to be broken into pieces".

> Too much of water hast thou, poor Ophelia,
> And therefore I forbid my tears. But yet
> It is our trick. Nature her custom holds,
> Let shame say what it will; when these are gone,
> The woman will be out.[1]

The last act opens with the scene with the grave-diggers, a scene in which Hamlet exhibits another accepted manifestation of his being the victim of melancholy adust as it is derived from the sanguine humour, for the sanguine adust turn tragedies into comedies as does Hamlet here while he jests with horror.

The arrival of the funeral procession of Ophelia changes this mocking of death, however, into something very different. And as the impetuous Laertes with his hyperboles leaps into her grave, Hamlet is once more moved in swift passion. Defiantly he also leaps into the grave, but as Laertes grapples with him, he cries out:

> I prithee, take thy fingers from my throat,
> For, though I am not splenitive and rash,
> Yet have I something in me dangerous,
> Which let thy wiseness fear.[2]

And later he makes good his hysterical boast, "Nay, an thou'lt mouth, I'll rant as well as thou".

We do not doubt Hamlet's love for Ophelia, nor yet his passionate grief, but the passion which makes him fly at Laertes is, indeed, the passion that has grown beyond all restraint into momentary madness, as he recognizes later. Even as he forecasts unconsciously the events of the last scene in his

> Our indiscretion sometimes serves us well
> When our deep plots do pall;[3]

---

[1] *Hamlet*, IV, vii, 186–90.
[2] v, i, 283–6.
[3] v, ii, 8, 9.

he seeks confirmation from Horatio of his own rightness in plotting to kill the King:

> He that hath kill'd my king and whor'd my mother,
> Popp'd in between the election and my hopes,
> Thrown out his angle for my proper life,
> And with such cozenage—is't not perfect conscience,
> To quit him with this arm? And is 't not to be damn'd
> To let this canker of our nature come
> In further evil?[1]

As Horatio advises him that the King must know soon of the trick which has sent his messengers to their death in England, Hamlet replies still:

> It will be short; the interim is mine,
> And a man's life's no more than to say "One".
> But I am very sorry, good Horatio,
> That to Laertes I forgot myself;
> For, by the image of my cause, I see
> The portraiture of his. I'll court his favours.
> But, sure, the bravery of his grief did put me
> Into a tow'ring passion.[2]

This same theme of his lapse from reason is developed as Hamlet meets Laertes with the foils:

> Give me your pardon, sir. I've done you wrong,
> But pardon't, as you are a gentleman.
> This presence knows,
> And you must needs have heard, how I am punish'd
> With sore distraction. What I have done
> That might your nature, honour, and exception
> Roughly awake, I here proclaim was madness....
> If Hamlet from himself be ta'en away,
> And when he's not himself does wrong Laertes,
> Then Hamlet does it not, Hamlet denies it.
> Who does it, then? His madness. If't be so,
> Hamlet is of the faction that is wrong'd;
> His madness is poor Hamlet's enemy.

[1] v, ii, 64–70.   [2] v, ii, 73–80.

> Sir, in this audience,
> Let my disclaiming from a purpos'd evil
> Free me so far in your most generous thoughts,
> That I have shot mine arrow o'er the house
> And hurt my brother.[1]

Laertes in his reply puts himself in the class of those not easily averted from anger:

> I am satisfied in nature,
> Whose motive, in this case, should stir me most
> To my revenge; but in my terms of honour
> I stand aloof,[2]

and until "elder masters of known honour" pronounce him free to accept peace, he will not accept the pronouncement of reason as sufficient. Furthermore, Laertes, punished for the excessive anger which has desired to make revenge more sure by the device of the poisoned foils, which Plutarch said were not needed by true courage, dying cries out:

> I am justly kill'd with mine own treachery.[3]

His punishment is the appropriate one of the poisoner poisoned. And as he explains the perfidy which has killed Hamlet, the Queen, and the King, he utters the great cry of the play, "the King, the King's to blame".

Then at last Hamlet in passionate anger at the King's treachery wounds him with the point which he has caused to be poisoned and forces him to drink from the cup which

---

[1] v, ii, 237–55. This figure is suggested several times in the literature of the period, but perhaps most strikingly in Nashe's *Terrors of the Night, Works,* pp. 234, 235, where it is used to explain the causes of dreams: "but the best reason among them all that I could ever picke out, was this, that as an arrow which is shot out of a bow, is sent forth manie times with such force, that it flyeth farre beyond the marke whereat it was assigned: so our thoughts intentively fixt all the day time upon a marke we are to hit, are now and then over drawne with such force, that they flye beyonde the marke of the day into the confines of the night".

[2] v, ii, 255–58.   [3] v, ii, 317.

he has made deadly to the others. "He is justly serv'd", according to all the thinking of Shakespeare's day.[1]

Hamlet and Laertes exchange forgiveness, but after Laertes dies, Hamlet bids Horatio live to tell his tale aright and to give his dying voice to Fortinbras as the new ruler. "The rest is silence", but Horatio has lived to tell the story, and he does not fail to moralize it:

> And let me speak to the yet unknowing world
> How these things came about. So shall you hear
> Of carnal, bloody, and unnatural acts,
> Of *accidental judgements, casual slaughters,*
> Of deaths put on by cunning and forc'd cause,
> And in the upshot, *purposes mistook*
> *Fallen on the inventors' heads*:[2]

And Fortinbras, to keep the joy-grief theme, proclaims "with sorrow I embrace my fortune".

If my analysis is correct, then, *Hamlet* becomes a study in the passion of grief. In Hamlet himself it is passion which is not moderated by reason, a passion which will not yield to the consolations of philosophy. And being intemperate and excessive grief, Hamlet's grief is, therefore, the grief that makes memory fade, that makes reason fail in directing the will, that makes him guilty of sloth. Yet Hamlet is capable of an anger that demands revenge. His blood answered the ghost's first demand with a swift promise; he could offend Ophelia, kill Polonius, escape on shipboard, insult Laertes, even kill the King in moments of unreasonable passion, but

> What to ourselves in passion we propose,
> The passion ending, doth the purpose lose,
> The violence of either grief or joy
> Their own enactures with themselves destroy.[3]

Because in our own day we are sentimental about grief and those that grieve, it is hard for us to get the Renaissance

---

[1] Cf. Section I, chapter i, especially pp. 9 and 21.
[2] v, ii, 390–96.   [3] Cf. p. 109, *ante.*

point of view in regard to grief, a point of view which was inherited from the Middle Ages as well as from the older classical philosophy. Shakespeare did not fail to see and to show the essential humanness of grief in its passionate refusal of the consolations of philosophy. Neither did he fail to show the destruction which followed Hamlet's sloth-fulness in executing what his reason had judged and com-manded him to do. Nor did he fail to show the destruction that came from his passionate and rash action when he acted from passion and not from reason.

Laertes, too, was the victim of excessive grief, but his grief was that which moved to rage. He, too, acted from passion and not from reason. Even in his killing of Hamlet he acted against the dictates of his own conscience, having promised to do so under the influence of violent passion, moved by grief to hate and by hate to revenge.

Ophelia is also the victim of excessive grief, her own and Hamlet's. And thus the toll of that passion which sins in failing to follow reason is complete.

There is still to be reckoned the sin which is mortal, the sin which has come as the effect of passion which has per-verted the will. Such is the acknowledged sin both of the King and the Queen. The King in his great soliloquy as he tries to pray sees himself accursed like Cain and yet hopeful of mercy. But he cannot be forgiven while yet he holds the rewards of his deed, "My crown, mine own ambition, and my queen". The three objects of his passion, in themselves sinful, are thus indicative of the mortally sinful nature of the King's passion. These ends could not have been approved by reason unless reason was perverted. But more than that, we see the King continuing to guide his passion and his action to the very last by a reason perverted to the choice of wrong ends. Ambition and lust have taken possession of the King until they have turned his reason into an instrument for their own uses, and until they have indeed turned his soul away from God into mortal sin. And though God's vengeance is slow, there is no doubt in the mind of any reader of *Hamlet* that the King has suffered punishment from the moment when he committed his crime,—in the fear and suspicion and unrest of his days, in the increasing battalions of his troubles, in the sick soul which could not rid itself of passion or of the fruits of passion to find peace with God. Nor can any reader doubt that the eternal vengeance of God is to fall upon the King.

Shakespeare's picture of the Queen is explained to us by Hamlet's speech to her in her closet. There we see again the picture of sin as evil willed by a reason perverted by passion, for so much Hamlet explains in his accusation of his mother:

> You cannot call it love, for at your age
> The hey-day in the blood is tame, it's humble,
> And waits upon the judgement; and what judgement
> Would step from this to this?...
> O shame! where is thy blush? Rebellious hell,
> If thou canst mutine in a matron's bones,
> To flaming youth let virtue be as wax
> And melt in her own fire. Proclaim no shame
> When the compulsive ardour gives the charge,
> Since frost itself as actively doth burn
> And *reason panders will.* [1]

And of the Queen's punishment as it goes on throughout the play, there can be no doubt either. Her love for Hamlet, her grief, the woes that come so fast that one treads upon the heel of another, her consciousness of wrong-doing, her final dismay are those also of one whose soul has become alienated from God by sin.

It is here, it seems to me, that we see the true significance of the play in its treatment of passion. Through passion which has warped reason, so that "reason panders will", the King and the Queen have come to the sin that is mortal.

[1] III, iv, 68–88.

Through passion undirected by reason, Hamlet, Laertes, and Ophelia have brought havoc into the world, but theirs is not mortal sin. Hamlet has failed to do what his reason has decreed that he should do; he has failed to kill the King.[1] His grief has made him sluggish, and he has allowed swift passion to seize him. The result is devastation but not eternal damnation. And at the end of the play Fortinbras and Horatio live to dominate the scene, Fortinbras and Horatio being the two characters in the play in whom reason has swayed passion. Fortinbras has been called to grief for a father whose honour he has undertaken to revenge, but his passion has yielded to reason, and his Poland expedition has been undertaken for "divine ambition" and honour's sake. Horatio is not passion's slave, but one in whom "blood and judgement are so well commingled" that he is not a mere pipe for Fortune to play upon. And this is but to say again that those who balance passion by reason are not Fortune's puppets. And such is the lesson of tragedy.

[1] For the discussion of revenge, see *ante*, pp. 19–24. Hamlet was apparently chosen to execute the public vengeance delegated by God to his representatives, the rulers.

CHAPTER XIII

Othello: *A Tragedy of Jealousy*

OTHELLO has suffered less in its modern interpretation than any other of Shakespeare's tragedies, it would seem. So insistently did Shakespeare keep this tragedy unified about the theme of jealousy and the central victims of the passion, so obviously did he mould his plot about the black Moor and the cunning Iago and the victims of their jealousy that no interpreter has been able to ignore the obvious intention of the author. Yet if we study the contemporary interpretations of the passion here portrayed, we find that Shakespeare was following in detail a broader and more significant analysis of the passion than has in modern days been understood. The play is, however, clearly a study in jealousy and in jealousy as it affects those of different races.

Jealousy was, in the thinking of the Renaissance, not one of the simple or elementary passions but a derivative or compounded passion. It is a species of envy, which is in turn a species of hatred. Hatred finds its opposite in love and is opposed to love. Envy is opposed to mercy. Yet while jealousy is opposed to love, it rises often from love. And like envy it has something of the grief or fear that comes from seeing another in possession of that which we would possess solely for ourselves, or from fearing that another may possess it. It is this curious mingling of love and hatred with grief or fear that we see in jealousy. As *The French Academie* explained:

Nowe if wee remember what hath beene declared unto us of the nature of Love, wee heard that true and pure love was without jealousie, and that this affection sprang of the love of concupiscence: and yet it was tolde us yesterday, that Jealousie was placed amongst the kindes of envy....I understand by Jealousie, a feare which a man hath, lest an other whome hee would not, should enjoy something.[1]

That jealousy brought distress or grief or pain to the mind was inevitable. Timothy Bright wrote thus of jealousy, which he discussed in connection with envy:

If it be such benefit as we enjoy, and are grieved it should be communicated with other, and wherein we refuse a partener, that is called jelousie.[2]

Though jealousy is thus compounded, it still partakes of the nature of hatred. And hatred brings in its wake anger and revenge. *The French Academie* says:

There are many that take Hatred to be an inveterate anger, because it is a habite of anger, wherby the heart escheweth something as evil, and desireth to repell & drive it away. Wherfore this affection is directly contrary to love, and so likewise is anger. For it is an offence rooted in the heart, which causeth it to wish greatly his hurt by whome it taketh it selfe to be offended.[3]

[So likewise do envy and jealousy bring anger and a desire for revenge.]

But since jealousy is also a species of envy, we need to examine the nature of envy. And of envy there are four kinds, according to *The French Academie* again: (1) the envy that we feel because the profit of others is so great as to hurt our own; (2) the envy that we feel because the welfare or profit of another has not happened to us (being in reality a kind of covetousness); (3) the envy which makes us unwilling any other should have a good which we desire or which we have wished for and could not get; and (4) the envy which makes us feel ourselves hurt when others receive any good.[4]

[1] *The French Academie*, 1594 ed. p. 320.
[2] Bright, *op. cit.* p. 83.
[3] *The French Academie*, 1594 ed. p. 313.
[4] *Ibid.* p. 316. This is, of course, an adaptation of Aristotle, *Rhetorica*, 1387^b, 21–1388^a, 28.

The most complete study of jealousy during the Renaissance was made in an Italian work by Varchi, which was translated into English and published with notes by Robert Tofte in 1615 as *The Blazon of Jealousie*. It was a work popular before the publication of the translation, however, as the editor of the English Arden *Othello* tells us.[1] And here again the fact that jealousy is a kind of envy is emphasized. That the kinds of jealousy are related to the kinds of envy is at once apparent from Varchi's analysis, for he classifies the kinds of jealousy:

(1) Eyther when wee would not have, that any one should obtayne, that which wee our selves have already gotten: (2) Or that which wee wish and desire to obtayne: (3) Or which wee have laboured and endevoured, following it in chase, and yet could never gayne the same.[2]

According to this author, jealousy comes by reason (1) of pleasure, (2) of passion, (3) of property or right, and (4) of honour. And he defines these terms in the passages which I quote:

Jealousie commeth of Pleasure, when wee estimate and prise the delight wee take in the Partie we love, at so high a rate, as we would engrosse it wholy unto our selves, and when wee thinke, or imagine, it will decrease and waxe lesse, if it should be communicated, or lent unto another:[3]

Jealousie proceedeth from Passion, when we covet to enjoy or possesse that which we most love and like, wonderfully fearing lest we should loose the possession thereof, as if our Mistresse should become a secret sweet Friend unto another man:[4]

Thirdly, Jealousie springeth from the Propertie or Right that wee have, when we (enjoying our Lady or Mistresse) would have her soly and wholy unto our selves; without being able (by any meanes) to suffer or endure, that another man should have any part or interest in her, any way, or at any time:[5]

[1] Cf. the foot-note on *Othello*, IV, i, 102, in the English Arden edition—H. C. Hart, editor.

[2] *The Blazon of Jealousie*, p. 16.

[3] *Ibid.* p. 16.

[4] *Ibid.* p. 18.

[5] *Ibid.* p. 19.

Lastly, *Jealousie* commeth in respect of a mans Reputation and Honour, according as his nature is, or as his Breeding hath beene, or after the fashion and manner of the Country, in which hee is borne and liveth, because (in this point) divers are the opinions of men, and as contrary are the Customes of Countries, whereupon they say, that the Southerne Nations, and such as dwell in hot Regions are very Jealous; eyther because they are much given and enclined unto Love naturally: or else for that they hold it a great disparagement and scandall, to have their Wifes, or their Mistresses taynted with the foule blot of Unchastitie: which thing those that are of contrary Regions, and such as live under the North-Pole, take not so deepe at the heart.... [1]

It is easily seen, then, why Shakespeare chose a story which could centre the study of jealousy about those of different races, and why[Othello's great defence of his own actions at the last is significant:

> For nought I did in hate, but all in honour.]

Just as the grief-oppressed Hamlet was the inevitable choice for the subject of a play in which revenge was motivated by a ghost and inhibited by the very passion which at the same time made possible the perception of the ghost and the inability to persist in a purpose, so Othello is the perfect choice for a study of the passion of jealousy, since in him we can see the working of the passion in one of a race to whom it is natural to be jealous.

Of the effects of "airs, waters, places", upon men's natures in general, I have spoken in an earlier portion of this book. Caxton's translation of *The Mirrour of the World* explained of Ethiopians:

In this contre of Ethiope the peple ben blacke for hete of the sonne; for it is so hoot in this contre that it semeth that the erthe shold brenne.

And of the characteristics of these men of hot complexion

---

[1] *The Blazon of Jealousie*, pp. 21–3.

I have already quoted the excellent summary in Davies's *Microcosmos*:

> For South-ward, Men are cruell, moody, madd,
> Hot, blacke, leane, leapers, lustfull, usd to vant,
> Yet wise in action, sober, fearfull, sad,
> If good, most good, if bad exceeding bad.[1]

It is in order, then, to see what Shakespeare has to say about Othello at the opening of the play. From the first we hear the fact insistently repeated that he is a Moor, that he has thick lips, that Desdemona has chosen to go to his sooty bosom. Yet we are told that he is of noble birth, that war and adventure have been his nurses, that he may be considered a barbarian and yet that the Venetian state has found him so valuable in action that he cannot be expelled, no matter what offence may be found in him. His vaunting has won him his wife; his actions have won him the confidence of the state. His noble nature is not questioned even by Iago.

Iago, it would seem, is of the melancholy humour, fitly chosen for the villain in a tragedy of jealousy. As Tofte says,

the sallow complectioned fellow, with a blacke beard, beeing hee that is most prone, as well to suspect, as to be suspected about Womens matters,[2]

and the *Optick Glasse of Humors* likewise testifies that the melancholy man

by his contemplative facultie by his assiduitie of sad and serious meditation is a brocher of dangerous machiavellisme, and inventor of stratagems,...[3]

---

[1] Cf. Section II, chapter v, p. 62.
[2] *The Blazon of Jealousie*, p. 21.
[3] Walkington, *op. cit.* p. 66. It must always be remembered that melancholy resulted both in "heavenly contemplation" and in cynical meditation.

But Iago is, as we might expect, not merely jealous. With him jealousy is but one phase of envy, and in his heart is perfect hatred. In him passion has already worked its destruction. And from the outset of the play we see evidence of the eternal truth of the statement found in *The French Academie*:

> Now as there is no wicked affection, which carrieth not about, it owne torment to take vengeance thereof by the just judgement of God, so this of envy passeth all the rest in this respect. Therefore it was well saide of them that taught, that envy is most just, because of it selfe it is the same punishment to the envious man, which it deserveth.[1]

Envy, this writer says, is vile and servile, and is moreover secretive:

> But the envious body is constrained to bite on his bridle, to chew and to devoure his envy within himselfe, and to locke up his owne miserie in the bottome of his heart, to the ende it breake not foorth and shew it selfe, whereby the body receiveth great detriment. For it becommeth pale, wanne, swart, and leane, the eyes sinke into the head, the lookes are askew, and the whole countenance is disfigured. And within the heart the furies are enclosed, which give him so small rest, that greater torment can not be imagined.[2]

It is then on a theme of hate that the play opens. It is a hate of inveterate anger. It is a hate that is bound up with envy. Othello has preferred to be his lieutenant a military theorist, one Michael Cassio, over the experienced soldier Iago, to whom has fallen instead the post of "his Moorship's ancient". Roderigo questions Iago:

> Thou told'st me thou didst hold him in thy hate.

And the reply is a torrent of proof of the hatred for Othello that has almost exceeded the envy of Cassio because he possesses the prize which Iago has sought to obtain for himself. There follows proof also of the vile and servile and

---

[1] *The French Academie*, 1594 ed. p. 317.
[2] *Ibid.* pp. 317, 318.

secretive nature of this envy, for Iago's speech is a full confession:

> In following him, I follow but myself;
> Heaven is my judge, not I for love and duty,
> But seeming so, for my peculiar end;
> For when my outward action doth demonstrate
> The native act and figure of my heart
> In compliment extern, 't is not long after
> But I will wear my heart upon my sleeve
> For daws to peck at. I am not what I am.[1]

Just as Iago is envious because Cassio possesses the prize which he had sought to get for himself, and as he hates Othello as the one who preferred Cassio to himself, so Roderigo is presented as one who is the victim of jealousy because Othello has got possession of the girl whom he has followed and could not gain. So much is apparent from Brabantio's hostile greeting to his first warning of Desdemona's departure:

> I have charg'd thee not to haunt about my doors.
> In honest plainness thou hast heard me say
> My daughter is not for thee;...[2]

And as the reluctant Brabantio is finally roused to take heed of the warning given by these two envious and jealous alarmers, we hear Iago reaffirm the nature of his envy and his hate as he decides it will not be well for him to be recognized as an agent in giving the alarm against the Moor:

> Though I do hate him as I do hell-pains,
> Yet, for necessity of present life,
> I must show out a flag and sign of love,
> Which is indeed but sign.[3]

And from hearing the rage of Brabantio at his daughter, we are transported to the hypocritical warnings of Othello by Iago concerning the danger to be feared from this very

[1] I, i, 58–65. [2] I, i, 96–8. [3] I, i, 155–58.

Brabantio. Then in the midst of the commotion brewed in the night by the news of war and the news of Othello's marriage, we find that, having begun the play on the note of hate and envy, Shakespeare is now balancing love and hate, and the whole of the first act is seen to be as well an anatomy of love as of hate. Brabantio cannot see love save as decorum decrees. The maxim of the philosophers is his guide:

Wee must avoide all disparitie of goods, of houses, of age, and especially of nature and manners.[1]

And in all possible ways he cries:

> ...and she, in spite of nature,
> Of years, of country, credit, everything,
> To fall in love with what she fear'd to look on![2]

He is struck with grief over such a love, and he can only look to hell and witchcraft for its causes. His grief is so excessive that the Duke counsels him in the manner of the King to Hamlet, with many apothegms, that he endure his grief when remedies are wanting.

The simple and noble love of Othello and Desdemona is known to us all, but it must be noted that Desdemona, like Cordelia, loves both her father and her husband in reason. She says to her father:

> My noble father,
> I do perceive here a divided duty.
> To you I am bound for life and education;
> My life and education both do learn me
> How to respect you; you are the lord of duty;
> I am hitherto your daughter. But here's my husband;
> And so much duty as my mother show'd
> To you, preferring you before her father,
> So much I challenge that I may profess
> Due to the Moor, my lord.[3]

---

[1] *The French Academie*, 1586 ed. p. 500. 1618 ed. p. 205.
[2] I, iii, 96–8.   [3] I, iii, 180–9.

That her love is that perfect love which philosophers found
to blend the love of body and of mind is evident also in the
familiar:

> That I did love the Moor to live with him,
> My downright violence and storm of fortunes
> May trumpet to the world. My heart's subdu'd
> Even to the very quality of my lord.
> I saw Othello's visage in his mind,
> And to his honours and his valiant parts.
> Did I my soul and fortunes consecrate.[1]

And she begs to be allowed to go with him as he goes to war.

That Othello's love too is a love that is noble and perfect
is evident in his simple:

> She lov'd me for the dangers I had pass'd,
> And I lov'd her that she did pity them.[2]

Furthermore he stresses the fact in his plea that her wish to
accompany him be granted that he does not make the plea
in lust or because love has mastered reason:

> Vouch with me, Heaven, I therefore beg it not
> To please the palate of my appetite,
> Nor to comply with heat, the young affects
> In my defunct and proper satisfaction,
> But to be free and bounteous to her mind;
> And Heaven defend your good souls, that you think
> I will your serious and great business scant
> When she is with me.[3]

Against this tempered and noble love is pictured the love
of Roderigo. His love is intemperate, he is over-fond, he
wishes to commit self-murder rather than to live in such
torment, he is ashamed and yet cannot find virtue to overcome that of which he is ashamed. Above all, he will secure
his love by foul means and shamefully. His passion controls
his will even though his judgment acts in opposition to it.

---

[1] I, iii, 249–55.   [2] I, iii, 167, 168.   [3] I, iii, 262–9.

To him Iago explains his philosophy of love, and because he explains also with absolute explicitness the Shakespearean villain, his words are of great import. To Iago love is merely "a lust of the blood and a permission of the will". Self-love, which is in the thinking of Shakespeare's day the mother of all vices, is the only love that Iago respects. To Roderigo's talk of virtue he exclaims:

> Virtue! a fig! 't is in ourselves that we are thus or thus. Our bodies are our gardens, to the which our wills are gardeners; so that if we will plant nettles, or sow lettuce, set hyssop and weed up thyme, supply it with one gender of herbs, or distract it with many, either to have it sterile with idleness, or manured with industry, why, the power and corrigible authority of this lies in our wills. If the balance of our lives had not one scale of reason to poise another of sensuality, the blood and baseness of our natures would conduct us to most preposterous conclusions; but we have reason to cool our raging motions, our carnal stings, our unbitted lusts, whereof I take this that you call love to be a sect or scion.[1]

It is thus that the villain is defined. Will is directed to the gaining of ends set by passion and judged by reason. The passion which escapes reason and leads men on to their destruction is the passion which marks the tragic hero. But the passion which sets the ends and has the means judged by reason is the passion which we have already seen is mortal sin. And such is the passion that has brought the judgment and the will into its service in Iago and in the other villains. In Roderigo even there is still a fight between passion and reason; in Iago there is no fight, for the higher is made to serve the lower.

As for Iago's analysis of the love of Othello and Desdemona, he advises Roderigo to put money in his purse and prepare for what must be; Desdemona as soon as her desire is sated will turn from the Moor; the Moors are changeable, and Othello will change. And he summarizes:

> If sanctimony and a frail vow betwixt an erring barbarian and a

[1] I, iii, 321–37.

super-subtle Venetian be not too hard for my wits and all the tribe of hell, thou shalt enjoy her;...Seek thou rather to be hang'd in compassing thy joy than to be drown'd and go without her.[1]

And the act closes with a return to the original theme of hate in Iago's speech to Roderigo:

I had told thee often, and I re-tell thee again and again, I hate the Moor. My cause is hearted; thine hath no less reason. Let us be conjunctive in our revenge against him.[2]

The final soliloquy of Iago rehearses his villainy. He makes the fool Roderigo his purse, and he uses him for a purpose. Moreover, Iago is full of hate and envy and jealousy by habit. He feeds his passion constantly:

> I hate the Moor;
> And it is thought abroad that 'twixt my sheets
> He has done my office. I know not if 't be true;
> But I for mere suspicion in that kind,
> Will do as if for surety.[3]

To get Cassio's place and to effect a double purpose he plots all then—to make the Moor believe that the charming Cassio is too familiar with Desdemona, and to take advantage of the "free and open nature" of the Moor, who can be led by the nose because he thinks men honest if they seem to be so.

The second act of *Othello* opens with the peace after war, the calm after the storm, perfect happiness after the evils that make happiness more prized. Othello is moved to exclaim:

> If it were now to die,
> 'T were now to be most happy; for, I fear,
> My soul hath her content so absolute
> That not another comfort like to this
> Succeeds in unknown fate.[4]

---

[1] I, iii, 361–8.   [2] I, iii, 371–4.
[3] I, iii, 392–6.   [4] II, i, 191–5.

And again he confesses, "I dote In mine own comforts". The love of Othello and Desdemona is quiet and safe and sure.

But peace and calm and love are all to be broken by the villainy which will lead its victims one by one to passion and thence to self-destruction. Iago reveals his machiavellianism *– scheme* insistently. First we see him watching Cassio's greeting of Desdemona and concluding:

> With as little a web as this will I ensnare as great a fly as Cassio.

Then we see him working upon Roderigo, urging that Desdemona loved the Moor but for his "fantastical lies", that she loved him too violently:

> When the blood is made dull with the act of sport, there should be, again to inflame it, and to give satiety a fresh appetite, loveliness in favour, sympathy in years, manners, and beauties; all which the Moor is defective in. [1]

And as he insinuates vileness into the friendliness of Desdemona's greeting of Cassio, he urges Roderigo to anger Cassio, warning him, however, that Cassio is "rash and very sudden in choler". And then in his great soliloquy he shows us his soul:

> The Moor, howbeit that I endure him not,
> Is of a constant, loving, noble nature,
> And I dare think he'll prove to Desdemona
> A most dear husband. Now, I do love her too;
> Not out of absolute lust, though peradventure
> I stand accountant for as great a sin,
> But partly led to diet my revenge,
> For that I do suspect the lusty Moor
> Hath leap'd into my seat; the thought whereof
> Doth, like a poisonous mineral, gnaw my inwards;
> And nothing can or shall content my soul
> Till I am even'd with him, wife for wife;

[1] II, i, 228–33.

Or failing so, yet that I put the Moor
At least into a jealousy so strong
That judgement cannot cure. Which thing to do,
If this poor trash of Venice, whom I trash
For his quick hunting, stand the putting on,
I'll have our Michael Cassio on the hip,
Abuse him to the Moor in the rank garb—
For I fear Cassio with my night-cap too—
Make the Moor thank me, love me, and reward me,
For making him egregiously an ass
And practising upon his peace and quiet
Even to madness.[1]

The hatred which he feels toward Othello demands revenge;
and revenge demands not only a wife for a wife; it demands
also that Othello shall feel this same gnawing jealousy which
is destroying him. He will use Cassio to this purpose, but
no sooner does he turn his thoughts to Cassio than he suspects him too and feeds his jealousy with thinking. The rest
of the play is taken up largely with the execution of his plan,
for he does indeed put the Moor "into a jealousy so strong
That judgement cannot cure" and swiftly we see him
practising upon Othello's "peace and quiet Even to madness".

Deliberately Iago proceeds in his villainy by stirring up
passions in his victims that lure them on to their own
downfall. Roderigo, the "sick fool", "whom love hath
turn'd almost the wrong side out", is roused to a jealousy
of Cassio; Iago now proceeds to use him as a decoy for
Cassio. Cassio, who is "rash and very sudden in choler",
and who has "very poor and unhappy brains for drinking",
is led against his judgment into drinking, and drink for him
quickly obscures reason and lets passion go unchecked. The
scene which follows is but a prelude to the angry entrance
of Othello as he comes to demand the cause of an unseemly
brawl among his soldiers that disturbs the peace of Cyprus.

[1] II, i, 297–320.

And the anger of Othello is but the beginning of his down-fall. He himself gives us the cue:

> Now, by heaven,
> My blood begins my safer guides to rule;
> And passion, having my best judgement collied,
> Assays to lead the way.[1]

Thus Iago, by skilfully rousing each victim to passion, prepares for his final plot which shall touch even Desdemona and "turn her virtue into pitch" to Othello's jaundiced sight. There is discourse of reputation and of the devil of drink, but the act ends with Iago's soliloquy, repeating the wisdom of *Hamlet* and of *Macbeth* in regard to the necessity for quick action:

> Two things are to be done:
> My wife must move for Cassio to her mistress;
> I'll set her on;
> Myself the while to draw the Moor apart,
> And bring him jump when he may Cassio find
> Soliciting his wife. Ay, that's the way;
> Dull not device by coldness and delay.[2]

Act III is the record of the success of the plots so devised. Cassio entreats Desdemona and is seen by Iago and Othello. Her entreaties to Othello win him to her opinion, it would seem, and he cries prophetically:

> Excellent wretch! Perdition catch my soul,
> But I do love thee! and when I love thee not,
> Chaos is come again.[3]

Then as Iago commences his subtle suggestion of evil, as he confesses that his jealousy often "shapes faults that are not", we find that he begins his attack on Othello to rouse his jealousy by talking about his good name. In other words, the fourth cause of jealousy as given in *The Blazon of Jealousie*, is appropriately chosen here to stir up passion

---

[1] II, iii, 204–7.   [2] II, iii, 388–94.   [3] III, iii, 90–2.

in this man of the black complexion. In the passage from this work quoted earlier in the chapter, it was said:

Jealousie commeth in respect of a mans Reputation and Honor, according as his nature is, or as his Breeding hath beene, or after the fashion and manner of the Country, in which hee is borne and liveth.... [1]

Tofte's note on this passage of Varchi said:

Honor, is the Reputation and Credit, or the good name and Fame, of a Man, which the generous Spirit priseth, at so high a rate, as before hee will have the same eclipst, hee will loose all his wealth, yea, and his dearest life.... [2]

It is at once perceived that the note struck by Cassio in the second act in his "Reputation, reputation, reputation!" speech is the same one that is now more significantly echoed by Iago:

> Good name in man and woman, dear my lord,
> Is the immediate jewel of their souls.
> Who steals my purse steals trash; 't is something, nothing;
> 'T was mine, 't is his, and has been slave to thousands;
> But he that filches from me my good name
> Robs me of that which not enriches him,
> And makes me poor indeed. [3]

This is the keynote of Othello's jealousy, as it should be the keynote of the jealousy of the alien black man who was general in the army of Venice. And Shakespeare characteristically harps the note, in Cassio, in Iago, in Othello.

The Blazon of Jealousie gives the reason also for the next speech of Iago in the passage, which, quoting Petrarch, [4] explains:

And partly it declareth the nature of this insatiable Monster, who

[1] *The Blazon of Jealousie*, pp. 21–3.

[2] The annotations of Varchi's work with which Tofte has surrounded the text usually reinforce the text, but this is an interesting English addition.

[3] III, iii, 155–61.

[4] The passage is instanced by the key line, *Vatene: a che piu fiera che non suole*, etc.

thinketh it not enough, to have infected and spoyled a man with her poyson on the sodayne: but shee must also turne backe againe, with divers and strange Apparisions and Shadows, that is, with new Fashions and Shapes, after a more cruell and fearefull manner every day more than other, and so encreaseth continually, to the greater discontentment of his minde.[1]

The much-discussed words of Iago echo the metaphor:

> O, beware, my lord, of jealousy;
> It is the green-ey'd monster which doth mock
> The meat it feeds on.[2]

But as Othello disclaims all possibility of being jealous, despising jealousy in his soul, he boasts, and his boast is a statement of the jealousy arising from pleasure:

> No, Iago;
> I'll see before I doubt; when I doubt, prove;
> And on the proof, there is no more but this,—
> Away at once with love or jealousy![3]

Then it is that the crafty Iago uses the argument most likely to cause fear in Othello, the argument of the unknown; for Desdemona is of a different race and nation:

> In Venice they do let Heaven see the pranks
> They dare not show their husbands. Their best conscience
> Is not to leave 't undone, but keep 't unknown.[4]

She deceived her father to marry Othello; therefore deceit is in her. And above all, the recurrent argument is heard:

> Not to affect many proposed matches
> Of her own clime, complexion, and degree,
> Whereto we see in all things nature tends.—[5]

Furthermore, Desdemona may repent:

> Her will, recoiling to her better judgement,
> May fail to match you with her country forms,
> And happily repent.[6]

---

[1] *The Blazon of Jealousie*, p. 51.
[2] III, iii, 165–7.
[3] III, iii, 189–92.
[4] III, iii, 202–4.
[5] III, iii, 229–31.
[6] III, iii, 236–8.

It would seem that Othello's reaction, "Why did I marry?" is too sudden to have come save that he was already angered by Cassio. Varchi explained:

Besides, the Minde and Condition of the Lover toward the Woman whom hee affecteth, importeth very much in this businesse; for if he be given to choler, or is (by any other Accident) discontent and displeased, hee will then quickly take occasion to be angry with her, and every mote (as the Proverbe goeth) is a Beame in his eye.... [1]

As Othello is left alone, the workings of the monster in his heart are apparent. It is now the jealousy that through pleasure and passion felt in and for the loved one advances to jealousy that is the jealousy of property. Varchi says:

And so puissant and potent is this our desire, which wee have to enjoy that Party (which wee love) soly and alone, without the societie and company of any other whatsoever, as that (many times) when this our high-pris'd Commoditie chanceth to light into some other merchants hands, and that this our private Inclosure proveth to be a Common for others, wee care no more for it, but give it altogether over, quite extinguishing and quenching in us, not alone the Jealousie wee had of the same, but likewise the hot love and affection wee bare it before.... [2]

Thus we hear Othello:

> I am abus'd; and my relief
> Must be to loathe her. O curse of marriage,
> That we can call these delicate creatures ours,
> And not their appetites! I had rather be a toad
> And live upon the vapour of a dungeon,
> Then keep a corner of the thing I love
> For others' uses. [3]

Now indeed Othello is become the man who is described by Varchi:

for this strange Maladie engendreth a continuall and a perpetuall discontentment and disquietnesse in the minde, for that hee is not able, nor hath any power to give over from vexing himselfe.... [4]

---

[1] *The Blazon of Jealousie*, p. 29.   [2] *Ibid.* p. 20.
[3] III, iii, 267–73.   [4] *The Blazon of Jealousie*, p. 45.

Othello himself cries:

> thou hast set me on the rack.
> I swear 't is better to be much abus'd
> Than but to know a little.[1]

And then we find him torturing himself with the thoughts of Cassio's kisses on Desdemona's lips, and he reiterates the property idea in his talk of being robbed.

From this time on, Othello has become the slave of passion. As he cries farewell to the tranquil mind, to content, to war and his occupation, as he demands that Iago prove his love a whore, as he threatens Iago and begs for proof at the same time, he is finally led almost to the verge of madness in his return to a discussion of honour, Desdemona's honour this time:

> Her name, that was as fresh
> As Dian's visage, is now begrim'd and black
> As mine own face. If there be cords, or knives,
> Poison, or fire, or suffocating streams,
> I'll not endure it. Would I were satisfied![2]

Iago says truly:

> I see, sir, you are eaten up with passion;

and it is well to recall that Othello's speech when he came to quiet the brawl of Cassio marked the beginning of his giving way to passion which is climaxed here.

From this time Othello lives in a world which has become chaos through his own passion. Now jealousy is seen in its close kinship with that anger which demands revenge. To Iago's tale of Cassio's dream, he exclaims only:

> I'll tear her all to pieces.

To Iago's suggestion concerning the handkerchief which was lost, and which we have already seen Iago seize for

[1] III, iii, 335–7.   [2] III, iii, 386–90.

his purposes, Othello replies in a torrent of passionate invective:

> O, that the slave had forty thousand lives!
> One is too poor, too weak for my revenge.
> Now do I see 't is true. Look here, Iago;
> All my fond love thus do I blow to heaven.
> 'T is gone.
> Arise, black vengeance, from the hollow hell!
> Yield up, O love, thy crown and hearted throne
> To tyrannous hate! Swell, bosom, with thy fraught,
> For 't is of aspics' tongues.[1]

In final and desperate avowal, he swears his vengeance even as he kneels to sanctify his oath:

> Even so my bloody thoughts, with violent pace,
> Shall ne'er look back, ne'er ebb to humble love,
> Till that a capable and wide revenge
> Swallow them up.[2]

To Iago he charges that Cassio be not alive in three days, and then to Iago's skilful cry that he let Desdemona live, he determines:

> Damn her, lewd minx! O damn her! damn her!
> Come, go with me apart; I will withdraw
> To furnish me with some swift means of death
> For the fair devil.[3]

And he adds the proof of Iago's victory over the Cassio whom he envied:

> Now art thou my lieutenant.

The last scene of Act III is the result of the jealousy that makes every mote a beam, that makes the lost handkerchief the cause of murder. As Emilia and Desdemona talk at the beginning of the scene, Desdemona affirms her faith in her husband:

> ...and, but my noble Moor
> Is true of mind and made of no such baseness

[1] III, iii, 442–50.   [2] III, iii, 457–60.   [3] III, iii, 475–8.

> As jealous creatures are, it were enough
> To put him to ill thinking.[1]

Emilia inquires, "Is he not jealous?" and again Desdemona replies:

> Who, he? I think the sun where he was born
> Drew all such humours from him.[2]

But the entrance of Othello, with his persistent quibbling about Desdemona's hand as hot and moist, and hence as joyous and lascivious, proves her faith ironically misplaced. Her frightened lie about the handkerchief brings him to such evidences of jealousy that Emilia can question again, "Is not this man jealous?" And Desdemona can but answer that she never saw this in her lord before.

The entrance of Cassio finds Desdemona still wondering at Othello's strange behaviour; and at Iago's praise of Othello's habitual calm and his wonder at his anger, she becomes at once, in contrast to Othello, merciful and kind in her judgment. It is some distressing business of state that has caused his apparent anger, she decides, and Emilia wishes it may be so. But the experienced Emilia comments from her wisdom:

> But jealous souls will not be answer'd so;
> They are not ever jealous for the cause,
> But jealous for they're jealous. It is a monster
> Begot upon itself, born on itself.[3]

Thus also *The Blazon of Jealousie* says:

Besides, it importeth very much to know of what nature the Jealous man is, because if hee be naturally suspitious, hee then will take every thing in the worse sense, interpreting all whatsoever he eyther heareth or seeth, in a sinister and bad sense or meaning, and so his Disease (in time) commeth to be desperate.[4]

[1] III, iv, 26–9.
[2] III, iv, 30, 31. The insistence upon the result of climate on temperament is significant.
[3] III, iv, 159–62.   [4] *The Blazon of Jealousie*, p. 24.

Act III ends with Cassio giving the handkerchief to Bianca, ignorant of its fateful story. Act IV begins with Iago calling the handkerchief to Othello's memory and suggesting images of Desdemona and Cassio that must rouse jealousy to desperation.[1] Then in the midst of his inarticulate raving, Othello falls into an epilepsy, and Iago explains to Cassio, who enters in untimely fashion:

> My lord is fallen into an epilepsy.
> This is the second fit; he had one yesterday.
>
> .   .   .   .
>
> The lethargy must have his quiet course;
> If not, he foams at mouth and by and by
> Breaks out to savage madness.[2]

It is the same plea that Lady Macbeth makes for her Lord as the fit seizes him at the feast on the dread night of Banquo's murder.

To Othello, likewise after the fashion of Lady Macbeth, Iago speaks his chiding:

> Whilst you were here o'erwhelmed with your grief—
> A passion most unsuiting such a man—
> Cassio came hither. I shifted him away,
> And laid good 'scuse upon your ecstasy.[3]

And as he plots the misleading conversation with Cassio, which Othello must overhear, he counsels still:

> Marry, patience;
> Or I shall say you're all in all in spleen,
> And nothing of a man.[4]

It is a strange Othello who replies:

> I will be found most cunning in my patience;
> But—dost thou hear?—most bloody.

---

[1] This use of false images is to be noted as one of the chief means used by Iago, and also as one of the characteristic features of Othello's jealousy. Cf. III, iii, 341; IV, i, 35–44; IV, i, 198–201, etc.
[2] IV, i, 51–6.   [3] IV, i, 77–80.   [4] IV, i, 88–90.

The plot which Iago frames is interestingly explained in his

> Othello shall go mad;
> And his unbookish jealousy must construe
> Poor Cassio's smiles, gestures, and light behaviours
> Quite in the wrong.[1]

Now it has been argued whether his reference is to such books as *The Blazon of Jealousie*, in which Othello might have been conspicuously unversed.[2] But a knowledge of jealousy would not have helped him to construe aright the words and gestures of Cassio. Cassio was not supposed to be jealous but rather lustful and scornful of his lust. If Othello had known the signs of the passions as they were explained in such books as dealt with the anatomy of the soul or of the passions in particular, he could not have been deceived. And this is what Shakespeare meant to have Iago say, I think. To argue concerning a possible knowledge of books of jealousy (of which Varchi's seems to have been the only one devoted wholly to the one passion) is beside the point. At any rate, Othello was not able rightly to distinguish the signs of passion in Cassio, and hence Iago found him pliable and open to his suggestion.

Now that Othello is roused by jealousy to anger and to a hungry desire for revenge, it is of anger that is opposed to love and of the impatient desire for revenge that we hear. His speeches are full of threats: "How shall I murder him, Iago", and "I would have him nine years a-killing". But as his thoughts turn to Desdemona, even as he decides that "she shall not live", grief overwhelms him, and he commences to rehearse her claims to being loved, and to lament "the pity of it".

But to Iago's suggestion that if her offence does not injure Othello, it injures no one, Othello cries:

> I will chop her into messes. Cuckold me!

[1] IV, i, 101–4.   [2] Cf. note 1 on p. 150.

His mind is again centred on his own injury. And it may be well to study the words of *The French Academie*:

For this cause when the heart is wounded with griefe by any one, it desireth to returne the like to him that hurt it, and to rebite him of whome it is bitten. This affection is a desire of revenge, which being put in execution, is revenge accomplished: namely, when wee cause him that hath offended us to suffer that punishment, which in our judgement he hath deserved.... Every offence therefore that ingendreth hatred, anger, envy or indignation bringeth with it a desire of revenge, which is to render evill for evill, and to requite griefe received with the like againe.

And when the offence is grown to that passe, that nothing can asswage the extremitie thereof, nor stay it from breaking foorth into revenge and hurting by all the meanes that may bee, then is this Revenge turned into Rage.[1]

The revenge of Iago has demanded that Cassio be punished and that Othello be made to feel the same madness of jealousy that he has felt. The revenge of Othello demands now that both Cassio and Desdemona die for having caused him grief, for daring to injure his honour, for having cuckolded him. He demands poison, but Iago is more just in his revenges:

Do it not with poison; strangle her in her bed, even the bed she hath contaminated.[2]

And Othello replies:

Good, good; the justice of it pleases; very good.

Thus revenge always cries for justice and for that cunning justice that fits punishment to offence.[3]

As Lodovico arrives to summon Othello to Venice and to bring word that the government of Cyprus shall be placed in Cassio's care, the angry Othello has advanced so far in anger and rage that he strikes Desdemona, mocks her grief

---

[1] *The French Academie*, 1594 ed. pp. 325, 326.
[2] IV, i, 220–1.
[3] Cf. the series of "tragedies" described in Section I, chapter i.

as "well-painted passion", and welcomes Lodovico with such
insane jibes that the astonished man can but question Iago:

> Is this the noble Moor whom our full Senate
> Call all in all sufficient? Is this the nature
> Whom passion could not shake? whose solid virtue
> The shot of accident nor dart of chance
> Could neither graze nor pierce?[1]

And then to Iago's wise grief he adds:

> Are his wits safe? Is he not light of brain?[2]

The vexing suspicions of the jealous man, his insistent
feeding of his jealousy with reiterated suspicions, are brought
out in the next scene, in which Othello first questions
Emilia and then turns upon Desdemona with his reproaches.
Always there are stressed the images which fantasy forges
in Othello's mad brain to goad his passion. Truly Desdemona
may say that she understands a fury in his words. His great
cry for revenge is a cry that makes his fury echo all the
different claims of jealousy—the jealousy for honour, the
jealousy for pleasure and passion, the jealousy for property:

> Had it pleas'd Heaven
> To try me with affliction; had they rain'd
> All kinds of sores and shames on my bare head,
> Steep'd me in poverty to the very lips,
> Given to captivity me and my utmost hopes,
> I should have found in some place of my soul
> A drop of patience; but, alas, to make me
> The fixed figure for the time of scorn
> To point his slow and moving finger at!
> Yet I could bear that too, well, very well;
> But there, where I have garner'd up my heart,
> Where either I must live, or bear no life;
> The fountain from the which my current runs,
> Or else dries up; to be discarded thence!
> Or keep it as a cistern for foul toads
> To knot and gender in.[3]

[1] IV, i, 275–79.   [2] IV, i, 280.   [3] IV, ii, 47–62.

Swiftly there follow the episodes that bring us to the end of the act: Othello crushing Desdemona with his final coarse taunts; Iago hypocritically comforting her; Iago plotting Cassio's death with Roderigo, his tool; Desdemona singing the wanton's song as she prepares to lie between her wedding sheets; Emilia uttering wise and bitter comment on the ways of men and women in their jealousies.

The last act but spreads before us the devastation wrought by passion. Roderigo is fatally wounded in the fray which comes as the result of his attempt to kill Cassio. The Moor goes to his task of killing his wife in the name of justice:

> Thy bed, lust-stain'd, shall with lust's blood be spotted.[1]

And in the second scene, the scene of the murder, he cries again as he looks upon the sleeping Desdemona and kisses her:

> Oh, balmy breath, thou dost almost persuade
> Justice to break her sword![2]

It is this insistence upon the passion which makes men try to take the place of God, and by private revenge execute the laws of God that makes *Othello* significant in the tragedy of its time. Othello sees his acts as the expression of justice, worked out in the most perfect balance of deed and punishment. And yet Shakespeare shows us the passion which impels him to revenge rather than the judgment which alone can mete out justice. Desdemona makes us see him indeed as passion's slave and not as the executioner of God's justice when she cries:

> Alas, why gnaw you so your nether lip?
> Some bloody passion shakes your very frame.[3]

As Desdemona denies her guilt, he himself exclaims:

> O perjur'd woman! thou dost stone my heart,
> And mak'st me call what I intend to do
> A murder, which I thought a sacrifice.[4]

---

[1] v, i, 36.   [2] v, ii, 16, 17.   [3] v, ii, 43, 44.   [4] v, ii, 63-5.

It is a significant cry, for Othello does think of himself as sacrificing Desdemona to his honour.

His revenge knows no bounds. Of Cassio he exclaims:

> Had all his hairs been lives, my great revenge
> Had stomach for them all.[1]

And as he hears the news of Roderigo's death and Cassio's escape, he utters a cry like that of Macbeth:

> Not Cassio kill'd! Then murder's out of tune,
> And sweet revenge grows harsh.[2]

The end of the play in its uncovering of villainy and its terrific exhibiting of grief and repentance need not be rehearsed in detail. But Othello's final defence must be carefully considered:

> An honourable murderer, if you will;
> For nought I did in hate, but all in honour.[3]

And at the last:

> Then must you speak
> Of one that lov'd not wisely but too well;
> Of one not easily jealous, but being wrought
> Perplex'd in the extreme; of one whose hand,
> Like the base Indian, threw a pearl away
> Richer than all his tribe.[4]

It must be remembered, however, that Othello executes the same justice upon himself that he had tried to execute upon Desdemona, that he kills himself and falls upon the murderous bed with the cry:

> I kiss'd thee ere I kill'd thee: no way but this,
> Killing myself, to die upon a kiss.[5]

And Cassio pays him his final tribute, "For he was great of heart".

At the close of the play Brabantio is dead of his grief over

---

[1] v, ii, 74, 75.   [2] v, ii, 115, 116.   [3] v, ii, 294, 295.
[4] v, ii, 343–8.   [5] v, ii, 358, 359.

the marriage of his daughter; Roderigo is dead through the retribution that has come upon him in his attempt to gain the means to his unholy love; Emilia is dead through the angry vengeance of her husband; Desdemona has been murdered in Othello's attempt to revenge his own jealous honour; Othello has killed himself in his final grief; Iago awaits his punishment. But most truly has the play pictured the fact that

> Now as there is no wicked affection, which carrieth not about, it owne torment to take vengeance thereof by the just judgement of God, so this of envy passeth all the rest in this respect.[1]

And we see the significance of Othello's last words to Iago:

> I'd have thee live;
> For, in my sense, 't is happiness to die.[2]

Again Shakespeare has pictured a passion in all its associations. Here jealousy, which is compounded of the hatred which is envy and of grief that must be associated with envy, is pictured in all of its phases. The variants of love are shown; the variants of envy are likewise depicted. Again the passion studied is shown in different people of different races.

The envious jealousy of Roderigo, the envy of Iago which has possessed his reason and converted his very judgment and his will to its uses; the jealousy of Othello which centres about his honour but includes his pleasure and his passion and his sense of property as ministering causes—all these are pictured. And again passion has wrought its deadly work: drink has ministered to passion and caused disaster; passion has resulted in epilepsy and then in fury and rage and finally in murder. And passion has again caused the innocent to suffer with the guilty.

[1] Cf. p. 153, *ante*. [2] v, ii, 289, 290.

CHAPTER XIV

King Lear: *A Tragedy of Wrath in Old Age*

WILLIAM BALDWIN, to illustrate the value of teaching by means of proverbs and adages, proposed:

As for an example this lyttle proverb.
>   Wrathe leadeth shame in a lease.

What myght there be sayde to cause a man more to refayne his wrath? For every man naturally hateth shame, whiche sith it is the folower and ende of anger, and thereto joyned inseperablye, even as the shadowe foloweth the body, what man considering the ende, wyl use hym selfe therto. And to make hym ashamed, loe here an other.

>   He that to his wrath and anger is thrall,
>   Over his wyt hath no power at all.

Nowe what maye make a man more ashamed of hym selfe, than to be thought a very foole? I suppose nothyng.[1]

The number of such popular sayings in regard to anger imbedded in the literature and the philosophy of the sixteenth century is astonishing, but it reflects an absorbing interest in this passion. For of all the subjects upon which men of the Renaissance exercised moral judgment, none seems to have been so universally and so exhaustively studied as anger.

The more learned centred their discussion about the general problem of whether anger is a passion to be wholly

---

[1] William Baldwin, *A Treatise of Morall Philosophie*, 1547. Cf. Section II, note 2 on p. 49, *ante*. Cf. also the following questions and answers of *The Nosegay of Morall Philosophie*, by T(homas) C(rewe), 1580:

"*Q*. What is that doctrine which we should necessarily forget?
"*A*. The vice of revengement.
"*Q*. What is anger or furie?
"*A*. A certaine briefe kind of rage or folly".

condemned or whether it is, when tempered and used to serve certain ends, justifiable. The moderate position of the Peripatetics and of Thomas Aquinas was thus opposed to that of Cicero and the Stoics, who condemned all anger as bad. But the position of the Peripatetics was reinforced by the reputation that the ancient Jehovah had for being an angry God. In any case, intemperate anger was considered in many profound treatises, as well as in popular sayings, to be both folly and madness and to bring shame in its inevitable train.

But it is always to be remembered that the Renaissance passion of anger had its mediaeval background in the deadly sin of wrath. And nowhere is this sin better set forth than in the *Parson's Tale* of Chaucer:

> This synne of ire, after the discryvyng of Seint Augustyn, is wikked wil to been avenged by word or by dede. Ire, after the philosophre, is the fervent blood of man y-quyked in his herte, thurgh which he wole harm to hym that he hateth. For certes, the herte of man, by eschawfynge and moevynge of his blood, wexeth so trouble that he is out of alle juggement of resoun.
>
> But ye shal understonde that ire is in two maneres; that oon of hem is good and that oother is wikked. The goode ire is by jalousie of goodnesse, thurgh which a man is wrooth with wikkednesse, and agayns wikkednesse;...
>
> Now understondeth that wikked ire is in two maneres, that is to seyn, sodeyn ire, or hastif ire withouten avisement and consentynge of resoun. The menyng and the sens of this is, that the resoun of man ne consente nat to thilke sodeyn ire; and thanne it is venial. Another ire is ful wikked, that comth of felonie of herte, avysed and cast biforn with wikked wil to do vengeance, and therto his resoun consenteth; and soothly this is deedly synne.

Chaucer's Parson makes pride, envy, and contumely contribute to wrath or ire. Of the deadly fruits of ire he lists "hate, that is oold wratthe"; "discord, thurgh which a man forsaketh his olde freend that he hath lovede ful longe"; and manslaughter, both spiritual and bodily.

The Renaissance passion of anger was considered, then,

much as was the mediaeval sin of wrath or ire in this tale. But it was also considered in its relation to the humour of choler, and especially to choler when through passion it became choler adust, or that sort of melancholy adust which rose from the adustion of choler. The three terms, then— anger, wrath, and choler—are often confusingly used as synonyms.

The authorities upon which the widely varying discussions of anger were based were almost infinite. The usual divisions of anger were those recorded by Thomas Adams in his *Diseases of the Soul*.[1] On the authority of Damascene he divided anger into three sorts or three degrees, translating *Bilem, Iracundiam, Insensionem*, as "choler", "wrath", and "heavy displeasure", which he then defined as being respectively anger that is soon kindled and soon extinguished, anger which is not so soon kindled but which takes a deeper hold in the memory, and anger which takes fire suddenly and will not desist until revenge is complete. To these three he would add also a fourth kind of anger which is moderate, slow, and quickly appeased.

The foundation of all Renaissance discussion of anger is to be found in Aristotle, however, as I have already said. And Aristotle defined anger as

an impulse, accompanied by pain, to a conspicuous revenge for a conspicuous slight directed without justification towards what concerns oneself or towards what concerns one's friends.[2]

Anger, according to Aristotle, always rises from injured self-esteem, from some slight inflicted upon the individual directly or indirectly, there being three kinds of slighting possible—contempt, spite, and insolence.

Since a man expects to be respected by his inferiors, he expects those to respect him to whom he is superior in birth,

---

[1] Cf. Cicero, *Tusculan Disputations*, III, especially Section v.
[2] *Rhetorica*, 1378[a], 31–34.

capacity, goodness, or anything else. Furthermore, he expects those whom he has treated well, as well as those whom he is now treating well, to respect him. According to Aristotle, then, the man who is slighted by those who he thinks ought to respect him and feel grateful toward him is the more easily offended.

Furthermore, Aristotle pointed out that the slight is most keenly felt if that aspect in which we think ourselves most worthy consideration is treated slightingly. Thus the sick man is most angered if his sickness is disregarded, a lover if his love is ignored, a generous man if his kindness is ungratefully received, etc. Anyone who shows in speech or action a tendency to slight rather than praise these qualities upon which we base our self-esteem will be the recipient of our anger. But we will be more angry with friends than with others, with those who have previously treated us becomingly and now change, and with those who do not adequately appreciate or return kindness.

Aristotle also says that the feeble are more given to anger than are the strong, and old men than young.

One important passage from the Stoic Seneca was so often referred to that it also should be given here, and I quote from the Lodge translation of *A Treatise of Anger*:

> Some therefore of the wiser sort have said that Anger is a short madnesse, for she is as little Mistresse of her selfe as the other: she forgetteth all respect, neglecteth friendships intent and obstinate in that she hath undertaken, and neglectful of reason, and incapable of counsaile. [1]

Moreover, the treatise of Plutarch, *Of Meeknes, or How a Man should Refraine Choler*, contributed to the Renaissance understanding of this passion in important passages:

> Nowe the continuall custome of anger and the ordinary or often falling into a chafe, breedeth in the minde an ill habit called wrathfulnesse, which in the end groweth to this passe, that it maketh a man

[1] Lodge transl. *op. cit.* pp. 510, 511.

cholericke and hasty, apt to be mooved at everything; and besides, it engendreth a bitter humor of revenge, and a testinesse implacable, or hardly to be appeased; namely, when the mind is exulcerate once, taking offence at every small occasion, quarreling and complaining for toies and trifles, much like unto a thin or a fine edge that entreth with the least force that the graver putteth it to.[1]

Also when I consider by what meanes choler is engendred: I see that one falleth into it upon this cause, another upon that: but in all of them, it seemeth this generall opinion there is, that they thinke themselves to be despised and naught set by.[2]

Plutarch's description of anger as, like the seed of generation which is compounded from all the elements of the body, a seed which is made of all the passions of the mind, is significant also.[3]

The French Academie again gives us a summary of contemporary opinion:

First then we must know, that *Anger* is a vehement motion of the heart, because it seeth those good things which it hath, to be contemned, whereas it judgeth them not to be such as ought to be so lightly set by. And herein it thinks it selfe despised. For every one valueth himself according to the opinion of those good things which he judgeth to be in himself: therefore there is no anger which commeth not of offence.... But there are many things that dislike us, with which notwithstanding we are not angrie, because there is no contempt of us joyned with them.... But when a man letteth loose the bridle unto this affection in such sort, that hee accustomes himselfe thereunto, this use and custome turneth it into rancour, which is an inveterate anger that hath taken roote in the heart. Nowe the better that a man thinkes of himselfe, the sooner hee is offended at every thing and the readier he is to bee mooved to anger, as taking himselfe to bee despised. This is a very vehement and violent affection. For it overthroweth very often the whole minde and soule, so that it forgetteth all right, justice and equitie, all good will and amitie, and pardoneth not, no not women or children, neither yet kinsfolkes or friends.... To bee short,

[1] Holland's Plutarch, *Morals*, pp. 119, 120.
[2] *Ibid.* p. 128.
[3] The description of the seed of generation as necessarily compounded of all the elements is regularly found. The seed is a smaller microcosmos. Anger is similarly a microcosmos of passion.

after that anger hath once got the bridle at will, the whole mind and judgement is so blinded and caried headlong, that an angry man thinks of nothing but of revenge, insomuch that he forgetteth himselfe, and careth not what he doeth, or what harme wil light upon himselfe in so doing, so that he may be avenged. And many times hee will murmure against heaven and earth, and against all the creatures, because they are not mooved to revenge his quarell: yea, which is worse, he despiteth God himselfe and waxeth wroth against him, blaspheming him, because he taketh not pleasure in serving his revenging minde. Which is as much as if he should spette against heaven: and therefore it is very necessarie, that his spettle, proceeding from such a stinking mouth, shoulde returne and fall backe upon his owne face. And when this passion of anger is verie vehement, it leadeth a man even to furie and rage, and procureth unto him not onely manie diseases, but oftentimes death it selfe. Therefore although wee knewe not what hurt this affection doeth to the soule, yet the evill which it bringeth to the bodie ought to bee of sufficient force to turne us from it.... Now because anger is a griefe proceeding of the contempt of those good thinges that are in a man, who thinketh that it ought not to be so, therefore hee desireth to shew that they are not lightly to be esteemed of, which he supposeth may be done this way, by making his power knowne, especially in hurting. Whereupon this appetite of revenge is engendered, which is common to anger with offence, hatred and envie: so that anger is alwayes mingled with sorow and with desire of revenge.[1]

This same work emphasizes also the pride that goes before anger and the shame that succeeds it.

Of the physical penalties of anger much was written, and the close kinship of anger and madness was constantly emphasized. Thus Newton wrote also:

Anger whiche is a passion so like to furye & madnes, as nothing in the world more) what force it hath, & how much it altereth the state & outward shew of the body, appeareth chieflye by countenaunce, coloure, grymme visage, cruell, and fiery eyes, puffing and wrinkled nosethrils, byting lippes, enraged mouth, trembling & shaking lymmes, unsteady gate, stammerynge and fearful voyce.

And Newton also explained that while anger harms those

[1] *The French Academie*, 1594 ed. pp. 308, 309.

ANGER.

The effects of Anger shew its nature. The eyes become red and enflamed, the eye-ball is staring and sparkling, the eye-brows are sometimes elevated, and sometimes sink down equally, the forehead is very much wrinkled between the eyes, the nostrils are open and enlarged, the lips pressing against one another, the under one rising over the upper one, leaves the corners of the mouth a little open, making a cruel and disdainfull grin.

PLATE XIII. Illustration from *Heads representing the various Passions of the Soul* as drawn by Le Brun (1619–1690). (Published *c*. 1800.)

against whom it is directed, it harms even more the person in whose heart the passion rises, and he concludes:

the mynd therfore must be reined by reason, and curbed by temperaunce, that it yelde not to affections, but procure to it self quietnes & tranquility, which (as Tullie witnesseth) is the chiefest poynt that helpeth us in this life to live wel and happely.[1]

In a very learned, exhaustive, and admonitory Christian work by John John Downame, anger is most thoroughly anatomized. The work was given a title fitting its age and its subject:

Spiritual physicke to cure the diseases of the soule, arising from superfluitie of choller, prescribed out of Gods word. Wherein the chollericke man may see the dangerousnesse of this disease of the soule unjust anger, the preservatives to keepe him from the infection thereof, and also fit medicine to restore him to health beeing alreadie subject to this raging passion. Profitable for all to use, seeing all are patients in this disease of impatiencie.[2]

The work does not add much that is new but sums up argumentatively all that was old, commenting on the bodily evils that arise from anger and adding:

But anger bringeth no lesse evils to the soule. First like a darke cloude it overshadoweth and blindeth the light of reason, and for the time maketh men as though they were distraught of their wits. Whereof it is that anger is called *Brevis furor*, a short madnesse, because it differs not from madnesse but in time.[3]

It must be evident, then, that there was in Shakespeare's day an old and firmly founded philosophy of anger, finding its sources in ancient medicine and ancient philosophy and in the mediaeval makings-over of those ancient sources as well. According to this philosophy, pride or self-esteem is the condition in which anger takes its rise, vengeance becomes its immediate object, and some slight, real or imagined, is its cause. Anger is folly; anger brings shame

[1] Newton, *op. cit.* p. 60.   [2] Published in 1600.
[3] *Ibid.* p. 53.

in its train. The sequence of passions is pride, anger, revenge, and unless madness clouds the reason altogether, shame. Anger hurts him who feels it even more than it hurts the one on whom he seeks revenge. In its train are shame on the one hand and rage, fury, frenzy, and madness on the other, not to speak of death and eternity in the reckoning. It is the most pernicious, the most destructive of passions; it has in it indeed something of the essence of all passions. And the feeble and the old are its most likely victims.

As we have seen, anger is not paired with any other passion in the table of passions. Patience is the complementary virtue of anger, but there is no complementary vice of excess or defect. Because it stands alone in the table of passions, it is therefore studied alone in *King Lear*.

In connection with the study of the passion of anger, however, Shakespeare has presented several of the problems of what I have termed practical philosophy, all of them problems such as can be most appropriately considered in connection with anger. The first is the problem of old age, for as we have seen, the feeble and the old are more subject to anger than are others, and the particular aspect of the problem of age which concerned Shakespeare at this time would seem to have been that which was treated by Plutarch under the title *Whether an aged Man Ought to Manage publike affaires*. Specifically Plutarch wrote:

But forasmuch as men ordinarily alledge many causes and pretenses, for to colour and cover their sloth & want of courage to undertake the businesse and affaires of State, & among others, as the very last, and as one would say, that which is of the sacred line & race, they tender unto us old age, & suppose they have found now one sufficient argument to dull or turne backe the edge, and to coole the heat of seeking honor thereby, in bearing us in hand & saying: That there is a certein convenient & meet end limited, not only to the revolution of yeeres, proper for combats and games of proofe, but also for publike affaires and dealings in State. [1]

[1] Holland's Plutarch, *Morals*, p. 383.

Such an attitude, Plutarch affirms, is really the result of sloth and voluptuousness. In reality the aged man should give his experience and wisdom to the state, and he is being led by "sloth & want of courage" or by voluptuousness when he lays down his burdens.

Thus Lear enters with his explanation:

> Know that we have divided
> In three our kingdom; and 't is our fast intent
> To shake all cares and business from our age,
> Conferring them on younger strengths, while we
> Unburden'd crawl toward death.[1]

And he concludes his speech by restating his intention and then appealing to his daughters:

> Tell me, my daughters,—
> Since now we will divest us both of rule,
> Interest of territory, cares of state,—
> Which of you shall we say doth love us most,
> That we our largest bounty may extend
> Where nature doth with merit challenge?[2]

It is apparent that Lear here is divesting himself of cares which he no longer wishes to carry. And it is equally apparent that he is doing it not in the interest of the recipients of his benefits but because he seeks release from duties that are burdensome.

With his appeal to his daughters to proclaim who loves him most, the King demonstrates the difficulties of another problem which was of great interest to the Renaissance philosophers and which they found well stated in another essay of Plutarch, *How a man may discerne a flatterer from a friend*. Self-love, Plutarch says, subjects a man to flattery, for he likes to have his good opinion of himself sustained. It is difficult to tell the flatterer from the friend, but the basis of judgment is to be found in the fact that the flatterer applies

[1] I, i, 38–42.   [2] I, i, 49–54.

himself to appeal to the passions of the one concerned, while the friend makes his appeal not to passion but to reason. Many specific differences are further to be observed, of course. The flatterer is inconstant, the friend constant; the flatterer always says and does what will give pleasure, the friend does not hesitate to give pain, to offer rebuke or correction, when it is necessary; the flatterer is always ready to speak, the friend is often silent; the flatterer is over-ready and excessive in his promises, the friend is temperate and just and reasonable; the flatterer bustles about but is not ready with genuine service, the friend will dissuade from unjust action but will serve even at great cost to himself.

The excessive and passionate speeches of Goneril and Regan are wordy speeches recited in answer to Lear's appeal; they are in all essentials the speeches of flatterers. But Lear, happy in his self-love, demands still more from his "joy, his youngest daughter":

> ...what can you say to draw
> A third more opulent than your sisters?[1]

Cordelia's reply is the appropriate one for the friend. She can say nothing that will draw a richer third of the kingdom. And to her father's hasty warning she can only add:

> Unhappy that I am, I cannot heave
> My heart into my mouth: I love your Majesty
> According to my bond; no more nor less.[2]

Then she speaks further a speech closely resembling that of Desdemona to her father, a speech that is clearly an appeal to reason rather than passion:

> Good my lord,
> You have begot me, bred me, lov'd me: I
> Return those duties back as are right fit;
> Obey you, love you, and most honour you.
> Why have my sisters husbands, if they say
> They love you all?[3]

[1] I, i, 87, 88.   [2] I, i, 93–95.   [3] I, i, 97–102.

And she proclaims the fact that when she marries, she will give her husband half her care and duty.

That it is self-love that makes a man susceptible to flattery is shown in the next speech, but the speech indicates much more than a susceptibility to flattery. In self-love and injured self-esteem anger takes its rise, as we have seen. To Cordelia's tempered and reasonable speech, the aged King breaks out at once in intemperate and almost frenzied anger:

> Let it be so; thy truth, then, be thy dower!
> For, by the sacred radiance of the sun,
> The mysteries of Hecate, and the night;
> By all the operation of the orbs
> From whom we do exist, and cease to be;
> Here I disclaim all my paternal care,
> Propinquity and property of blood,
> And as a stranger to my heart and me
> Hold thee, from this, forever. The barbarous Scythian,
> Or he that makes his generation messes
> To gorge his appetite, shall to my bosom
> Be as well neighbour'd, piti'd, and reliev'd,
> As thou my sometime daughter.[1]

Then it is that another friend dares to speak to dissuade from unjust action, but the good Kent's interruption is checked by Lear's

> Come not between the dragon and his wrath.
> I lov'd her most, and thought to set my rest
> On her kind nursery.[2]

And thus in the beginning of his wrath we see Lear demonstrating what we know to have been an accepted principle, that a man is angered by an injury to his self-esteem, that he is soonest angered when that respect in which he has thought himself most worthy seems to be disregarded, that he is soonest angry with friends, with those who have previously treated him becomingly and now change, and with those

[1] I, i, 110–22.   [2] I, i, 124–6.

who do not appreciate his kindness. Cordelia, most loved and most loving heretofore, to whom he intended the greatest favours, is at once the easy victim of the aged Lear. And as is the manner of the angry man, he at once seeks to have revenge, to show his power, and to injure the one from whom he conceives himself to have received an injury. At once he adds to the dowers of his two flattering daughters all the third that should have been Cordelia's. It must be noted, however, that while he gives away the burdens of the state, he retains

> The name, and all the addition to a king;

and thus we see that pride will still be panoplied with the trappings of a king. His monthly progress between the divided halves of his kingdom with his extensive retinue evidently pleases him as he pictures it. His pride and self-esteem are so mingled with his anger and his desire for revenge in this speech that they become one.

Again Kent will show that he is a true friend by attempting to check the rashness of his king, but Lear again rebuffs him:

> The bow is bent and drawn; make from the shaft.[1]

Now Kent becomes the man of righteous anger, angry not at the doer, but at the deed; further, he is the true friend opposing himself to the flatterer as he replies:

> ...be Kent unmannerly
> When Lear is mad. What wouldst thou do, old man?
> Thinkst thou that duty shall have dread to speak
> When power to flattery bows?[2]

And he begs Lear to check his "hideous rashness", even as he pleads the love of Cordelia. And even to the King's threat of his life, he will not yield his right to try to protect

[1] I, i, 145.   [2] I, i, 147–50.

him from himself. Even as the King lays his hand upon his sword, Kent exclaims again:

> Kill thy physician, and thy fee bestow
> Upon the foul disease. Revoke thy gift;
> Or, whilst I can vent clamour from my throat,
> I'll tell thee thou dost evil.[1]

And now, just as Lear has turned in his pride to try to revenge himself for the injury to his self-esteem inflicted by Cordelia's refusal to offer flattering vows and promises, he turns likewise at once in pride and outrageous anger to revenge himself on his most loyal friend, who likewise has refused to play the part of flatterer but has instead insisted upon trying to save him from evil and folly by telling him the truth. At once Lear shows his power in ordering the faithful Kent to turn his "hated back" upon his kingdom by the sixth day, the forfeit of his life to be exacted if he fail to accept his brutal banishment.

Then the angry King turns to scoff again at Cordelia. To Burgundy he offers her as

> Unfriended, new-adopted to our hate,
> Dower'd with our curse, and stranger'd with our oath,[2]

and France he beseeches to avert his love

> ...a more worthier way
> Than on a wretch whom Nature is asham'd
> Almost to acknowledge hers.[3]

Finally, to Cordelia's plea that he explain to her suitors that his changed attitude is not the result of murder or unchastity on her part, he replies:

> Better thou
> Had not been born than not to have pleas'd me better.[4]

But Cordelia is as temperate in her sorrow as in her love, and to France's injunction to bid her sisters farewell,

[1] I, i, 165–8.   [2] I, i, 206, 207.
[3] I, i, 214–6.   [4] I, i, 236, 237.

"though unkind", even to her father's final rebuffs, she replies only by indicating that she knows what sort of persons she is leaving her father with, and she departs sounding almost like a daughter of the good Polonius:

> Time shall unfold what plighted cunning hides;
> Who covers faults, at last shame them derides.
> Well may you prosper![1]

That Lear's anger has led him to a course that is both evil and foolish is at once evident in the discussion between Goneril and Regan that follows the departure of Cordelia. It is apparent that Lear has always been something of a problem at home, and that, in this fatal outburst of anger, he has but shown the results of a temperament given to habitual anger. Goneril observes:

You see how full of changes his age is; the observation we have made of it hath not been little. He always lov'd our sister most; and with what poor judgement he hath now cast her off appears too grossly.[2]

To which daughter's wisdom Regan adds:

'Tis the infirmity of his age; yet he hath ever but slenderly known himself.[3]

And Goneril reasons well:

The best and soundest of his time hath been but rash; then must we look from his age to receive not alone the imperfections of long-engraffed condition, but therewithal the unruly waywardness that infirm and choleric years bring with them.[4]

Regan instances this "inconstant start" of Kent's unjust banishment, and Goneril arrives at the main point that something must be done, for

if our father carry authority with such disposition as he bears, this last surrender of his will but offend us.[5]

And they proceed to remove the sting from the adder.

[1] I, i, 283–5.   [2] I, i, 291–5.   [3] I, i, 296, 297.
[4] I, i, 298–303.   [5] I, i, 308–10.

It is thus apparent that we have in Lear the habitually wrathful man, advanced by years to that age when his self-esteem takes offence suddenly, easily, without reason and without regard to justice. He is indeed the slave of habitual wrath.

The second scene of the first act of *Lear* repeats the same philosophical themes that were introduced in the first scene. Again a father is moved by a sense of injured self-esteem to anger which demands revenge, and seeks to find revenge in an immediate use of power to hurt the one who is supposed to be the author of the injury. Again a father is moved by the flattery of an undeserving child to cast off the loyal child and prefer the flatterer in his place. And again there enters the question of old age and its continued guidance of affairs.

Even as we see Edmund forging his plot, Gloucester comes on the stage regretting the deeds of the King:

> Kent banish'd thus! and France in choler parted!
> And the King gone to-night! subscrib'd his power!
> Confin'd to exhibition! All this done
> Upon the gad![1]

But he proceeds to illustrate dramatic irony by falling himself into the same pitfall of anger. Edmund shows him the forged letter which suggests that Edgar finds "an idle and fond bondage in the oppression of aged tyranny" and expresses the wish that he might enjoy the estate now kept in the hands of his father.[2] The insistence upon this theory of old age as retaining too long its possessions is, of course, an interesting foil for the action of the King in the first

---

[1] I, ii, 23–6.

[2] Cardan's *Comforte* says in this connection:

"But as it is the part of an ungracious sonne to hate the lyfe of his parentes, so it is the part of a wise sonne paciently to take theyr deathes, and to turne the same to his commoditye. . . .

"The authoritye of fathers contayneth in it somewhat more then service, and hindereth the execution of great thinges, be it in warres, learning or administration of the common wealth".

scene in dividing his kingdom. At any rate the suggestion
of disloyalty on Edgar's part is enough to cause Gloucester
to break into invectives:

> O villain, villain! His very opinion in the letter! Abhorred villain!
> Unnatural, detested, brutish villain! worse than brutish! Go, sirrah,
> seek him; I'll apprehend him. Abominable villain! Where is he?[1]

Yet he still speaks of his tender love for the son whom he
has just cursed so thoroughly. And he proceeds to blame
the heavens for the unnatural conduct of father against child
and child against father, of the King against Cordelia, of
Edgar against himself.

Edmund left alone comments cynically upon this convenient theory by which men blame the stars for their evil
deeds and dispositions; then he proceeds to the completer
revelation of his own evil nature and the unsuspecting
goodness of his father and his brother. His comments are
exactly like those of Iago in this respect, even as he proceeds
similarly to stir up evil. Now having roused his father to
anger, he proceeds with "villanous melancholy" to set his
plot going by urging Edgar to keep away from his father
and not to stir abroad without being armed.

In the third scene we hear more of King Lear and his
habits from Goneril, whose gentleman the King has just
struck for reproving his fool:

> By day and night he wrongs me; every hour
> He flashes into one gross crime or other
> That sets us all at odds. I'll not endure it.
> His knights grow riotous, and himself unbraids us
> On every trifle.[2]

Our sympathy cannot go with her, however, when she gives
permission to Oswald for him and his fellows to put on what
"weary negligence" they please in their obedience to the
King. She feels confidence in her sister's like-mindedness

[1] I, ii, 80–4. [2] I, iii, 3–7.

with her in the matter. But it must be noted that she comments on her father as one

> That still would manage those authorities
> That he hath given away.[1]

The picture of the group is further developed in the fourth scene. The good Kent is proved the true friend in his return in disguise to serve one who unjustly turned him away. He is proved a friend too in that he speaks at once when he sees the King apparently wronged in the falling off of the services rendered him. His steadfast loyalty and his patience are put into relief by the picture of the King, who is calling impatiently for his dinner and his fool in turn, who is raging about the compliant Oswald as "that mongrel" and "the slave", and who is in general justifying the description which we have just heard Goneril give of him. Typically the reappearance of Oswald, whose presence he has been demanding, is greeted by,

> O, you sir, you, come you hither, sir. Who am I, sir?[2]

Oswald's reply, "My lady's father", but sets him in a rage again, and he seems fairly to scream his words:

"My lady's father"! My lord's knave! You whoreson dog! you slave! you cur![3]

His striking of Oswald is augmented by Kent's tripping up the unfortunate steward, who leaves as the fool enters. The threat of the whip cannot keep the fool from enlarging upon the folly of the King, however.

Goneril's entrance to make further complaint needs to be considered carefully. The charges that she makes at first are borne out by what we have seen:

> Not only, sir, this your all-licens'd Fool,
> But other of your insolent retinue
> Do hourly carp and quarrel, breaking forth
> In rank and not-to-be-endured riots.[4]

[1] I, iii, 17, 18.   [2] I, iv, 85.   [3] I, iv, 87–9.   [4] I, iv, 220–3.

And her suggestion that if such actions are allowed or encouraged by her father, he is not without blame, would seem fair enough.

But Lear is at once outraged again, and when Goneril suggests that he should be wise as he is old and reverend, that her house has become through his followers more like a tavern or a brothel, and that he must "a little disquantity" his train and let those whom he retains be such as befit his age, he cries out violently:

> Darkness and devils!
> Saddle my horses; call my train together!
> Degenerate bastard![1]

Goneril continues the quarrel by charging that he has struck her people, while his retainers have made servants of their betters.

Then it is that, as Albany enters, Lear bursts out into his first apostrophe to ingratitude. And since this play has been so often called a play of ingratitude, it is perhaps well to pause to consider what Shakespeare's age thought on the subject.

The source of most of the Renaissance ideas on gratitude seems to have been *The woorke of the excellent Philosopher Lucius Annaeus Seneca concerning Benefyting, that is too say the dooing, receyving, and requyting of good Turnes,*—a treatise popular in the English translation of Arthur Golding published in 1578.[2] The work explains:

I may well saie, there is in a maner nothyng more hurtfull, than that wee knowe not, either how too bestow, or how too take good turnes. For it foloweth of consequence, that the good turnes which are ill bestowed should bee il owed. And therefore if thei bee not requited, it is too late for us to complayn, for asmucheas thei were lost in the verie bestowing of them. And it is no marvell that among so

---

[1] I, iv, 273–5.
[2] Wright, *op. cit.* ed. of 1604, added a long treatment of the various sorts of love and their relation to benefits bestowed and received.

many and so greate vyces, there is none more ryfe than unthankful-
nesse. I see many causes thereof.[1]

The first cause of unthankfulness Seneca found to be "that
wee choose not worthie persones too bestowe upon", as was
indicated above. And it would seem that here was indeed the
first cause of unthankfulness in the life of King Lear, for he
did not choose worthy persons upon whom to bestow his
favours, and his benefits were lost in the giving.

But Seneca said also:

> No man keepes a register of his benefites: neither dooth the covetous
> Userer call dayly and howrely uppon his detter. A good man never
> thinketh upon the good tournes he hath doon, except he bee put in
> mynde by him that requyteth. For otherwyse they pass intoo the nature
> of dettes.[2]

And still more explicitly he wrote:

> For the Lawe of benefyting betweene men is this: That the one
> must foorthwith forget that he hathe given, and the other must never
> forget what he hath received. For the ofte rehearsall of good deser-
> vinges, dooth greatly frette and greeve the mynd.[3]

Thus in *King Lear* we find that the law of benefiting is not
observed by either party, for the King never ceases to
recount the good he has done and the gratitude that is owed
him, while his undutiful daughters forget altogether the
benefits they have received and fail to be grateful for them.

Both the giver and the receivers are here guilty, then.
And of the giver it is necessary to ask further with Seneca
for what reason he did the good turn for which gratitude is
due. Did he do it to profit the one benefited? Or did he
do it to delight himself? In the case of Lear there can be no
doubt that he gave, not that which he prized for himself,
but that which he wished to be rid of. Gratitude was not,
therefore, due to him for his good turn.

[1] *Ibid.* fol. i.   [2] *Ibid.* fol. 2 *verso.*
[3] *Ibid.* fol. 15.

On the other hand, "Not to bee thankfull for a good turne", Seneca says, "is bothe a shame, and so counted emong all men".[1] And the ungrateful daughters of Lear are indeed counted shameful in that they were ungrateful.

Since it is ingratitude that particularly injures our self-esteem, it is ingratitude that rouses to violent anger the one who feels his own good deeds not appreciated. In anger at Cordelia's slighting of him, Lear revenged himself by turning her undowered from his kingdom. Now at Goneril's first suggestion that he restrain his followers and "dis-quantity his train" a little, he feels contempt thrown upon his own goodness:

> Ingratitude, thou marble-hearted fiend,
> More hideous when thou show'st thee in a child
> Than the sea-monster![2]

To gentle Albany's "Pray, sir, be patient!" he but breaks out anew in a torrent of rage against the "detested kite" and then turns to his thoughts of Cordelia and her slight fault of ingratitude which drew from his heart all love and added to the gall. Again, he reproaches the folly of his own anger. And to Albany's further assertion that he is ignorant of the cause of such distress, Lear but turns to the business of cursing his daughter more thoroughly:

> Hear, Nature! hear, dear goddess, hear!
> Suspend thy purpose, if thou didst intend
> To make this creature fruitful!
> Into her womb convey sterility!
> Dry up in her the organs of increase,
> And from her derogate body never spring
> A babe to honour her! If she must teem,
> Create her child of spleen, that it may live
> And be a thwart disnatur'd torment to her!
> Let it stamp wrinkles in her brow of youth,
> With cadent tears fret channels in her cheeks,

[1] Golding's trans., *op. cit.* p. 28.   [2] I, iv, 281–3.

> Turn all her mother's pains and benefits
> To laughter and contempt, that she may feel
> How sharper than a serpent's tooth it is
> To have a thankless child![1]

Lear departs, Albany questions Goneril and is assured that her father's actions are but the result of dotage, but as Albany, full of "milky gentleness", continues to ask questions, Lear re-enters, having discovered that his retainers are reduced to fifty. Now he curses, rages, and threatens vengeance in turn:

> Blasts and fogs upon thee!
> The untented woundings of a father's curse
> Pierce every sense about thee! Old fond eyes,
> Beweep this cause again, I'll pluck ye out,
> And cast you, with the waters that you loose,
> To temper clay. Ha! is it come to this?
> Let it be so: I have another daughter,
> Who, I am sure, is kind and comfortable.
> When she shall hear this of thee, with her nails
> She'll flay thy wolvish visage. Thou shalt find
> That I'll resume the shape which thou dost think
> I have cast off for ever.[2]

But Goneril is not to be stayed from sending messages to Regan, even by her husband's typical fondness for wise sayings:

> Striving to better, oft we mar what's well.[3]

And the preparations of Lear for an immediate departure are interrupted with ejaculations from his own musings on himself:

> I did her wrong—
>
> .   .   .   .   .
>
> I will forget my nature. So kind a father!
>
> .   .   .   .   .
>
> Monster ingratitude![4]

[1] I, iv, 297–311.   [2] I, iv, 321–32.
[3] I, iv, 369.   [4] I, v, 25–44.

At last he cries prophetically:

> O, let me not be mad, not mad, sweet heaven!
> Keep me in temper; I would not be mad![1]

The two stories of fathers wounded in their self-love and casting off in anger the children who would have befriended them are thus begun separately in Act I of *King Lear*. In Act II the two stories are woven together with the coming of the Duke of Cornwall and Regan, his duchess, to seek hospitality in Gloucester's castle, where they hope to avoid the imminent visit of Lear. Thus they become party to the vengeance Gloucester seeks for Edgar's treachery, which he has unquestionably accepted as fact on Edmund's unsupported word.

And Cornwall is likewise party to the quarrel between the messenger Oswald and the messenger Kent. Upon an Oswald whose one desire is to get away from Kent, whom he does not recognize but who recognizes him, there flows a torrential stream of impromptu invective in answer to his simple question, "What dost thou know me for?"

Interrupted, Kent pleads that he may be allowed to "tread this unbolted villain into mortar", and to Cornwall's reprimand offers the excuse that "anger hath a privilege".

Cornwall asks, "Why art thou angry?"

And again Kent bursts into a flood of invective, explaining that Oswald is a rogue and a coward and a pander to his master's passions, bringing oil to fire, snow to colder moods, etc.[2]

Cornwall is led to ask, apparently in all sincerity, "What, art thou mad, old fellow?" And then he turns to question Oswald as to his offence.

It is well to note that as Oswald explains to Cornwall that Kent's former conduct came by his flattering the King's displeasure in adding a kick to a blow, and as he tells the

[1] I, v, 50, 51.   [2] II, ii, 14–77.

absolute truth about the unprovoked nature of the present assault, Kent remarks:

> None of these rogues and cowards
> But Ajax is their fool.[1]

N w it will be remembered that Ajax was during the Renaissance constantly referred to as typical of the foolish anger that was in reality a short madness, and it is, therefore, apparent that Kent is uttering a profound truth when he says that the angry man becomes the fool of cowards and rogues.

Cornwall orders Kent to be put in the stocks, and the order is executed in spite of Gloucester's protests against so insulting the King's messenger and hence the King.

Next we see the fruit of Gloucester's anger in the fleeing Edgar, who has determined to seek safety in the likeness of a Bedlam beggar.

Then again we turn to Lear, newly wrathful as he encounters Kent in the stocks. So angry does he grow that his wrath almost smothers him with choking:

> O, how this mother swells up toward my heart!
> *Hysterica passio*, down, thou climbing sorrow,
> Thy element's below.[2]

He meets the suggestion of the weariness of Cornwall and Regan with cries for vengeance. To Gloucester's pacifying words he replies with bitter anger. Then for a moment he does try to calm himself, but it is only a moment until he again shows his mounting anger:

> Give me my servant forth.
> Go tell the Duke and's wife I'd speak with them,

---

[1] II, ii, 131, 132. Cf. p. 29 for a typical description.

[2] Drayton's *Poly-olbion*, Song VII, 11, 19–26, is usually instanced for a description of a fit of the mother. The descriptions are frequent in the case of pregnant women, but I have not been able to find any other reference such as this in *Lear*, and I am inclined to think the *hysterica passio* is the important part of the description as far as naming the disease is concerned.

> Now, presently. Bid them come forth and hear me,
> Or at their chamber-door I'll beat the drum
> Till it cry sleep to death.[1]

And then again he cries:

> O me, my heart, my rising heart! But, down![2]

To Regan's specious reasonableness concerning Goneril, and to her insistent stressing of the decorum belonging to old age, he cries that Goneril has reduced his train by half, has "look'd black" upon him, struck him with her tongue, "serpent-like". And therefore he will have it:

> All the stor'd vengeances of heaven fall
> On her ingrateful top! Strike her young bones,
> You taking airs, with lameness![3]

And he adds the paternal

> You nimble lightnings, dart your blinding flames
> Into her scornful eyes! Infect her beauty,
> You fen-suck'd fogs, drawn by the powerful sun,
> To fall and blast her pride![4]

As Regan says that he will wish such things for her also, he assures her that it is not so. But the reasons for his reassurance are not in himself; they are in her. She will never be so unnatural, so unfilial, so ungrateful as to grudge him his pleasures, scant his train, give him hasty words, and shut him out. She cannot have forgotten his benefits:

> Thy half o' the kindgom hast thou not forgot,
> Wherein I thee endow'd.[5]

As Goneril arrives and the two daughters join forces against him, the King becomes for the first time pitiful. His wrath has become impotent. And again he tries to avert madness by crying out against it:

> You heavens, give me that patience, patience I need!
> You see me here, you gods, a poor old man,

[1] II, iv, 116–20.   [2] II, iv, 122.   [3] II, iv, 164–6.
[4] II, iv, 167–70.   [5] II, iv, 183, 184.

As full of grief as age; wretched in both!
If it be you that stirs these daughters' hearts
Against their father, fool me not so much
To bear it tamely; touch me with noble anger,
And let not women's weapons, water-drops,
Stain my man's cheeks! No, you unnatural hags,
I will have such revenges on you both
That all the world shall—I will do such things,—
What they are, yet I know not; but they shall be
The terrors of the earth. You think I'll weep:
No, I'll not weep.
I have full cause of weeping; but this heart
Shall break into a hundred thousand flaws
Or ere I'll weep. O, Fool! I shall go mad![1]

He has run nearly the whole gamut of the passions in this speech.

As the King goes out into the stormy night, we hear from Gloucester, "The King is in high rage".[2]

But as Cornwall and Regan retire out of the storm, Regan utters more truly than kindly the bit of wisdom made apparent in the wrath of Lear:

O, sir, to wilful men,
The injuries that they themselves procure
Must be their schoolmasters.[3]

In the terrible third act we hear through Kent's informer of the King out in the storm who

tears his white hair,
Which the imperious blasts, with eyeless rage,
Catch in their fury, and make nothing of;
Strives in his little world of man to out-scorn
The to-and-fro-conflicting wind and rain.[4]

Thus we see another of the Renaissance doctrines ex-emplified. The tempest in the elements is reflected in the mind of the man, for the tempestuous winds enter into the

[1] II, iv, 274–89.   [2] II, iv, 299.
[3] II, iv, 305–7.   [4] III, i, 7–11.

spirits of the man who breathes the air thus tempest-tossed, and he too becomes mad.

Then we ourselves see Lear raging at the elements, madly complaining of his own woes. But we can see that it is still his own unappreciated goodness that moves him:

> Rumble thy bellyful! Spit, fire! Spout, rain!
> Nor rain, wind, thunder, fire, are my daughters.
> I tax not you, you elements, with unkindness;
> I never gave you kingdom, call'd you children;
> You owe me no subscription.[1]

Yet even as the King calls upon heaven to avenge the enemies of the gods, he cries out as though in self-defence, "I am a man More sinned against than sinning".[2]

Even as we see Gloucester determining that the King must be relieved, ironically we see his own abused son, Edgar, disguised as Tom of Bedlam, sharing the sufferings of the King. But Shakespeare still drives home the cause of Lear's madness:

> When the mind's free,
> The body's delicate; the tempest in my mind
> Doth from my senses take all feeling else
> Save what beats there. Filial ingratitude!
> Is it not as this mouth should tear this hand
> For lifting food to't? But I will punish home.
> No, I will weep no more. In such a night
> To shut me out! Pour on! I will endure.
> In such a night as this! O Regan, Goneril!
> Your old kind father, whose frank heart gave all,—
> O, that way madness lies; let me shun that;
> No more of that.[3]

The mingled ravings of Edgar and of Lear are interrupted by Gloucester come on his secret errand of mercy to offer shelter to the King, and we hear then this second father's grief:

> Thou say'st the King grows mad; I'll tell thee, friend,
> I am almost mad myself. I had a son,

[1] III, ii, 14–18.   [2] III, ii, 59, 60.   [3] III, iv, 11–22.

an in the Moon drinks Claret,

owder-Beef Turnip and Carret.

Tune is, Grays-Inn-Mask.

fome Cell,　　Laft Night I heard the Dog-ftar bark,

Hell,　　Mars met Venus in the dark ;

Wold again,　　Limping Vulcan beat an Iron-bar,

PLATE XIV. Illustration from *New Mad Tom of Bedlam*, no. 51 of *Bagford Ballads*.

> Now outlaw'd from my blood; he sought my life,
> But lately, very late. I lov'd him, friend,
> No father his son dearer; true to tell thee,
> The grief hath craz'd my wits.[1]

A conversation between Cornwall and Edmund reveals to us the penalty to be meted out to Gloucester for his having comforted the King. Then the scene of the play returns again to the shelter provided by the pity of Gloucester, and we hear Kent explaining of Lear:

> All the power of his wits have given way to his impatience.[2]

The King who enters the hovel is still raving in his madness of his cruel daughters, wishing to bring them to trial, to anatomize them to find whether there is "any cause in nature that makes these hard hearts". Kent will not have him troubled, for "his wits are gone".[3] And Edgar, finding companionship in his misery, can but comment, "He childed as I fathered".[4]

The almost intolerable scene in which Gloucester is blinded shows anger and desire for revenge further at work. Cornwall will have revenge for Gloucester's help to the King. It must be noted that the angry Cornwall, like the angry Lear of the first scene of the play, is interrupted in his fury by a servant who in the office of friend cries,

> Hold your hand, my lord!
> I have serv'd you ever since I was a child;
> But better service have I never done you
> Than now to bid you hold.[5]

And as Cornwall and Regan both reply in anger, he like Kent ventures again his

> Nay, then, come on, and take the chance of anger.[6]

Again the good servant is punished for daring to rebuke his master for wrong-doing. He is killed by Regan, even as

[1] III, iv, 170–5.   [2] III, vi, 4, 5.   [3] III, vi, 94.
[4] III, vi, 117.   [5] III, vii, 72–5.   [6] III, vii, 79.

Cornwall puts out the other eye of Gloucester with his horrible, "Out, vile jelly!"

It is then as at last Gloucester learns the truth from the angry Regan that he cries, like Lear:

> O my follies! then Edgar was abus'd.
> Kind gods, forgive me that, and prosper him.[1]

Cornwall, injured in the fight with his servant, is led off by Regan as the servants, struck with horror at the sight of such crimes, cry out for justice on such wickedness lest all do evil seeing it go unpunished. Meanwhile a second servant suggests getting "the Bedlam" to lead Gloucester from his gate, whence he is banished, while a third servant goes to find healing remedies for his bleeding eyes.

Act IV opens with Edgar musing on the eternal theme of tragedy:

> The lamentable change is from the best;
> The worst returns to laughter.[2]

And even then the blind Gloucester is led on by the old servant, crying out in the hearing of his disguised son:

> O dear son Edgar,
> The food of thy abused father's wrath![3]

It is thus that Shakespeare insists upon the destruction caused by the passion which he is portraying in the play. The poor Bedlam beggar, who is Edgar, is the result of the evil wrath of Gloucester. But Gloucester himself is paying the even heavier penalty for the folly of his anger which has made him seek revenge on Edgar by preferring the unworthy Edmund. And this folly now leads him to the very brink of self-destruction.

Then we see Goneril and Edmund in their plotting, in contrast to the just and temperate Albany, who dares to call his wife and her sister "tigers, not daughters", and to

[1] III, vii, 91, 92.   [2] IV, i, 5, 6.   [3] IV, i, 23, 24.

denounce the evil they have done. We hear Goneril calling him a "moral fool", and yet we see him restraining his anger and refusing because she is a woman to put into action his passionate hatred of such deeds as hers.

The theme of angry vengeance still is emphasized. A messenger reports the death of Cornwall from the wound inflicted by his servant, against whom he had rushed "enrag'd" because of his reproof. The same messenger reports the blinding of Gloucester, and again belief in God as the God of vengeance is heard in the cry of Albany:

> This shows you are above,
> You justicers, that these our nether crimes
> So speedily can venge! But, O poor Gloucester![1]

But yet he adds, at the further news of Edmund's guilt, as though he would not trust all to heaven's vengeance:

> Gloucester, I live
> To thank thee for the love thou show'dst the King,
> And to revenge thine eyes.[2]

And now we are given a picture of the virtue that is opposed to the vice of wrath, a picture of patience opposed to anger, of reason opposed to passion. For we have pictured for us the scene when Cordelia received the news of her father's sufferings. Kent and the gentlemen who has served as messenger converse:

Kent. Did your letters pierce the Queen to any demonstration of grief?
Gent. Ay, sir; she took them, read them in my presence;
    And now and then an ample tear trill'd down
    Her delicate cheek. It seem'd she was a queen
    Over her passion, who, most rebel-like,
    Sought to be king o'er her.
Kent.   O, then it mov'd her.
Gent. Not to a rage; patience and sorrow strove
    Who should express her goodliest.[3]

[1] IV, ii, 78–80.　　[2] IV, ii, 95–7.　　[3] IV, iii, 11–19.

And as we hear them talk, we are brought to the knowledge also that the King is paying the penalty of anger which was traditional in the old adage quoted by Baldwin, "Wrath leadeth shame in a lease", for though Lear is in the same town, he will not see Cordelia, and Kent explains to the gentleman:

> A sovereign shame so elbows him. His own unkindness,
> That stripped her from his benediction, turn'd her
> To foreign casualties, gave her dear rights
> To his dog-hearted daughters,—these things sting
> His mind so venomously, that burning shame
> Detains him from Cordelia.[1]

The scene contains almost the heart of the mystery. Cordelia is mistress over passion. Lear has been mastered by passion. It cannot be over-emphasized, I think, that Shakespeare's picture is of a Lear whose wrath has made him guilty of deeds both evil and foolish. It is not primarily ingratitude that has caused his downfall; rather it is his wrath over ingratitude. It must be remembered that his wrath over Cordelia's ingratitude was just as great as his wrath over the ingratitude of his other daughters. If Lear had accepted the slight to his self-esteem as Cordelia or as Kent accepted the insults and injuries which he heaped upon them, there would have been no tragedy. And now we have Cordelia still bearing grief patiently, as she bore earlier wrongs, while Lear is paying with madness and shame the penalty of his continued wrath.

But it must be noted that there is possible a righteous indignation, according to Shakespeare. It is righteous anger that moves Kent to protest his master's deeds, it is righteous anger that moves Albany against his wife and Edmund, it is righteous anger that now makes Cordelia and France fight their battle for the restitution of the rights of the old and now mad King.

[1] IV, iii, 44–9.

As we hear Cordelia speaking with the doctor of her father's madness and begging for man's aid in curing his madness, we hear an echo of Macbeth's plea, but this time the doctor can give hope, for there is not on Lear's conscience as there was on that of Lady Macbeth the stain of mortal sin:

> There is means, madam.
> Our foster-nurse of nature is repose,
> The which he lacks; that to provoke in him,
> Are many simples operative, whose power
> Will close the eye of anguish.[1]

But Cordelia urges haste in finding the King,

> Lest his ungovern'd rage dissolve the life
> That wants the means to lead it.[2]

And after a scene showing the new passion of jealousy which has sprung up between the evil daughters over Edmund, we are transported to the scene where Gloucester, unable to endure affliction, tries to kill himself. But he in his failure is made to cry at last:

> Henceforth I'll bear
> Affliction till it do cry out itself,
> "Enough, enough," and die.[3]

It is again the lesson of patience that he has had to learn. And as he meets the King in his mad wandering, uttering his "reason in madness", Gloucester again prays:

> You ever-gentle gods, take my breath from me;
> Let not my worser spirit tempt me again
> To die before you please.[4]

Then as the unrecognized Edgar again starts to lead his sightless father, Oswald comes to meet his fate by trying to oppose him. Thus Edgar is moved also to kill in righteous anger.

[1] IV, iv, 11–15.   [2] IV, iv, 19, 20.
[3] IV, vi, 75–7.   [4] IV, vi, 221–3.

When next we see Lear as he is brought on to the stage to be awakened after his healing sleep, the doctor explains to Cordelia:

> Be comforted, good madam; the great rage,
> You see, is kill'd in him. [1]

The fifth act is a chaos of passion. The jealousy of the two sisters leads to an angry revenge that makes each slay the other. The fortunes of war go against Cordelia and Lear and put them in the power of Edmund. The interlude of their happiness in being reunited even in prison but interrupts the progress of horror momentarily. Edmund commands their death. Then in the meeting of Edgar and Edmund we hear again the theme of tragedy as Edgar speaks:

> My name is Edgar, and thy father's son.
> The gods are just, and of our pleasant vices
> Make instruments to plague us.
> The dark and vicious place where thee he got
> Cost him his eyes. [2]

In his lust Gloucester begot his destroyer; in his anger he gave him power to destroy. His death came also from passion, for the recognition of his injured son as his guide overcame him finally:

> ...but his flaw'd heart
> Alack, too weak the conflict to support!
> 'Twixt two extremes of passion, joy and grief,
> Burst smilingly. [3]

The bodies of Goneril and Regan are brought on the stage as evidence of "the judgement of the heavens". As Edmund dies, he tries in vain to do some good yet by commanding a reprieve for Lear and Cordelia. But it is too late, for even as the body of Edmund is carried off, Lear enters bearing the body of Cordelia. And it is now a Lear who is forever mad that we see. His renewed anger at the slave who killed

[1] IV, vii, 78, 79.   [2] V, iii, 169–73.   [3] V, iii, 196–99.

Cordelia gave him strength to kill the slave, but he comes on the stage to die in pitiful madness. And with his dying speech he tells us his fool has been hanged.

Thus at the close of the play we have alive only Edgar, Albany, and the dying Kent, whose master is even then calling him. And it is on the note of youth and old age that the play ends:

> The oldest hath borne most; we that are young
> Shall never see so much, nor live so long.[1]

King Lear as the tragedy of wrath, then, was planned as a tragedy of old age. In Lear and Gloucester Shakespeare represented old men bestowing benefits unjustly, led by flattery to give unwisely, led by anger to withhold unjustly and to seek revenge for imagined slights. Both the evil and the folly[2] of their anger are brought out. The evil lay in their inflicting evil on others. The folly lay in the evil they brought upon themselves. Even Kent, the friend and loyal follower, is led in anger to go beyond the command of reason in his treatment of Oswald and hence to bring further misfortune on the King. Cornwall is killed in an angry fight with his servant, but the servant is also killed for his righteous anger. The whole is a welter of passion. But the picture is relieved by Cordelia, who cannot be moved by passion; by Edgar, who acts as reason dictates even in the guise of a madman; and by Albany, who at the last is the calm arbiter of the "gor'd state".

The play at times becomes inarticulate, but its meaning can never be in doubt.

---

[1] v, iii, 325, 326.
[2] Hardin Craig, "The Ethics of King Lear", in the *Philological Quarterly*, vol. IV, pp. 97–109, stresses this quality of folly, but it will be seen that the reason for its prominence in the play is simply that it was habitually regarded as the accompaniment of anger.

CHAPTER XV

Macbeth: *A Study in Fear*

IT is usual to refer to *Macbeth* as a tragedy of ambition, and with a certain justification, for ambition does act as a determining passion in the play. This passion *The French Academie* described as "an unreasonable desire to enjoy honours, estates, and great places".[1] Such is the passion which moves Macbeth and Lady Macbeth to the murder of Duncan, but it is not ambition that is anatomized in the tragedy of *Macbeth*.

The play is really a study in fear. And since fear is but one of a pair of passions, Shakespeare, according to his habit, paints the passion studied against the background of its opposite. Just as *Romeo and Juliet* sounds its love-hate theme at the beginning, as *Hamlet* stresses the joy-grief pair of passions, as *Othello* develops the love-hatred of jealousy, so *Macbeth* develops the study of fear against a background of its opposite.

The pair of passions here studied, then, is a pair that were variously named during the English Renaissance. Wylkinson's Aristotle called them "fear and hardines"; Holland's Plutarch named them "Cowardice and rash Audacitie". *The French Academie* entitled the chapter dealing with them "Of Timorousnesse, Feare, and Cowardlinesse, and of Rashnesse".[2] Bryskett called them fury and fear. But however they were named, they are the passions which represent the excess and the defect of the virtuous mean which was known

[1] 1618 ed. p. 92. It is interesting to note that according to Bartlett's *Concordance* "ambition" is mentioned three times in *Macbeth*, and "fear" forty-two times.

[2] 1618 ed. p. 114, 1586 ed. p. 277.

generally as fortitude or courage or strength. Wylkinson
translated Aristotle:

feare & folyshe hardinesse corrupteth the valiantnes of man, for
whi? the fearefull fleeth from everye thyng. And the hardye assaileth
every thyng, beleving in himselfe to bring it to passe; nother in the one
nor in the other there is no doutinesse, for prudence is in keping the
meane betwene fear and folyshe hardynes. For a man ought to fle
& assail there where it is to assail.[1]

Defining fortitude as "a meane betwene feare and hardines", the *Ethiques* also explained in regard to false courage:

Strength is in five sortes, the first is civil strength, because that
menne of Citees suffre muche and many perels to have honor and
to bee blameles of their citezens. The second sort is by wit and policie
that a manne hath in his office: As we se of men that be wise in feactes
of armes, that do great thynges trustyng in their Science, and bee not
strong accordyng to the truthe, bycause that when thei se the daunger
of battaill, thei flee beeyng more afraied of death then of shame....
The thirde sorte is by furye as we se in wylde strength, that be
strong and hardy by the great furor that is in theim, this is not the very
strength, for who so ever putteth hymself in perel by ire or furye, is
not to bee called strong....
The fourth sort is by strong movyng of concupiscence, as we maie
se of brute beastes....
The fifth sorte is by suretie wher a man hath had oft tymes victory....[2]

In a modern translation this passage explains:

There are five kinds of courage, so named from a certain analogy
between them; for they all endure the same things but not for the same
reasons. One is a civic courage, due to the sense of shame; another is
military, due to experience and knowledge, not (as Socrates said)
of what is fearful, but of the resources they have to meet what is
fearful. The third kind is due to inexperience and ignorance....Another
kind is due to hope, which makes those who have often been fortunate,
or those who are drunk, face dangers—for wine makes them sanguine.
Another kind is due to irrational feeling, e.g. love or anger...for
passion is beside itself. Hence wild boars are thought to be brave
though they are not really so, for they behave as such when beside

[1] Wylkinson, *op. cit.* chapter viii.   [2] *Ibid.* chapter xvi.

themselves, but at other times are variable, like confident men.... But in truth none of these forms is courage, though all are useful for encouragement in danger.[1]

It seems vague to conjecture where Shakespeare got his special knowledge of this false courage, but in the various writers of his day who derived their analysis directly or indirectly from Aristotle these various sorts of specious courage were discussed: the civic courage resulting from the sense of shame; military courage; courage that came as ignorance of what was rightly to be feared; drunken courage; and the courage that is best described by Shakespeare in *Antony and Cleopatra*:

> To be furious,
> Is to be frighted out of fear; and in that mood
> The dove will peck the estridge.[2]

Of false courage *The French Academie* said:

No doubte but Rashnesse is that vice which falsely shrowdeth it selfe under the title of Fortitude and Valure.[3]

And it is with these various manifestations of that excess of fortitude, of which the defect is fear, that we have to do in the study of "brave Macbeth" and his lady.

The complementary passion of fear, which furnishes the great central study of *Macbeth*, is most exhaustively treated in Aristotle's *Rhetoric*, which it will be remembered Bacon said was the best storehouse of knowledge of the passions to be found in the works of Aristotle. There Aristotle stressed three things in his definition of fear: it is painful; it has to do with the future rather than the present; it arises from some mental picture of an evil that is painful or

---

[1] *Ethica Eudemia*, De Virtutibus et Vitiis, transl. by J. Solomon, 1229^a, 12–31. Cf. also *Ethica Nicomachea*, 1116^a, 15–1117^a, 28, etc.

[2] *Antony and Cleopatra*, III, xiii, 195–7.

[3] 1586 ed. p. 285, 1618 ed. p. 117.

destructive. Following Aristotle, then, *The French Academie* explained that what hope is to joy, fear is to sorrow:

Nowe, as sorrow is a griefe for some evil which a man presently feeleth, shutting up the heart as unwilling to receive it: so feare is a sorrow, which the heart conceiveth of some looked for evill, that may come unto it....So that we may well say, that Feare is not onely a fantasie and imagination of evill approaching, or a perturbation of the soule proceeding from the opinion it hath of some evill to come, but it is also a contraction and closing up of the heart.... [1]

Aristotle further commented on the causes of our fear, listing many sorts of people whom we fear. He noted that we fear the enmity and anger of those who have power to do us harm; we fear injustice in the possession of power; we fear outraged virtue; we fear those who have us at their mercy, and therefore we fear those who share a secret with us lest they betray us; we fear those that have been wronged lest they seek retaliation; we fear those that have done wrong, since they stand in fear of retaliation; we fear those who have shown their power by destroying those stronger than we are; we fear those who are our rivals for something which we cannot both have at once. [2] And the table stands as a pattern for the fears and murders and revenges of *Macbeth*.

It must, of course, be noted that everywhere and always superstition and fear are considered as related. Aristotle continually affirmed that a man was a madman not to fear those superhuman terrors (such as thunder and lightning) which he ought to fear.

Plutarch, however, showed that it was a want of true knowledge of the gods that led men of gentle and tender spirits to superstition. In the words of his Renaissance translator, he said:

As for superstition, according as the nature of the Greeke word (which signifieth *Feare of the Gods*) doth imply, is a passionate opinion

[1] 1594 ed. pp. 260, 261.
[2] Cf. *Rhetorica*, transl. by W. Rhys Roberts, 1382ᵃ, 19 ff., and 1382ᵇ.

and turbulent imagination, imprinting in the heart of a man a certaine fearfulnesse, which doth abate his courage and humble him downe to the verie ground....[1]

But in the Renaissance study of fear and superstition the question became, as we have seen in the first part of this book and in the chapters of *Hamlet*, a question as to the physical cause or the metaphysical cause of the appearances which caused superstitious terror in men's hearts. And of this aspect of *Macbeth* I shall speak again. But I want to quote here one further passage from Plutarch relative to superstition and sleep:

Sleepe easeth the cheines, gives and fetters, of those that ly by the heeles bound in prison....But superstition will not give a man leave thus to say: For it alone maketh no truce during sleepe; it permitteth not the soule at any time to breath and take rest,...but as if the sleepe of superstitious folke were a verie hell and place of damned persons, it doth present unto them terrible visions and monstrous fansies; it raiseth divels, fiends and furies, which torment the poore and miserable soule; it driveth her out of her quiet repose by her owne fearfull dreames, wherewith she whippeth, scourgeth, and punisheth herselfe (as if it were) by some other, whose cruell and unseasonable commandements she doth obey....[2]

Such was the general background of thinking in regard to the passions of fear and rash courage in Shakespeare's day. And that Shakespeare patterned his study upon the edicts of the philosophers in their anatomies of the passions here studied seems obvious. But his method is that which he regularly used. A passion is studied with its opposite. The same passion is studied in different persons. Fear and courage are studied in the play as opposites, the defect and the excess of true fortitude. Ambition has no opposite and is here used without an opposite and is used only as a supplementary passion in any case. But passion is studied as it affects two

[1] "Of Superstition", in Holland's Plutarch, *Morals*, p. 260.
[2] *Ibid.* p. 261.

different people especially—a man and a woman, Macbeth and Lady Macbeth.

In both Macbeth and Lady Macbeth there is seen the ambition which moves to rash deeds; in both there is seen the gradual dissolution of fear, the one being led to final self-destruction, the other to the final fury of despair.

Yet it is of "brave Macbeth" that we first hear, for as I have said, the study of fear is placed against a background of its opposite. The bleeding captain tells of Macbeth, who is "Valour's minion", fighting Macdonwald,

> Till he unseam'd him from the nave to the chaps,
> And fix'd his head upon our battlements.[1]

Moreover, a fresh assault failed to dismay Banquo and Macbeth, so that the captain reports to Duncan:

> If I say sooth, I must report they were
> As cannons overcharg'd with double cracks; so they
> Doubly redoubled strokes upon the foe.
> Except they meant to bathe in reeking wounds,
> Or memorize another Golgotha,
> I cannot tell.[2]

Macbeth is, indeed, "Bellona's bridegroom", though critics seem rather at a loss to know just who Bellona's bridegroom may have been. At any rate, we have pictured at the outset the military courage which in the captain's report seems bloody and rash and definitely pictured as an excess of fortitude, and which may well be ranked as one of the types specially listed by Aristotle as false courage.

In the next scene it is, however, a very different Macbeth who, with Banquo, meets the three witches on the blasted heath in the thunder that appropriately heralds the appearance of the supernatural on the stage. Now it is Banquo who boldly challenges the witches, while Macbeth can but feebly echo his question to them. And as they hail Macbeth in turn

[1] I, ii, 22, 23.　　　[2] I, ii, 36–41.

as thane of Glamis, thane of Cawdor, and King hereafter,
his actions call reproof from Banquo:

> Good sir, why do you start, and seem to fear
> Things that do sound so fair?[1]

And still Macbeth stands—so that Banquo says "he seems rapt
withal"—while the bold Banquo continues to question the
witches as to whether they are real or fantastical (created by
the fantasy), and to challenge them:

> Speak then to me, who neither beg nor fear
> Your favours nor your hate.[2]

It is necessary to note carefully that this scene emphasizes
from the beginning, therefore, the fear that appears in
Macbeth just as his rash military courage appeared in the
preceding scene. And this fear still holds him as the witches
reply to Banquo in the final oracular:

> Thou shalt get kings, though thou be none;

and as they vanish while Macbeth tries to detain them with
tardy questions.

But even as the witches vanish, we are faced with the problem of the supernatural as the result of physical or metaphysical causes. And it is always to be borne in mind that
according to King James, one of the two great passions that
led men into temptation, that made them fit subjects for the
Devil's work, was ambition. It is clear again that Shakespeare
was writing with authority when he portrayed Macbeth
as subjected by the passion of ambition to the temptation
of what appears to be the supernatural.[3] Banquo, however,
first utters the familiar question:

> Were such things here as we do speak about,
> Or have we eaten on the insane root
> That takes the reason prisoner?[4]

---

[1] I, iii, 51, 52.   [2] I, iii, 60, 61.
[3] Cf. pp. 88, 89, *ante*.   [4] I, iii, 83–5.

And as Ross and Angus enter to announce to Macbeth the reward of his having been "nothing afeard" of death, and even as Ross hails Macbeth thane of Cawdor, Banquo continues the argument:

> What, can the devil speak true?

As Macbeth utters his, "The greatest is behind", and turns to question whether Banquo too has had ambition roused by the fulfilment of prophecy, Banquo still carries on the same old argument, familiar from *Hamlet*, as he says:

> But 't is strange;
> And oftentimes, to win us to our harm,
> The instruments of darkness tell us truths,
> Win us with honest trifles, to betray 's
> In deepest consequence.[1]

Then, while Macbeth reveals his hungry ambition already pressing on to the "imperial theme", we hear him taking up the argument as though to echo the thought of Banquo:

> This supernatural soliciting
> Cannot be ill, cannot be good. If ill,
> Why hath it given me earnest of success,
> Commencing in a truth? I'm thane of Cawdor.
> If good, why do I yield to that suggestion
> Whose horrid image doth unfix my hair
> And make my seated heart knock at my ribs,
> Against the use of nature? Present fears
> Are less than horrible imaginings.
> My thought, whose murder yet is but fantastical,
> Shakes so my single state of man that function
> Is smother'd in surmise, and nothing is
> But what is not.[2]

And such is his appearance still that Banquo calls attention to him:

> Look, how our partner's rapt.

[1] I, iii, 122–6.   [2] I, iii, 130–42.

And such is the fear that has kept him rapt that for the moment fear has conquered ambition, and Macbeth decides even as he apologizes for his having appeared rapt:

> If chance will have me King, why, chance may crown me,
> Without my stir.

In the next scene Duncan bestows the title of Prince of Cumberland upon young Malcolm, even as he also gives thanks to Macbeth for his valour. And as Macbeth hears the title given to Malcolm, he shows again the conflict within him between ambition and fear:

> The Prince of Cumberland! That is a step
> On which I must fall down, or else o'erleap,
> For in my way it lies. Stars, hide your fires;
> Let not light see my black and deep desires;
> The eye wink at the hand; yet let that be
> Which the eye fears, when it is done, to see.[1]

As we see Lady Macbeth in the scene which follows reading her lord's letter in which he tells her of the witches' prophecies and of their strange fulfilment, not failing to mention that he stood rapt with the wonder of it, we hear her but emphasize this conflict of fear and ambition that must always characterize Macbeth. But she embroiders her theme:

> Yet do I fear thy nature;
> It is too full o' the milk of human kindness
> To catch the nearest way. Thou wouldst be great,
> Art not without ambition, but without
> The illness should attend it. What thou wouldst highly,
> That wouldst thou holily; wouldst not play false,
> And yet wouldst wrongly win. Thou'dst have, great Glamis,
> That which cries, "Thus thou must do, if thou have it";
> And that which rather thou dost fear to do
> Than wishest should be undone. Hie thee hither
> That I may pour my spirits in thy ear,

[1] I, iv, 48–53.

> And chastise with the valour of my tongue
> All that impedes thee from the golden round
> Which fate and metaphysical aid doth seem
> To have thee crowned withal.[1]

At the news of Duncan's approach, which follows the letter swiftly, Lady Macbeth offers her frightful invocation that she may be unsexed, cruel, remorseless, to do the deed that is fitting night and hell. Then, as Macbeth himself arrives, she bids him to put all in her hands; for him her only command is:

> Only look up clear;
> To alter favour ever is to fear.[2]

But with Duncan as his guest in his castle, Macbeth starts to argue the deed in his mind. And here we find in *Macbeth* the persistent theme of tragedy that we have heard so often:

> If it were done when 't is done, then 't were well
> It were done quickly. If the assassination
> Could trammel up the consequence, and catch
> With his surcease success; that but this blow
> Might be the be-all and the end-all here,
> But here, upon this bank and shoal of time,
> We'd jump the life to come. But in these cases
> We still have judgement here, that we but teach
> Bloody instructions, which, being taught, return
> To plague the inventor. This even-handed justice
> Commends the ingredients of our poison'd chalice
> To our own lips.[3]

This deep fear of heaven's justice, of the unknown decrees of justice, of retribution in the now, as well as in the hereafter, is but the prologue to Macbeth's argument; on the one side are Duncan's claims as King and kinsmen and guest, Duncan's virtues, and above all pity, while on the other there is only "vaulting ambition" as the spur to his intent.

---

[1] I, v, 17–31.   [2] I, v, 72, 73.
[3] I, vii, 1–12.

For the time being ambition loses the argument, and Macbeth declares:

> We will proceed no further in this business.[1]

But Lady Macbeth will have nothing of such temporizing. Her taunts again centre about the same question of fear and ambition:

> Art thou afeard
> To be the same in thine own act and valour
> As thou art in desire? Wouldst thou have that
> Which thou esteem'st the ornament of life,
> And live a coward in thine own esteem,
> Letting "I dare nót" wait upon "I would",
> Like the poor cat i' the adage?[2]

Macbeth's reply is ironically the very definition of the man of fortitude given by the moral philosophers:

> I dare do all that may become a man;
> Who dares do more is none.[3]

But Lady Macbeth scorns such a definition. Was he then less than man, a beast, when he proposed the enterprise? Rather he was then a man, and to be more would be to be more than man. Time and place, then wanting, now make themselves. And again she argues on the basis of her sex, as before; she would as a mother have killed her child at her breast rather than to have failed in such an oath as he has sworn. And to Macbeth's timid,

> If we should fail?

she replies passionately:

> We fail!
> But screw your courage to the sticking-place,
> And we'll not fail.[4]

It is she who plans the deed—the drunken chamberlains, the death of Duncan, the guilt laid on others.

---

[1] I, vii, 31.   [2] I, vii, 39–45.
[3] I, vii, 46, 47. [4] I, vii, 59–61.

Then again Macbeth sounds the sex note so often repeated in the play:

> Bring forth men-children only;
> For thy undaunted mettle should compose
> Nothing but males.[1]

But in his admiration he has not forgotten fear, and he questions the surety with which the guilt may be attached to the chamberlains. Then at last, at the close of the act, he utters his determination in which the resolve of ambition is seen brought to the courage that is the fear of shame and is, indeed, a fearful courage:

> I am settled, and bend up
> Each corporal agent to this terrible feat.[2]

In order to see the significance of much of the second act of *Macbeth*, it is necessary to remember that according to Lavater:

> That whiche we have hytherto spoken concerning melancholicke men, and men out of their witts, may also be understood of timorous and fearefull men. For if any man be timorous by nature, or subject to feare through great daungers, or by some other wayes, he also imagineth straunge things whiche in deede are not so, especially if he have in him any store of melancholie.[3]

As the terrors of the night begin in this act, it is Banquo who curiously if not craftily speaks of having dreamt of the three weird sisters, but Macbeth replies that he thinks not of them. Then, as Macbeth is left alone, the vision of the dagger appears, and he reasons in the traditional strain of the melancholy man questioning his illusions:

> Is this a dagger which I see before me,
> The handle toward my hand? Come, let me clutch thee.
> I have thee not, and yet I see thee still.

[1] I, vii, 72–4.   [2] I, vii, 79, 80.
[3] Lavater, *op. cit.* p. 14. Cf. Section II, chapter ix, p. 86.

> Art thou not, fatal vision, sensible
> To feeling as to sight? or art thou but
> A dagger of the mind, a false creation,
> Proceeding from the heat-oppressed brain?[1]

And then, as he sees the blood upon the dagger, he exclaims:

> There's no such thing.
> It is the bloody business which informs
> Thus to mine eyes.[2]

But he closes the soliloquy in fear and horror, his imagination playing with the ideas of night and witchcraft and murder until the bell tolls which is to act as Duncan's knell.

The next scene reveals the first sign of fear in Lady Macbeth, for her admission that she would herself have killed Duncan had he not resembled her father as he slept is an admission of weakness she would earlier have scorned. Moreover, her courage now is admittedly the sort of false courage listed by Aristotle as achieved by drink, for she says:

> That which hath made them drunk hath made me bold;
> What hath quench'd them hath given me fire.[3]

But as the terror-stricken Macbeth comes from doing the deed with his fearful whimperings about the grooms' "Amen" and "God bless us", she answers prophetically:

> These deeds must not be thought
> After these ways; so, it will make us mad.[4]

It is then that Macbeth introduces the theme of sleep which is always found in any study of fear, and he speaks again by the book:

> Methought I heard a voice cry, "Sleep no more!
> Macbeth does murder sleep,"—the innocent sleep,
> Sleep that knits up the ravell'd sleave of care,
> The death of each day's life, sore labour's bath,

[1] II, i, 33–9.
[2] II, i, 47–9.
[3] II, ii, 1, 2.
[4] II, ii, 33, 34.

> Balm of hurt minds, great nature's second course,
> Chief nourisher in life's feast,—[1]

But Lady Macbeth reproves him for his "brainsickly" talking about these things. Her fear is more active and more provident. She will have him wash his hands; she will have him carry back the daggers to the King's chamber and smear the grooms with blood.

Macbeth is fearful beyond care, however:

> I'll go no more.
> I am afraid to think what I have done;
> Look on 't again I dare not.[2]

And Lady Macbeth with her chiding "Infirm of purpose!" goes to the practical task of smearing the grooms with blood, while Macbeth can but look at his hands and wonder at the endless red of the blood thereon as the loud knocking commences and he exclaims:

> Whence is that knocking?
> How is 't with me, when every noise appalls me?[3]

As Lady Macbeth comes from her task in the King's chamber with reassuring suggestions for washing away the blood and getting into a nightgown, Macbeth hears only the knocking:

> Wake Duncan with thy knocking! I would thou couldst!

The recital of the night's ominous horrors in the scene which follows is interrupted by Macduff's shrill cry:

> O horror, horror, horror!

But even in the midst of the confusion which ensues upon the news of Duncan's murder the note of sex decorum is again sounded. All that a woman should be and all that

---

[1] II, ii, 35–40.   [2] II, ii, 50–2.
[3] II, ii, 57, 58.

Lady Macbeth is not is suggested in Macduff's gentle care for his hostess:

> O gentle lady,
> 'T is not for you to hear what I can speak;
> The repetition in a woman's ear
> Would murder as it fell. [1]

The awful news is, indeed, greeted by Lady Macbeth with a feeble, "What, in our house?" while with bitter irony her lord exclaims:

> The wine of life is drawn, and the mere lees
> Is left this vault to brag of. [2]

In what follows we discover that Macbeth has already shown his fear in one of the traditional ways, for he has killed the grooms, fearing those who had him in their power through sharing perchance his secret. He apologizes:

> Who can be wise, amaz'd, temperate and furious,
> Loyal and neutral, in a moment? No man.
> The expedition of my violent love
> Outrun the pauser, reason. [3]

And as Lady Macbeth is helped from the room, we see fear working in the others. Banquo admits that fears and scruples shake them all, even while he proclaims his enmity to treason. But Banquo fears rightly the anger or hatred of the Macbeth who has power to do him harm. And Malcolm and Donalbain flee quickly from the Macbeth who has destroyed one stronger than they in Duncan, even as Malcolm explains:

> This murderous shaft that's shot
> Hath not yet lighted, and our safest way
> Is to avoid the aim. [4]

Ironically the last scene tells us that the sons are suspected of having done the deed for ambition's sake and that Macbeth is already crowned.

[1] II, iii, 88–91. [2] II, iii, 100, 101.
[3] II, iii, 114–7. [4] II, iii, 147–9.

Yet it must be noted that while these first two acts of the play are taken up with the struggle of two passions for victory, while that struggle has been resolved by the deed which fear was not quite able to keep ambition from accomplishing, yet in the very moment when ambition seems to have won, fear has in reality taken possession of the victim. After the murder of Duncan, the whole play is motivated by the increasing passion of fear. Nowhere is there more clearly evidenced the truth of Plutarch's statement:

but wickednesse ingendering within it selfe...displeasure and punishment, not after a sinfull act is committed, but even at the very instant of committing, it beginneth to suffer the pain due to the offence.... [1]

Macbeth has been forced to "bend up Each corporal agent to this terrible feat". At the very moment when the deed is committed, the wine of life is indeed drawn, and fear takes complete possession of the guilty souls. From the murder of Duncan onward, it is not ambition but fear that terrorizes its victims into action. The death of the grooms is but the first of the fear-provoked acts.

The third act begins with a soliloquy spoken by Banquo, a soliloquy which shows that suspicion of Macbeth and ambition roused by the prophecy of the witches have both found lodgement in him, so that it is not without cause that Macbeth reasons in his next soliloquy:

> To be thus is nothing;
> But to be safely thus. Our fears in Banquo
> Stick deep; and in his royalty of nature
> Reigns that which would be fear'd. 'T is much he dares;
> And, to that dauntless temper of his mind,
> He hath a wisdom that doth guide his valour
> To act in safety. [2]

[1] Cf. p. 21, *ante*.   [2] III, i, 48–54.

It is this wisdom in Banquo that makes Macbeth, who can act only in passion, envy him his superiority:

> There is none but he
> Whose being I do fear; and, under him,
> My Genius is rebuk'd, as, it is said,
> Mark Antony's was by Caesar.[1]

If the witches have spoken as truly to Banquo as to him, Macbeth sees that he wears a "fruitless crown" and carries a "barren sceptre" in his hand; he has indeed given peace and immortality to make the race of Banquo kings. And he proceeds to his interview with the murderers, plotting what he dare not do openly, for the fear that comes when we are rivals for a thing and cannot both have it makes it seem to Macbeth:

> That every minute of his being thrusts
> Against my near'st of life;[2]

and he will kill his fear by having Banquo and Fleance both put to death.

When we hear Lady Macbeth speak in the next scene alone, we know that to her, too, ambition has brought only unquiet as its reward:

> Nought's had, all's spent,
> Where our desire is got without content.[3]

But to Macbeth she advises:

> Things without all remedy
> Should be without regard; what's done is done.[4]

Such an attitude is impossible to Macbeth, however. His danger constantly haunts him, and, moreover, he has grown desperate:

> But let the frame of things disjoint, both the worlds suffer,
> Ere we will eat our meal in fear, and sleep

[1] III, i, 54–7. [2] III, i, 117, 118.
[3] III, ii, 4, 5. [4] III, ii, 11, 12.

> In the affliction of these terrible dreams
> That shake us nightly. Better be with the dead
> Whom we, to gain our peace, have sent to peace,
> Than on the torture of the mind to lie
> In restless ecstasy. Duncan is in his grave;
> After life's fitful fever he sleeps well.[1]

Macbeth is proving with Thomas Nashe that

The table of our hart is turned to an index of iniquities, and all our thoughts are nothing but texts to condemne us.[2]

But it must be noted that by this time the earlier signs of melancholy which Macbeth showed have now become more pronounced. Passion has wrought havoc in him. He is the victim of dreams, he keeps alone, he envies the dead, his thoughts are of black night. His invocation to night closes with the vain hope:

Things bad begun make strong themselves by ill.[3]

But that such hope is vain is proved by the next scene, in which Banquo is murdered only to charge young Fleance with his death cry, "Thou mayst revenge". And Fleance escapes.

Thus it is even as the King gathers his friends about the banquet table, the first murderer appears to tell him of Banquo's death and the escape of Fleance. Again safety has eluded his grasp, and fear again seizes him as he exclaims, "Then comes my fit again".

Now it will be remembered that Lavater cited from other familiar writers the instances of those guilty persons who framed to themselves out of their melancholy and their fear fantastical accusers of their guilt.[4] Tales of such appearances

[1] III, ii, 16–23.

[2] Nashe, *Terrors of the Night*, p. 220.

[3] This whole invocation, III, ii, 46–55, is one of the most interesting adornments of the play, since it carries on the association of fear and night.

[4] Cf. p. 86 *ante.*

at table, causing the guilty one to reveal his hidden guilt to the guests, suited the Renaissance theory of sin and were frequent. Therefore, Shakespeare again is refashioning a traditional story of fear and guilt when he makes Macbeth see the ghost of Banquo as he approaches the feast with his guests. In the traditional way he cries out:

> Thou canst not say I did it; never shake
> Thy gory locks at me. [1]

The explanation which Lady Macbeth offers to the guests must be well listened to:

> Sit, worthy friends; my lord is often thus,
> And hath been from his youth. Pray you, keep seat;
> The fit is momentary; upon a thought
> He will again be well. If much you note him,
> You shall offend him and extend his passion.

It will be remembered that Macbeth did stand "rapt" at the appearance of the witches. The fit which now seizes him is apparently the fit of passion which he was subject to—the fit of fear which he could still by thought but which would truly be extended if it was noted by others. And Lady Macbeth tries to rouse him to the thought or reason which can get mastery over passion as she says, "Are you a man?" And she continues in significant fashion to emphasize the fantastical nature of the apparition and the feminine quality of his fear:

> This is the very painting of your fear;
> This is the air-drawn dagger which, you said,
> Led you to Duncan. O, these flaws and starts,
> Impostors to true fear, would well become
> A woman's story at a winter's fire,
> Authoriz'd by her grandam. Shame itself!
> Why do you make such faces? When all's done,
> You look but on a stool. [2]

[1] III, iv, 50, 51.   [2] III, iv, 61–8.

As the ghost vanishes, the cry of Macbeth seems to be more full of horror than any other in this play of horror:

> The time has been,
> That, when the brains were out, the man would die,
> And there an end; but now they rise again,
> With twenty mortal murders on their crowns,
> And push us from our stools.[1]

And even as Macbeth gains control of his passion, even as he apologizes for his "strange infirmity", even as he speaks of Banquo to wish that he were present, he again sees the ghost and cries out to it in terror. While Lady Macbeth again apologizes, he reiterates his manly fortitude in the old definition of fortitude:

> What man dare, I dare.

And like Othello, he affirms his ability to meet any test but this.[2] To Lady Macbeth's further reproof, he can only reply in amazement:

> You make me strange
> Even to the disposition that I owe,
> When now I think you can behold such sights,
> And keep the natural ruby of your cheeks,
> When mine is blanch'd with fear.[3]

When the guests have been hastily despatched, he can but continue to talk of the belief that "blood will have blood", and to give instances of strange phenomena which have been called to the revealing of guilt. His fear will not let him rest. Though Macduff has refused his invitation, he has spies in all their houses. He will visit the weird sisters on the morrow, though he undoubtedly ranks them as evil. His cry is despairful:

> I am in blood
> Stepp'd in so far that, should I wade no more,
> Returning were as tedious as go o'er.

---

[1] III, iv, 78–82.   [2] Cf. *Othello*, IV, ii, 47–55.
[3] III, iv, 112–16.

And as Lady Macbeth urges his need of sleep, the scene closes with his,

> We are but young in deed.

The act closes with the satirical conversation between Lennox and another lord, in which we discover the knowledge which is abroad of the murders of Duncan, of the grooms, of Banquo. But we learn, too, that Malcolm and Donalbain and Fleance and Macduff have cause to fear; that injury has also flown to seek help in vengeance. Now our attention is for the moment centred upon the "suffering state" and the tyrant that Macbeth has become. And we remember that the true man of fortitude is tested by his ability to remain unchanged by the changes of fortune, so that the tyrant is the man who cannot stand the test of prosperity but is ruled by passion in his prosperity rather than by reason.

If we accept Scene v of Act III as canonical, we must accept it as a prologue to Act IV, and if we accept it, much of the mystery of the witches is gone.[1] We are not allowed to be in doubt concerning the evil intention of Hecate, and we hear the ideas of King James re-echoed in her proposal further to raise "such artificial sprites" as shall draw Macbeth on "to his confusion".

As Act IV opens and the witches appear, we are prepared for the "artificial sprites" which shall draw Macbeth on. But as we saw in Act III, Macbeth's fear has driven him to seek certainty as his one objective. He wants certainty from the witches, howsoever they may come to know it, and at whatever cost. His fear of the unknown has cast out all fear of the witches themselves.

In this scene Shakespeare has given us much reason to defend a notion that the witches and their "sprites" need

[1] On this point see the Introduction and the foot-note on this scene by Henry Cunningham in the English Arden edition of *Macbeth*.

not have been completely objective, for curiously Macbeth's fears point the direction to their prophecies. The first apparition warns him:

> Macbeth! Macbeth! Macbeth! beware Macduff!
> Beware the thane of Fife.

And Macbeth answers:

> Thou hast harp'd my fear aright.

The second apparition bids him be bold,

> for none of woman born
> Shall harm Macbeth.

And Macbeth thinks yet of Macduff:

> Then live, Macduff; what need I fear of thee?
> But yet I'll make assurance doubly sure,
> And take a bond of fate. Thou shalt not live;
> That I may tell pale-hearted fear it lies,
> And sleep in spite of thunder.

The third apparition bids him be proud and careless, for

> Macbeth shall never vanquish'd be until
> Great Birnam wood to high Dunsinane hill
> Shall come against him.

And Macbeth cries in relief, "That will never be", but still he yearns to know whether Banquo's issue shall ever reign. And as the answering procession of kings passes before him and he seems to see "the blood-bolter'd Banquo" pointing them out for his, apparently his fit comes on him again, for the first witch says:

> ...but why
> Stands Macbeth thus amazedly?

This time the witches appear only to Macbeth. Lennox, who enters to announce the flight of Macduff, has not seen them. The news that Lennox brings is enough to spur

Macbeth to immediate action. Now he speaks the very theme of *Hamlet*:

> The flighty purpose never is o'ertook
> Unless the deed go with it. [1]

And he plans the death of Macduff's wife and children with a grim

> This deed I'll do before this purpose cool.

Whether Shakespeare could write badly enough to write the second scene of the fourth act of *Macbeth* I shall leave others to dispute. That it offers opportunity for ringing further changes on the theme of fear is evident throughout. Lady Macduff is distinctly of the opinion that her husband fled the land from fear, even without having done anything which should make him fear retribution. To Ross she says:

> His flight was madness. When our actions do not,
> Our fears do make us traitors. [2]

As Ross argues that she cannot know whether it "was his wisdom or his fear", she very pertinently argues against the wisdom that will make a man fly from the place in which he leaves his wife and children, and she instances the courage of the wren that will make it fight the owl to protect its young ones in proof that Macduff's fear has made him unnatural in his actions. She concludes:

> All is the fear and nothing is the love;
> As little is the wisdom, where the flight
> So runs against all reason. [3]

Her statement as to the wisdom that acts in accordance with reason and not against it must be reckoned as a part of the analysis of passion in the play.

---

[1] Cf. *Hamlet*, III, ii, 204, 205.   [2] IV, ii, 3, 4.
[3] IV, ii, 12–14.

Ross argues vaguely that Macduff "is noble, wise, judicious", and that the times are cruel,

> ...when we hold rumour
> From what we fear, yet know not what we fear,[1]

but he departs sadly even as Lady Macduff sentimentalizes further with her son:

> Poor bird! thou'dst never fear the net nor lime,

and as the messenger enters grieving that he has to "fright" her thus. It must be noted, too, that Lady Macduff stresses her sex in the whole scene even to the final "womanly defence" that she has done no harm and in her outcry of defiance as the murderers enter to do their horrible work.

Whether the scene be worse than Shakespeare, it is at any rate a development of the same theme of fear. These new murders are the new results of Macbeth's fear; they are also laid to the fear of Macduff which made him escape and leave his wife and children unprotected. And they add a melodramatic horror to the horrors already piled on horrors in the play.

The next scene, between Malcolm and Macduff, emphasizes the tyranny of Macbeth in contrast to the virtues that become a King. The scene is weak and obvious, but it affords opportunity for Shakespeare to give one of those lists of kingly virtues and vices that were so popular in the books of moral philosophy. As Ross comes with the news of the slaughter which was portrayed in the preceding scene on the stage, Malcolm becomes the leader. His words are reminiscent of *Hamlet*, emphasizing the grief of Laertes as against the grief of Hamlet himself:

> Be comforted.
> Let's make us medicines of our great revenge,
> To cure this deadly grief.[2]

[1] IV, ii, 19, 20.   [2] IV, iii, 213–15.

And again as Macduff grieves that his wife and children
were slaughtered because of him, Malcolm cries:

> Be this the whetstone of your sword; let grief
> Convert to anger; blunt not the heart, enrage it. [1]

That grief does blunt the heart was evident in *Hamlet*, that
anger enrages it is evident both in *Hamlet* and in the suc-
ceeding scenes of *Macbeth*.

The act closes with the words of Malcolm that reiterate
the general notion of God's vengeance:

> 　　　　　　　　　　　　　　　Macbeth
> Is ripe for shaking, and the powers above
> Put on their instruments. Receive what cheer you may;
> The night is long that never finds the day. [2]

Act v presents swiftly and relentlessly the results of
passion, of the passion which has become mortal sin. First
it is Lady Macbeth that we see enduring the fate of the sinful
in whom fear and remorse have already begun to effect
the punishment for evil. That Shakespeare chose to manifest
Lady Macbeth's melancholy as a disturbance in her sleep
shows that he was a student of the moral philosophy of the
time, for as we have seen earlier, all the accounts of fear
are concerned with the effect of fear on sleep. Macbeth's own
cry, "Macbeth hath murdered sleep" was but the statement
of the realized truth of philosophy. Nashe's *Terrors of the
Night* said truly:

> In the daye time wee torment our thoughts and imaginations with
> sundry cares and devices; all the night time they quake and tremble
> after the terror of their late suffering, and still continue thinking of the
> perplexities they have endured. [3]

But Lady Macbeth's sleep has been troubled as only the
sleep of those can be troubled who have been led by passion
into melancholy, whose minds have become "infected

---

[1] iv, iii, 228, 229. Cf. the chapter on *Hamlet*, p. 114 of this study.
[2] iv, iii, 237–40.　　　　　　　　[3] p. 235.

minds". She walks and talks in her sleep. Thus Nashe explained in accordance with the popular belief of the day that we make for ourselves "images of memory" and some superfluous humour in the night erects a puppet stage for these images. It is thus that Lady Macbeth shows the images of memory which have been most deeply etched by fear. She sees the spot of blood which will not out. She sees again the murdered Duncan. Yet who would have thought the old man to have had so much blood in him? She recalls Lady Macduff. She recalls her husband's dangerous starting. She smells blood still. She remembers her fearful admonition to Macbeth on the night of the murder to put on his night-gown, on the night of the feast to put away his imagination of Banquo's ghost. Then it is the knocking at the gate that she hears again.

Anyone who does not believe that Lady Macbeth as well as her husband is the victim of fear should study these images of memory, for they reveal horror and fear. She does not dwell upon the havoc wrought by such deeds; she rather recalls those images associated with her extreme moments of terror and fear: the blood upon her hands, her husband's starting that endangered all, the old man bleeding so much blood, the feast marred by Banquo's ghost, and then the awful knocking that summoned fear on the night of Duncan's murder. All this is not remorse but fear. And in the last act we see the pitiful results of the fear that conquered finally the reason that so long held it in abeyance. It was long before Lady Macbeth's reason gave way before the reiterated fears of her imperial ascent, but at last passion has conquered reason fully, it would seem.[1] Futhermore, it must be noted that even as Macbeth revealed his guilt at the

---

[1] From the first of the play, Lady Macbeth's reason was subdued by passion. Passion determined the end. Reason but determined the means to that end. Now Reason no longer functions at all. Passion reigns alone.

feast to those who were his guests, so Lady Macbeth finally
revealed her guilt to the watchers. It is thus that the old
themes of tragedy are newly spoken by Shakespeare. And
it is the theme of moral philosophy which is spoken as well
in the doctor's words:

> More needs she the divine than the physician.[1]

In the next scenes we turn again to Macbeth. First we
hear of the revenges which burn in those who lead on the
English power to Macbeth's destruction. And then we hear
reports of the results of passion within the man himself.
Caithness reports:

> Some say he's mad, others that lesser hate him
> Do call it valiant fury;

Angus explains the fear and uncertainty that hedge him
about; and Menteith questions:

> Who then shall blame
> His pester'd senses to recoil and start,
> When all that is within him does condemn
> Itself for being there?

And then we see the shattered Macbeth fighting fear. He
reassures himself:

> Till Birnam wood remove to Dunsinane
> I cannot taint with fear. What's the boy Malcolm?
> Was he not born of woman?

And he rehearses the words of the witches, concluding:

> The mind I sway by and the heart I bear
> Shall never sag with doubt nor shake with fear.

[1] Wright wrote, *op. cit.* 1604 ed. p. 2: "The Divine herein may first
challenge his parte, because the inordinate motions of Passions, their
preventing of reason, their rebellion to virtue are thornie briars sprung
from the infected root of original sinne...." Cf. Thomas Adams,
Diseases of the Soule, 1616, for a detailed application of the general
idea.

As the servant enters to tell of the oncoming host, Macbeth rages at him, calling him "lily-liver'd boy" and "whey-face" and bidding him "over-red" his fear. But in a moment of realization he becomes sad, counting the things fit for age which are not for him. He speaks truly when he says:

> I am sick at heart.

But as he turns to fevered activity, the doctor reports concerning Lady Macbeth:

> Not so sick, my lord,
> As she is troubled with thick-coming fancies,
> That keep her from her rest.[1]

And Macbeth gives in his reply a complete picture of the effects of passion:

> Canst thou not minister to a mind diseas'd,
> Pluck from the memory a rooted sorrow,
> Raze out the written troubles of the brain,
> And with some sweet oblivious antidote
> Cleanse the stuff'd bosom of that perilous stuff
> Which weighs upon the heart?[2]

The doctor replies as any doctor of the time would have replied:

> Therein the patient
> Must minister to himself.

But Macbeth still urges some physical remedy if possible. Then as the doctor admits having heard of the coming of the English, Macbeth again proclaims:

> I will not be afraid of death and bane,
> Till Birnam forest come to Dunsinane.

The Macbeth who is preparing to meet the siege must first meet other disaster, however. The cry of the women within only recalls him to his earlier fears:

> I have almost forgot the taste of fears,
> The time has been, my senses would have cool'd

[1] v, iii, 37–9. [2] v, iii, 40–45.

> To hear a night-shriek, and my fell of hair
> Would at a dismal treatise rouse and stir
> As life were in 't. I have supp'd full with horrors;
> Direness, familiar to my slaughterous thoughts,
> Cannot once start me.[1]

And at the news of the death of the Queen he has scarcely time to rail at life in the great speech ending with the final estimate of life:

> It is a tale
> Told by an idiot, full of sound and fury,
> Signifying nothing.[2]

As the theorists of fear have pointed out, there cannot be fear where we have experienced every horror already; there is some hope necessary to fear. But from this point on, we see Macbeth who has "supp'd full with horrors", advancing to that despair which is the final stage of fear and which manifests itself as fury. On the news of the death of the Queen there follows fast the news of the advance of Birnam wood. And Macbeth advances to defend his castle with his thoughts full of the witches and their promise, furiously crying:

> Ring the alarum-bell! Blow, wind! come, wrack!
> At least we'll die with harness on our back.[3]

When next we see Macbeth in battle, he reasons concerning his fortune:

> They have tied me to a stake; I cannot fly,
> But, bear-like, I must fight the course. What's he
> That was not born of woman? Such a one
> Am I to fear, or none.[4]

The Macbeth here is the Macbeth of the first scenes of the play, the Macbeth in military action, the Macbeth who recalls the "brave Macbeth" with which the play opened. But here

[1] V, v, 9–15.
[2] V, v, 26–8.
[3] V, v, 51, 52.
[4] V, vii, 1–4.

again he fights irrationally, not with the fortitude of the man controlling his passion by reason, but rather with the courage of the animal that fights without reason when there is no choice but to fight for its life. Shakespeare could not say more clearly that this apparent courage is that of the beast and not of the man.

But Macbeth's final ground for hope is taken away. Just as the advance of Birnam wood has made him doubt the assurance of the witches, so now the parley with Macduff in the next stage of the battle makes it apparent that their warning to beware Macduff and their promise that Macbeth should not yield to one of woman born are not irreconcilable. To Macduff's statement concerning his birth, Macbeth replies:

> Accursed be that tongue that tells me so,
> For it hath cow'd my better part of man![1]

And as he renounces faith in the witches, he cries in despair, "I'll not fight with thee".

But as Macduff calls him coward and demands that he yield, he cries again in utter despair:

> I will not yield,
> To kiss the ground before young Malcolm's feet
> And to be baited with the rabble's curse.
> Though Birnam wood be come to Dunsinane,
> And thou oppos'd being of no woman born,
> Yet I will try the last.[2]

Yet Shakespeare gives us another picture of true fortitude before the play closes, in the picture of Siward, who meets the news of the death of his son in battle with a refusal to grieve unduly.

The entrance of Macduff with Macbeth's head comes as evidence of the final end of the "dead butcher" who was

---

[1] v, viii, 17, 18.   [2] v, viii, 27–32.

Macbeth, and we hear from the newly proclaimed King
of the end also of "the fiend-like queen":

> Who, as 't is thought, by self and violent hands
> Took off her life. [1]

According to this analysis, then, *Macbeth* is a study in the
complementary pair of passions of rash courage and fear.
It begins with the courage that is not real courage and ends
with the courage that is not real courage. It pictures in turn
the military courage of Macbeth, his excited valour and
excessive bravery in action, the drunken courage of Lady
Macbeth, the bravery of passion, the fury of despair, and the
courage of desperation. It pictures as well superstitious fear,
melancholy fear, the fear of those who share our secrets, the
fear of those who are our rivals, the fear of those whom we
have harmed, all the fears that lead to murder after murder,
that result in melancholy, in sleeplessness, in disturbing
dreams, in ghosts and visions, in fits of passion, in frenzy, in
sleep-walking, in self-destruction; fears that destroy peace
and happiness and honour and hope; fears that make ambition fruitless and success a mockery.

But the study is also a study of man and woman. Lady
Macbeth is pictured as sinning partly, I think, in that she
is false to herself as woman. [2] She is pictured as consciously
unsexing herself, as converting all that is womanly into the
courage and determination to be cruel. Even more than
Macbeth, she wills to do evil. She dyes her will in her
ambition. Because her will is strong and directed by passion
and not by reason, the fear that is her punishment is more
terrible than that of Macbeth and brings her even to the
despairful sin of self-destruction.

Macbeth is, however, not only a study of fear; it is a study

---

[1] v, viii, 70, 71.
[2] Cf. Section I, chapters x and xi, for the discussion of decorum
as morality, especially pp. 98 and 104.

in fear. The sounds and images in the play combine to give the atmosphere of terror and fear. The incantation of the witches, the bell that tolls while Duncan dies, the cries of Duncan, the cries of the women as Lady Macbeth dies, the owl, the knocking at the gate, the wild horses that ate each other, the storm, the quaking of the earth—all of these are the habitual accompaniments of the wilfully fearful in literature. *Macbeth* might well have shared Nashe's title, *The Terrors of the Night*.

APPENDIX A

Bradley Revisited: Forty Years After[1]

ORE than forty years ago, in 1904, Professor A. C. Bradley published his *Shakespearean Tragedy*. It was a mighty book, taking Shakespearean criticism again into the realm of the universal and the significant. I well remember the enthusiasm of my teachers when they read it, for I was at an age when I wondered at their excitement. To the younger teachers of Shakespeare, willing or anxious to lay aside the analyzing of his plays according to Freytag and to cease following him "Out of the depths" and "On the heights" with Dowden, salvation seemed to come with their new leader. So great was their enthusiasm that, to explain Shakespeare, they took to explaining Bradley, and they oriented all Shakespeare studies to the new sun. But the young scholars of the first decade of the twentieth century are those who now attend the Old Guard dinners of the Modern Language Association, and it is as dangerous in scholarship as in politics to stop thinking new ideas and reconsidering old ones. Some of the political progressives of 1906 have died thinking they were still progressive because they still believed what they did in 1906. Among Shakespearean scholars there are still many who regard the dicta of Bradley as having been brought down to the people from Sinai, and who demand that each new interpretation be tested by whether it can be reconciled with what Bradley says. It seems to me that the time has come to re-examine Bradley's book in the light of what we have learned during these forty years, obeying the first law of honest criticism, that we prove all things and hold fast to that which is good.

[1]Reprinted from *Studies in Philology*, XLIV, 2, April, 1947, with the special permission of the publishers.

Professor C. H. Herford in presenting *A Sketch of Recent Shakespearean Criticism* wrote of Bradley in 1925:

The current doctrine, rapidly hardening into dogma, that Shakespeare, like lesser men, can be interpreted only through the historic conditions in which he wrote, went by the board. Bradley's instrument of interpretation was the intuitive insight of a trained, alert, and kindled imagination.

But if he thus openly attached himself to the aesthetic tradition of Coleridge and Hazlitt, he used this instrument of interpretation with a methodical precision which reflected the more scientific temper of the Elizabethan scholarship of his own period.

To many critics still following this aesthetic tradition, historic criticism seems to confine genius within narrow boundaries of time and place, to substitute facts for truth, to center attention upon the dross rather than upon the refined gold of great art. But they still cannot escape their own environing ideas of art and psychology and economics and religion. The conviction grows as we study their criticism that a universal critic is the only possible complement to a universal artist.

Indeed, modern psychological teaching makes inevitable our concern with interpreting Shakespearean drama in the light of the customs, attitudes, and ideas of Shakespeare's England, for we have extended to our historical studies our acceptance of the fact that the individual is conditioned by his environment. If such a psychological theory interferes with the older idea of the universal artist as one whose interpretations of life are made without regard to time and place and circumstance, it seems to me that, rather than deny our newer understanding, we must look to future studies of the nature of genius to throw further light on the way in which the great artist transmutes the passing into the eternal, the local into the universal.

Bradley could no more than lesser critics rid himself of the preconceptions resulting from the environing ideas which conditioned his thought. As a result of his letting Elizabethan ideas go by the board, he frequently concerned himself with problems that were irrelevant or ignored the significance of evidence important to the tracing of the moral pattern in the plays, to which task he had set himself. It seems to me desirable to study in detail certain of these interpretations of Shakespearean tragedy which have focused attention upon misleading issues. I hope in the near future to survey in turn several of the major criteria advanced by Bradley. As a first step I propose to reexamine his discussion of the moral responsibility of the tragic heroes in relation to what he calls the "additional factors" in tragedy—abnormal conditions of mind, the supernatural, and accidents. I am going to repeat some things I have said before, but it seems necessary to do so in order to make plain the issues.

Bradley's definition of a Shakespearean tragedy is "a tale of suffering and calamity conducting to death," and ultimately "a story of exceptional calamity leading to the death of a man in high estate." Such tragic calamity he conceives to proceed mainly from the actions of men, so that the tragic hero contributes "in some measure to the disaster in which he perishes." And the hero's deeds issue from his character. "The centre of the tragedy," he concludes, therefore, "may be said with equal truth to lie in action issuing from character, or in character issuing in action," so that his final definition affirms "that the story is one of human actions producing exceptional calamity and ending in the death of such a man." However, there are in Shakespearean tragedy "beside the characteristic deeds, and the sufferings and circumstances of the persons, three "additional factors" which he lists as abnormal conditions of mind, the supernatural, and chance or accident.[1]

Overpassing his definition of tragedy, let us consider what he has to say about these "additional factors,"

[1] Pp. 7, 11, 12, 16. All references are to the 1911 edition.

though it may be noted at the outset that his discussion of them consists of an attempt to prove that they are not really *factors* at all. Of the first of them he writes:

> Shakespeare, occasionally and for reasons which need not be discussed here, represents abnormal conditions of mind; insanity, for example, somnambulism, hallucinations. And deeds issuing from these are certainly not what we called deeds in the fullest sense, deeds expressive of character.

Here, it seems to me, is a prime illustration of a nineteenth-century mind imposing a moral pattern upon the work of a sixteenth-century mind. Bradley chose to ignore the all-important reasons which made these abnormal mental conditions an essential part of the moral pattern of tragedy and instead discussed the problem of moral responsibility, legalistically interpreted. He considers these abnormal conditions of mind only to prove, however, that they are "never introduced as the origin of deeds of any dramatic moment." And he argues the matter in regard to each specific case:

> Lady Macbeth's sleep-walking has no influence whatever on the events that follow it. Macbeth did not murder Duncan because he saw a dagger in the air: he saw the dagger because he was about to murder Duncan. Lear's insanity is not the cause of a tragic conflict any more than Ophelia's; it is, like Ophelia's, the result of a conflict; and in both cases the effect is mainly pathetic. If Lear were really mad when he divided his kingdom, if Hamlet were really mad at any time in the story, they would cease to be tragic characters.[2]

This is the point with which he is concerned, the moral responsibility of the characters for the deeds which lead to tragic conclusions. In discussing *Hamlet* he avers of Hamlet's melancholy (or melancholia):

> But this melancholy is something very different from insanity, in anything like the usual meaning of that word. . . . It is a totally different thing from the madness which he feigns; . . . Nor is the

[2] Pp. 13-14.

dramatic use of this melancholy, again, open to the objections which would justly be made to the portrayal of an insanity which brought the hero to a tragic end. The man who suffers as Hamlet suffers—and thousands go about their business suffering thus in greater or less degree—is considered irresponsible neither by other people nor by himself: he is only too keenly conscious of his responsibility. He is, therefore, so far, quite capable of being a tragic agent, which an insane person, at any rate according to Shakespeare's practice, is not.[3]

And of *King Lear* he says:

The first lines tell us that Lear's mind is beginning to fail with age.

But he adds a footnote:

Of course I do not mean that he is beginning to be insane, and still less that he is insane (as some medical critics suggest).[4]

A little later, in speaking of Lear's condition, he again stresses the fact of his moral responsibility:

Our consciousness that the decay of old age contributes to this condition deepens our pity and our sense of human infirmity, but certainly does not lead us to regard the old King as irresponsible, and so to sever the tragic *nexus* which binds together his error and his calamities.[5]

Incidentally, Bradley notes as the first characteristic of Lear's later insanity "the domination of a fixed idea,"[6] an interpretation which would certainly not have been clear to Lear's creator. But the important point is that he argues persistently that such things as Hamlet's melancholy, Lear's insanity, and Lady Macbeth's sleep-walking can be disregarded in the moral pattern of the tragedies because they are "never introduced as the origin of deeds of any dramatic moment." This is like saying that a physician should disregard fever in diagnosing a disease because fever does not cause the disease.

In the first place, Bradley is merely arguing in a circle. He makes his own definition of tragedy as centering

[3] Pp. 121-22.   [4] P. 281.   [5] P. 282.   [6] P. 288.

about action issuing from character or character issuing in action. Then he makes his own definition of such action as consisting of "deeds in the fullest sense, deeds expressive of character," excluding all that are done while the doer is the victim of any abnormal state of mind. Having established these two premises by definition, he proves that Hamlet was not mad and that Lear was not senilely insane when he divided his kingdom because then "they would cease to be tragic characters." In other words, he by definition makes a tragic hero set the tragic circle in motion while he is morally responsible and then proves that he must have been morally responsible when he set the forces of destruction at work or else he could not have been a tragic hero.

In the second place, Bradley ignores the Elizabethan acceptance of these abnormal states of mind as resulting from the unchecked domination of passion over reason and hence confuses cause and effect. Shakespeare wrote in an age that continually used Ajax as an arch example of a tragic hero and his tragedy as an outstanding instance of the effectiveness of tragedy as a moral teacher, an age also that understood a prosecution claim in court that a man who committed a criminal act while drunk should, as Aristotle advised, be considered doubly guilty, of being drunk and of having committed the act.[7] The Elizabethan attitude is typified in Sidney's defence of tragedy as a moral teacher superior to philosophy and history:

Anger, the *Stoicks* say, was a short madness: let but *Sophocles* bring you *Aiax* on a stage, killing and whipping Sheepe and Oxen, thinking them the Army of Greeks, with theyr Chieftaines *Agamemnon* and *Menelaus*, and tell mee if you haue not a more familiar insight into anger then finding in the Schoolmen his *Genus* and difference.[8]

[7] Edmund Plowden, *The Commentaries or Reports of* (trans. fr. French) (1779), p. 19. The argument was used in the case of Reniger versus Fogasso, temp. Ed. VI. Plowden dated his work 20 October, 1578, from the Middle Temple.

[8] G. G. Smith, *Elizabethan Critical Essays* (Oxford, 1937), p. 165.

Sidney was not concerned with whether Ajax committed his tragic acts when he was morally responsibile, but he was concerned with the ultimate moral responsibility of Ajax when he allowed anger so to dominate him that he could be led to complete unreason and insane acts.

The fact that Bradley argued in a circle when he argued for legal and moral responsibility as a necessary condition for tragic acts, and the fact that he confused cause and effect in his argument are both due, it seems to me, to his failure to consider Elizabethan ideas. "Shakespeare," he said, "occasionally and for reasons which need not be discussed here, represents abnormal conditions of mind." I contend that it is beside the point to find that these abnormal conditions of mind are "never introduced as the origin of deeds of any dramatic moment," but that it is important to understand the reasons which led Shakespeare to introduce them. It is just as destructive to the moral significance of the great tragedies to fail to reckon the part which Hamlet's melancholy (or melancholia) and Lear's insanity and Lady Macbeth's sleep-walking play in the moral structure as it would be to the theatrical effectiveness of the plays to omit these scenes from the stage presentations.

Now medical jurisprudence was not developed in the sixteenth century to its present complexity and deviousness, but a man *"non sanis memoriae,"* it was said, could not break the law, of which, because of his condition, he was unaware.[9] Sir William Hale in the mid-seventeenth century codified the ideas that had been current in a chapter "Concerning the defect of ideocy, madness and lunacy, in reference to criminal offenses and punishments" in his *History of the Pleas of the Crown.* He notes that "tho by the law of *England* no man shall avoid his own act by reason of these defects, . . . yet as to capital offenses these have in some cases

[9] Plowden, p. 19.

the advantage of this defect or incapacity," which he calls *dementia*. Among its subdivisions he lists *dementia accidentalis, vel adventitia*, which he describes as proceeding "sometimes from the distemper of the humours of the body, as deep melancholy or adust choler" and sometimes from a disease, or a concussion or hurt of the brain. It may be intermittent or varying in degree, and he explains that that which differs in degree obtains in melancholy persons "who for the most part discover their defect in excessive fears and griefs, and yet are not wholly destitute of the use of reason" so that "this particular insanity seems not to excuse them in the committing of any offense for its matter capital." Yet he advises that the merits of each individual case be decided by the jury.[10]

It is, of course, these cases of *dementia accidentalis, vel adventitia* that Bradley is discussing, but Shakespeare does not seem to me to be sitting as a judge, nor does he ask the audience to sit as a jury on their sanity. What he shows us is the dominance of passion which brought them to the state in which we see them so theatrically manifesting their *dementia*. Choler adust (or melancholy adust, as it was more often called), is such an unpoetic and unliterary phrase that most critics will have none of it, but in Elizabethan philosophy it is the key to this distempered state in which we find Hamlet and Othello and Macbeth and Lear.

Shakespearean tragedy made concrete Elizabethan moral teaching, and that teaching was centered about the conflict of passion and reason in man's soul. When passion rather than reason controls his will, man errs or sins. And the punishment for error and for sin is first of all seen in the turbulence of soul created by passion. The disintegration and turmoil grow. Death

[10] *Historia Placitorum Coronae. The History of the Pleas of the Crown.* Ed. by Sollom Emlyn (1736), Vol. I, chap. iv. Hale lived 1609-1676.

itself is not so terrible as the loss of the will to live which we see in each of the great tragic heroes of Shakespeare. Hamlet begs Horatio:

> If thou didst ever hold me in thy heart,
> Absent thee from felicity awhile,
> And in this harsh world draw thy breath in pain,
> To tell my story.[11]

Othello anathematizes Iago in like words:

> I'd have thee live;
> For, in my sense, 't is happiness to die.[12]

Macbeth rages at life, for as he sees it,

> It is a tale
> Told by an idiot, full of sound and fury,
> Signifying nothing.[13]

Kent bids Edgar not to try to recall the dying Lear:

> Vex not his ghost: O! let him pass; he hates him
> That would upon the rack of this tough world
> Stretch him out longer.[14]

It is not the death of Hamlet or Othello or Macbeth or Lear that awes and horrifies us but the despair and disillusion that grows within his soul as he views the desolation and confusion to which he has contributed. He is "the branch that might have grown full straight," and our pity overwhelms us.

But the way to the final disillusion of the tragic hero is marked by stages. The melancholy of Hamlet, the "epilepsy" of Othello, the sleep-walking of Lady Macbeth and the hallucinations of her husband, the temporary insanity of Lear, are landmarks on the inevitable progress to doom. They were clearly understood by Shakespeare's contemporaries as signs of that distem-

---

[11] *Hamlet*, V. ii. 357-60. I quote from the English Arden texts throughout.

[12] *Othello*, V. ii. 287-88.

[13] *Macbeth*, V. v. 26-8.   [14] *King Lear*, V. iii. 314-16.

perature of the humors which was called melancholy adust, and they were regularly discussed among the diseases of the soul. Always we find the great Shakespearean tragedies tracing the same path to catastrophe and despair.[15] When we understand their most theatrically effective scenes as essential parts of the moral pattern which they exhibit, we are brought to a new appreciation of Shakespeare's mastery of his artistic medium, the drama.

The second additional factor in tragedy listed by Bradley is the supernatural, under which heading he considers "the ghosts and witches who have supernatural knowledge." He refuses to explain away the ghosts and witches as illusions in the minds of the characters, and he admits their contribution to the action. "But," he affirms, "the supernatural is always placed in the closest relation with character":

> It gives a confirmation and a distinct form to inward movements already present and exerting influence; to the sense of failure in Brutus, to the stifled workings of conscience in Richard, to the half-formed thought or the horrified memory of guilt in Macbeth, to suspicion in Hamlet.[16]

Moreover, he insists that the supernatural is never compulsive, so that we are never allowed to feel that it has removed the hero's capacity or responsibility for dealing with the problem that he has to face. His discussion of the supernatural throughout the series of lectures is thin and rather vague, but his objective is not vague. He is again primarily interested in proving that the tragic hero is morally responsible for his deeds, for otherwise he would cease to be a tragic hero—according to the premise laid down by definition.

[15] I have discussed these matters at some length in my *Shakespeare's Tragic Heroes* (Cambridge, 1930), Chaps. vii and viii and Section III.

[16] P. 14.

With the great Greek tragedies and their Senecan recensions the familiar and accepted ideals of tragedy during the Renaissance, it is highly improbable that the Elizabethans made an issue of the degree of moral responsibility involved when the gods and other supernatural agencies intervened in very compelling ways. And so far as I can discover, they did not discuss it. Bradley is again forcing a nineteenth-century legalistic interpretation upon sixteenth-century material. But the Elizabethans were interested in the *why* of supernatural manifestations, as I shall demonstrate later.

Meanwhile, in his study of individual plays Bradley's discussion of the ghosts in *Hamlet* and *Macbeth* is largely given over to proving the objectivity of these apparitions. The earlier appearances of the ghost in *Hamlet* he assumes to have been objective because they were witnessed by others than Hamlet. That the second return to earth was also not an hallucination he argues on the basis of two points. First, he says, Hamlet's state of mind when he was chiding his mother was "such that we cannot suppose the Ghost to be meant for an hallucination." In this judgment he certainly disagrees with Hamlet's mother.[17] Second, he finds that "the Ghost proves, so to speak, his identity by showing the same traits as were visible on his first appearance—the same insistence on the duty of remembering and the same concern for the Queen." I should think that if the ghost had said something new, Hamlet's mind would have been less likely to create it, but

> Alas, how is't with you,
> That you do bend your eye on vacancy
> And with the incorporal air do hold discourse?
> Forth at your eyes your spirits wildly peep;
> And, as the sleeping soldiers in the alarm,
> Your bedded hair, like life in excrements
> Starts up and stands on end.

[17] The queen describes Hamlet's appearance as she speaks to him (III. iv. 116-122):

I do not think the matter arguable. However, Bradley continues:

The idea of later critics and readers that the Ghost is an hallucination is due partly to failure to follow the indications just noticed, but also to two mistakes, the substitution of our present intellectual atmosphere for the Elizabethan, and the notion that, because the Queen does not see and hear the Ghost, it is meant to be unreal.

Then he fills in the Elizabethan atmosphere as follows:

But a ghost, in Shakespeare's day, was able for any sufficient reason to confine its manifestation to a single person in a company; and here the sufficient reason, that of sparing the Queen, is obvious.[18]

Of course, the ghost had refused to speak to anyone but Hamlet on its first appearance, and such particularity was a well-known habit of these returned travellers. There is surely no reason for bringing chivalry in to account for it. And I note that Bradley does not attribute any such motive to the ghost of Banquo when it remains invisible to Lady Macbeth. However, his interest is in proving the external reality of the ghost.

This preoccupation is repeated in the discussion of the ghost of Banquo in *Macbeth*. Bradley seems to have felt that the subject was important, for he devoted a longish note to it in the appendix. His conclusion is that:

On the whole, and with some doubt, I think that Shakespeare (1) meant the judicious to take the Ghost for an hallucination, but (2) knew that the bulk of the audience would take it for a reality. And I am more sure of (2) than (1).[19]

How a stage manager would arrange the production for a mixed audience of the judicious and otherwise I cannot imagine. And I suggest that the presentation of the supernatural on the stage is a matter for the producer to decide. The audience must be made in some fashion to understand that ghosts and witches appear to certain people and convey certain messages. The

[18] Pp. 139-40.   [19] Pp. 492-93.

how is a matter of more importance in the theatre than in the drama.

It is difficult to see why Bradley paid such particular heed to this very minor matter of the objectivity of the ghosts in these plays. It would have been more to the point, it seems to me, had he questioned the validity of the ghost's commands to Hamlet. But that they were valid he accepts without discussion, asserting that Hamlet's expressed doubts were mere fictional excuses. Since Hamlet's "sacred duty" obliged him to obey the ghost in seeking revenge, the only real problem in the play according to Bradley is the reason for his delay. The problem is one which he inherited from his literary forbears, but it is a misleading center about which to arrange an analysis of the play, for it ignores Elizabethan ideas about (1) revenge and (2) the authenticity of ghosts.

There is nothing more certain than that the law, the church, the historian, the moralist, and the popular pamphleteer in Elizabethan England were at one in teaching that God had decreed that "Vengeance is mine," that he would surely exact vengeance for sin, but that he was jealous of his prerogative. To rulers and magistrates he delegated the execution of public justice, but private revenge was forbidden to all and was sure to bring God's vengeance upon anyone engaged upon it, even though the avenger might be used as the instrument of God's vengeance.[20] That Shakespeare's *Hamlet* followed the pattern of what we have come to call the revenge play is not disputed by anyone. From the ghost crying for revenge to the play within the play the dramatic and theatrical devices were familiar to theatergoers when Shakespeare used them. But the ghost which Shakespeare presented was an Elizabethan

[20] I have developed these ideas in "Theories of Revenge in Renaissance England," *MP*, XXVIII (1930-31), 281-296 and *Shakespeare's Tragic Heroes*, Chap. I.

rather than a Senecan ghost, and Christian rather than
pagan morals gave meaning to the plot.

It can be argued that Hamlet was, in fact, the public
executioner of God's justice as he is represented as being
in the Belleforest version of the story, but the proof is
inadequate. Horatio recognizes the ghost of the late
king in arms as a portent of "fierce events"[21] in the
state, Hamlet speaks of King Claudius as having
"Popp'd in between the election and my hopes,"[22] and
he accepts the command of the ghost as though it were
more than a personal burden:

> The time is out of joint;—O cursed spite,
> That ever I was born to set it right!—[23]

But on the other hand the main theme of all his musing
and his talk with Horatio is that King Claudius has
"killed my king and whored my mother."[24] And on the
whole, I think we feel that it is private revenge that
Hamlet is called upon to execute.

It is important, above all, however, to remember
that at the last Hamlet kills his uncle-father, not to
avenge his father's wrongs, but to punish the treachery
of the poisoned dagger and the poisoned cup.[25] He does
not mention his father as he does the deed, nor does he
speak of him as he asks Horatio to live to tell his story.
And as Horatio tells the story, it ends as an account

> Of deaths put on by cunning and forced cause,
> And, in this upshot, purposes mistook
> Fall'n on the inventors' heads.

Nevertheless God's vengeance has been exacted to the
full for the "carnal, bloody, and unnatural acts," which
had been the theme of the ghost's recital. The pity of
it lies in the "accidental judgments, casual slaughters,"
which have littered the path of Hamlet's revenge.[26]

[21] *Hamlet*, I. i. 121.
[22] V. ii. 65.   [23] I. v. 189-90.   [24] V. ii. 64.   [25] V. ii. 330-38.
[26] V. ii. 391-96.

Viewed against a background of Elizabethan teaching about revenge this play becomes much more than a study of Hamlet's "delay" in carrying out his "sacred duty."

The unquestioning acceptance of the "sacred duty" of revenge derives, of course, from an almost child-like belief in the authenticity of the ghost, the second point on which Bradley ignored Elizabethan teaching. *Hamlet* mirrors the conflicting judgments of the time. Recent historical research has demonstrated that there were actually three schools of thought existent concerning ghosts. The orthodox Catholic position was that ghosts might return from purgatory "partly for the comfort and warning of the living, and partly to pray aide of them." The Protestant position was not official and therefore not uniform, but there were many who, like King James, thought ghosts to be the feignings of the devil (or perhaps even of the good angels), appearing frequently in the form of a parent or a friend, which form the devil chose the more surely to entice his victim to destruction. The third group, of those whom we should term scientists, attributed the seeing of ghosts to physiological or psychological causes, generally melancholy adust. I have discussed these three schools of thought elsewhere,[27] but I must again point out that the good Catholic could certainly have recognized Hamlet's father's ghost as released temporarily from purgatory by its description of its abode and by the usual tests to which it answers. King James would have approved of Horatio's efforts to keep Hamlet from fol-

---

[27] *Shakespeare's Tragic Heroes*, Chap. IX. See also W. C. Curry, "The Demonic Metaphysics of *Macbeth*," *SP*, XXX (1933), 395-426 (reprinted in *Shakespeare's Philosophical Patterns*, Baton Rouge, 1937); the introduction by Dover Wilson and the essay by May Yardley on the Catholic position in their edition of Lewes Lavater, *Of Ghostes and Spirites Walking by Night* (Oxford, 1929); and a more exhaustive treatment in R. H. West's *The Invisible World* (Athens, Ga., 1939). Professor West appends a bibliography.

lowing it to a remote part of the platform lest it lure
him to madness or self-destruction. Hamlet himself
argues:

> The spirit that I have seen
> May be the devil; and the devil hath power
> To assume a pleasing shape; yea, and perhaps
> Out of my weakness and my melancholy,
> As he is very potent with such spirits,
> Abuses me to damn me.[28]

And as he bids Horatio watch his uncle during the play,
he protests that if guilt is not then made manifest, "It
is a damned ghost that we have seen."[29] Shakespeare
gives his Elizabethan audience full opportunity to interpret the ghost, each according to his preconceived
opinions.

But since Bradley did not question the authority of
the ghost, he had none of Hamlet's qualms about what
he called Hamlet's "appointed duty," and he was therefore driven to explain them as "an unconscious fiction,
an excuse for his delay—and for its continuance." [30]
Yet neither dialogue nor plot gives us a hint of any fic-
tion-mongering in Hamlet's speeches, and he was uttering the alternate theories that were current in the literature of the time.

The same arguments that characterize the discussion
of the ghost, it must be noted, attend the appearance
of the witches to Macbeth and Banquo. Macbeth demands, "Live you? or are you aught /That man may
question?" Banquo presses the question, "Are ye fantastical, or that indeed /Which outwardly ye show?" [31]
And in turn he suggests the three possible explanations:

> The earth hath bubbles, as the water has,
> And these are of them.
> Were such things here, as we do speak about,
> Or have we eaten on the insane root,

[28] *Hamlet*, II. ii. 637-42.   [30] Pl 131.
[29] III. ii. 90.   [31] *Macbeth*, I. iii. 42-3; 53-4.

That takes the reason prisoner?
And oftentimes, to win us to our harm,
The instruments of darkness tell us truths;
Win us with honest trifles, to betray's
In deepest consequence.—[32]

There is no doubt that King James, whose predelictions seem to have been definitely in the mind of the author when he wrote *Macbeth*, would have strongly endorsed the last of these views, for he was always the devil's advocate in such matters. But there were others who would have favored some natural explanation or alternately an explanation which accounted for witches also as creations of the mind. Shakespeare, then, did not settle the matter of the objectivity of these supernatural manifestations, either ghosts or witches, but chose rather to throw out suggestions which might satisfy those members of his audience who followed any one of the three schools of thought on the subject. And he made his presentation consistent by portraying the effect of the apparitions on characters who were already victims of melancholy adust, the one having been brought to this state by grief and the other by the conflict of ambition and fear. These were the passions that King James and other writers picked out as most likely to be attended by such visitations. A wider acquaintance with what Professor Robert H. West calls the "pneumatology" of the period proves, as he says it does, that "Shakespeare's was the most extensive use of it," and what is more important, that Shakespeare

---

[32] I. iii. 79-80: 83-5: 122-26. Bradley (pp. 342-43 n. 3) rationalizes his peculiar Elizabethan lore to harmonize with his own preconceptions of Shakespeare: "Of course in the popular notion the witch's spirits are devils or servants of Satan [Cf. *Macbeth*, IV. i]. If Shakespeare openly introduces this idea only in such phrases as 'the instruments of darkness' and 'what can the devil speak true?' the reason is *probably his unwillingness to give too much prominence to religious ideas.*" The italics are mine. On this subject see below, pp. 263 ff.

"employed it integrally and fully, not ornamentally or incidentally, in three of his greatest plays." [33]

That Bradley was feeling for some truth beyond his inadequate explanations of the supernatural is apparent from passing remarks. In the last paragraph of his discussion of the witches, in which he has dwelt on the moral responsibility of Macbeth (since the witches do not have compulsive power over him), he says:

The words of the Witches are fatal to the hero only because there is in him something which leaps into light at the sound of them; but they are at the same time the witness of forces which never cease to work in the world around him, and, on the instant of his surrender to them, entangle him inextricably in the web of Fate. [34]

But he does not search for that "something which leaps into light" in Macbeth at the sound of the witches' words. And because he does not do so, he never finds the ultimate cause of the tragedy. The villain Edmund gave cynical expression to a truth which Bradley might have quoted:

This is the excellent foppery of the world, that, when we are sick in fortune, often the surfeit of our own behaviour, we make guilty of our disasters the sun, the moon, and the stars as if we were villains on necessity, fools by heavenly compulsion, knaves thieves and treachers by spherical predominance, drunkards liars and adulterers by an enforced obedience of planetary influence; and all that we are evil in, by a divine thrusting on: an admirable evasion of whoremaster man, to lay his goatish disposition to the charge of a star! [35]

But this is only the negative aspect of the problem. To say that it is not the sun or the moon or the stars or ghosts crying "Revenge!" or witches prophesying of things to come is not to trace tragedy to its source, which in Shakespeare always goes back to the failure of reason to win the battle with passion for man's soul.

[33] *Op. cit.* p. x.   [34] P. 349.
[35] *King Lear*, I. ii. 131-42.

However, in the last two paragraphs of his last lecture on *Hamlet* Bradley's deepening knowledge of the play made him add a significant comment. He had come to feel that the ghost in *Hamlet* and, to a somewhat lesser degree, the ghost in *Macbeth* bring "an intimation of a supreme power concerned in human evil and good." By this time the ghost of the late King of Denmark,—majestic, solemn, impersonal—seems to him not only a spirit intent upon serving its own purposes, but also "the messenger of divine justice set upon the expiation of offences which it appeared impossible for man to discover and avenge, a reminder or a symbol of the connexion of the limited world of ordinary experience with the vaster life of which it is but a partial appearance." [36] Bradley's intuition here was reaching out toward an Elizabethan commonplace, though it was one which had been uttered many times since the Lord said unto Cain, "The voice of thy brother's blood crieth unto me from the ground." But it was never repeated in more ways and with more illustrative examples, I think, than during the period when Shakespeare was writing. In a universe where divine justice rules, it is inevitable that as Hamlet says,

> foul deeds will rise,
> Though all the earth o'erwhelm them, to men's eyes. [37]

Sermons were preached and pamphlets written, stories from classical history and literature were retold and modern instances cited, to prove that no man can fly from God, that the murderer will reveal himself when there is no one to accuse him. Macbeth recalls these tales when the ghost of Banquo has made him reveal his guilt to his now departed guests:

> It will have blood, they say; blood will have blood:
> Stones have been known to move, and trees to speak;

[36] P. 174.
[37] *Hamlet*, I. ii. 256-57.

> Augurs, and understood relations, have
> By magot-pies, and choughs, and rooks, brought forth
> The secret'st man of blood.[38]

In demonstrating the truth that "murder, though it have no tongue, will speak with most miraculous organ," [39] the ghost of Banquo is quite as useful as is the ghost in *Hamlet*, but Bradley does not comment on the fact.

Nor does he note that the tragedies and histories of Shakespeare reveal the supernatural in omens as well as in ghosts and witches.[40] He does not even note that the ghost in *Hamlet* is first regarded as an omen. Horatio marks it as a "precurse of fierce events," an omen of disaster in the state. I do not propose here to supply Bradley's omission but only to suggest that no evaluation of the supernatural in Shakespearean tragedy can be complete without due attention to the omens which Bradley mentions only in connection with the general atmosphere they help to produce.

Though here and there, as I have indicated, Bradley seems to be reaching toward a more integrated philosophy in the tragedies than that which he expounds in fragments, his discussion of the third of the additional factors in tragedy, chance or accident, reveals his failure to meet the problem with the clarity of real conviction. He admits that chance or accident does "have an appreciable influence at some point in the action" in most of Shakespeare's tragedies.

An accident he defines as "any occurrence (not supernatural, of course) which enters the dramatic sequence neither from the agency of a character, nor from the

[38] *Macbeth*, III. iv. 122-26.

[39] *Hamlet*, II. ii. 632-33.

[40] In regard to the omens in *Macbeth* he says (p. 337): "In nature, again, something is felt to be at work, sympathetic with human guilt and supernatural malice. She labours with portents."

obvious surrounding circumstances," and he would even admit as an accident "the deed of a very minor person whose character had not been indicated." Since the operation of accident is a fact in human life, it cannot be omitted, he says. "And, besides," he continues, "it is not merely a fact. That men may start a course of events but can neither calculate nor control it, is a *tragic* fact." The dramatist may use it to produce this effect or for other dramatic uses (unspecified). But ultimately, firm in his belief that the center of the tragedy lies "in action issuing from character, or in character issuing in action," he is driven to offer a sort of *apologia* for the admission of accident into Shakespeare's tragedies:

On the other hand, any *large* admission of chance into the tragic sequence would certainly weaken, and might destroy, the sense of the causal connection of character, deed, and catastrophe. And Shakespeare really uses it very sparingly. We seldom find ourselves exclaiming, "What an unlucky accident!" I believe most readers would have to search painfully for instances. It is, further, frequently easy to see the dramatic intention of an accident; and some things which look like accidents have really a connection with character, and are therefore not in the full sense accidents.

And at last he gets back to his moral responsibility argument:

Finally, I believe it will be found that almost all the prominent accidents occur when the action is well advanced and the impression of the causal sequence is too firmly fixed to be impaired.[41]

Arguing that there are few accidents, that some are put in for "dramatic" purposes, that those related to character are not really accidents, and that the prominent accidents do not often impair the causal sequence of the action is certainly going off in a good many directions at once. The very multiplicity of such arguments suggests that Bradley did not satisfy his own questions

[41] Pp. 14-16 and n. 1 on p. 15.

with any of his answers. And he contradicts these
general statements when he comes to a consideration
of the individual plays. In the passage quoted he avers
that Shakespeare uses accident "very sparingly," and
presses the point: "We seldom find ourselves exclaiming 'What an unlucky accident!' I believe most readers
would have to search painfully for instances." But in
discussing *Othello*, he admits the contrary:

This influence of accident is keenly felt in *King Lear* only once, and
at the very end of the play. In *Othello*, after the temptation has
begun, it is incessant and terrible. The skill of Iago was extraordinary, but so was his good fortune. Again and again a chance word
from Desdemona, a chance meeting of Othello and Cassio, a question which starts to our lips and which anyone but Othello would
have asked, would have destroyed Iago's plot and ended his life.
In their stead, Desdemona drops her handkerchief at the moment
most favorable to him, Cassio blunders into the presence of Othello
only to find him in a swoon, Bianca arrives precisely when she is
wanted to complete Othello's deception and incense his anger into
fury.[42]

We are almost led to feel that there is no escape from
fate, or even "that fate has taken sides with villainy,"
he confesses, though somewhat hesitatingly he affirms
that Shakespeare succeeded in toning down this impression. He notes as an accident Edgar's delay in
rescuing Lear and Cordelia[43] and the accident "introduced into the plot in its barest and least dramatic
form, when Hamlet is brought back to Denmark by
the chance of the meeting with the pirate ship." [44]
Of Duncan's decision to visit Macbeth at the very time
when the witches have given impetus to his ambition,
of Fleance's escape and the events which many readers
would class as accidents in all the tragedies Bradley
has nothing to say.

But the final paragraphs of his last lecture on *Hamlet*
show that he was in reality drawing away from a truth

[42] Pp. 181-82.   [43] P. 15.   [44] P. 173.

which he felt but could not bring himself to admit. He writes:

In *Macbeth* and *Hamlet* not only is the feeling of a supreme power or destiny peculiarly marked, but it has also at times a peculiar tone, which may be called, in a sense, religious. I cannot make my meaning clear without using language too definite to describe truly the imaginative impression produced; but it is roughly true that, while we do not imagine the supreme power as a divine being who avenges crime, or as a providence which supernaturally interferes, our sense of it is influenced by the fact that Shakespeare uses current religious ideas here much more decidedly than in *Othello* or *King Lear*.[45]

Then he mentions the "accident" in *Hamlet* which he thinks probably "is meant to impress the imagination as the very reverse of accidental," and Hamlet's own feeling in this connection that he was in the hands of Providence.

To explain this unwilling admission it is necessary to turn back to the first lecture, "On the Substance of Tragedy," where we find another premise accepted without argument as axiomatic:

The Elizabethan drama was almost wholly secular; and while Shakespeare was writing he practically confined his view to the world of non-theological observation and thought, so that he represents it substantially in one and the same way whether the period of the story is pre-Christian or Christian.

Apparently further living with the tragedies made him uneasy about this passage, for he added a footnote to it when the lectures were published:

I say substantially; but the concluding remarks on *Hamlet* will modify a little the statements above.[46]

Now when Bradley intimates that an accident is not an accident if providence had a hand in it, when he seems to confuse Hamlet's fatalism with the concept

[45] P. 172.
[46] P. 25 and n. 1. It should be noted that Bradley confuses Shakespeare's religious or non-religious interpretation of events with that of the characters in his plays.

of a divinely ordered universe, when he refers to an accident as "any occurrence (not supernatural, of course)" he is certainly not thinking with any great degree of clarity. The Elizabethans may have thought wrongly, but they did not run to vagueness in their philosophies, and they certainly did not have Bradley's hesitation about mentioning God. I cannot think of anything less Elizabethan and less Shakespearean, for that matter, than Bradley's recognition in *Hamlet* and *Macbeth* of a "feeling of a supreme power or destiny peculiarly marked," that has "at times a peculiar tone, which may be called in a sense religious." I do not understand what "a destiny peculiarly marked" is, but I can see nothing peculiar about a religious tone produced by the realization in the plot of a play that God is at work in human affairs. Just in what sense it would be "in a sense" religious, however, I do not know. Bradley's expressed fear that he would use language that was too definite seems to me to have been unwarranted when he wrote:

it is roughly true that, while *we* do not imagine the supreme power as a divine being who avenges crime, or as a providence which supernaturally interferes, our sense of *it* is influenced by the fact that Shakespeare uses current religious ideas here much more decidedly than in *Othello* or *King Lear*.

If I were sure about the antecedents of the *we* and the *it* which I have here underlined, I should be on firmer ground. If he means to include Shakespeare in the *we* and to refer to the divine being as *it*, then I cannot see why Shakespeare did *not* imagine the supreme power as a divine being, or as a providence which supernaturally interferes, because apparently even Bradley is admitting that these were religious beliefs of the time. If he excludes Shakespeare from his *we*, the sentence grows more bewildering still. And it is bewildering because he was mindful of his earlier generalization about Shakespeare and could not bring himself to deny it.

He therefore in these last remarks on *Hamlet*, added like a postscript and not integrated with the discussion of the play as a whole, suggested vaguely what his study of the supernatural and the accidents in the plays was driving him to see, however darkly.

Apparently he thought to have done with this disturbing sense of more things in heaven and earth than he had dreamt of in his philosophy when he quitted *Hamlet* and *Macbeth*, where Shakespeare used "current religious ideas much more decidedly than in *Othello* or *King Lear*." However, when he comes to discussing *King Lear* he finds that "References to religious or irreligious beliefs and feelings are more frequent than is usual in Shakespeare's tragedies, as frequent perhaps as in his final plays."[47] But he still insists that in *King Lear* as in all the tragedies, "Any theological interpretation of the world on the author's part is excluded," and more particularly that "their effect would be disordered or destroyed equally by the ideas of righteous or of unrighteous omnipotence." [48] I do not wish to go at this time into the question of the "mystery" which he demands for tragedy, and which he gets at the price of a universe which the mind of no Englishman before the Romantic Movement could have created.

Rather, I want to go back to my original criticism, that Bradley by discussing the three "additional factors" in tragedy—abnormal conditions of mind, the supernatural, and accidents—only to prove that they were not really factors at all because none of them served to remove the moral responsibility of the characters for their actions was proving something irrelevant. Lady Macbeth's sleepwalking was not the source of any tragic act. True, but it is an important part of the tragedy because it is part of her punishment. The witches may not compel Macbeth to act. True, but he would not have been chosen by the witches had

[47] P. 271.   [48] P. 279.

his soul not been prepared for them. "A man that fortune's buffets and rewards /Hath ta'en with equal thanks," does not have his life controlled by accidents. These are the important things to understand if we are to see the tragedies as artistic wholes.

Furthermore I must in closing again point out that Bradley constantly argues in a circle that these conditions could not have determined the actions of the tragic heroes because then they would not be tragic characters according to his premised definition.

Finally I want to stress again that Bradley's discussion of the last two of these additional factors brought him to the very brink of a more integrated philosophy in the plays, but that he never permitted himself to gaze into its depth.

Concerning Bradley's *Shakespearean Tragedy* [1]

IN 1948 there was published a new edition of Professor A. C. Bradley's *Shakespearean Tragedy*, the first edition of which appeared in 1904. During those forty-four years it remained probably the most influential book of Shakespearean criticism. . . . the enthusiasm of many critics for Bradley has made them demand that every new interpretation of Shakespeare be oriented to his *Shakespearean Tragedy*. To me it seems that the development of critical thought is no more possible than the development of scientific thought if there are certain *a priori* assumptions that are never to be challenged. Bradley confessed that he "worshipped" Shakespeare, and the intensity of his feeling inspired his readers, sometimes to worship not only Shakespeare but also Bradley. Yet I am convinced that Bradley set up certain stumbling blocks to a progressive knowledge of the subject of his adoration, and that it is desirable to see just what they are.

Professor H. B. Charlton in his recent book *Shakespearian Tragedy*, proclaiming himself "a devout Bradleyite," considers modern trends in Shakespearean criticism:

In the field of interpretation, the most striking trend of the last generation has been the assault on Andrew Bradley. On the one hand, we are told, he is too little of a historian and too much of a philosopher; he lifts Shakespeare out of his Tudor theatre, making no allowance for Elizabethan stage conventions, and assuming in his innocence that words and scenes mean what they seem to mean. On the other hand, he is assailed because he takes Shakespeare's dramas as plays and not as poems; he accepts the persons of them

[1] Reprinted from *The Huntington Library Quarterly*, 7, November, 1949, with the special permission of the publishers.

at their face value as semblable men and women, and not as plastic symbols of esoteric imagery, nor as rhythmic ripples in a chromatic ritual. The position of these neo-Shakespearians disturbs me because I cannot understand it.[2]

Professor Charlton has as well as anyone summarized the claims of Bradley to the devotion of his followers. (1) He was a philosopher, and as Professor Charlton says later, "a psychological naturalist" or a "natural psychologist." (2) He read Shakespeare "assuming in his innocence that words and scenes mean what they seem to mean." (3) He read Shakespeare's plays as dramas and accepted the persons of the plays as real men and women.

It is in the last of these claims that I think we find the first stumbling block to understanding Shakespeare's plays when we follow Bradley, for he failed to distinguish between a dramatic character and a person in real life of whom one may have had occasional revealing glimpses. Though he does occasionally remind us that Shakespeare's characters are dramatic creations, he in fact treats them not as artistic creations but as real people, following Coleridge's dictum that "the characters of the *dramatis personae*, like those in real life, are to be inferred by the reader;—they are not told to him." [3] Now in my opinion this is a fundamental critical fallacy. A dramatist may fashion a character as he will. He may outline a figure in the manner of a cartoon, or he may etch in every detail with infinite care. But the artistic representation stops just where the author chooses. The spectator may imagine that he can actually see the colors and the rounded forms of such figures as appear in a Rembrandt etching; but the minute he takes his little brush in hand and paints them in, he has destroyed the integrity of the etching

[2] H. B. Charlton, *Shakespearian Tragedy* (Cambridge, 1948), p. 1.
[3] D. Nichol Smith, *Shakespearean Criticism* (The World's Classics), p. 270.

as a work of art. Bradley is forever busy with his paint brush, filling in what is not there in Shakespeare's portraits, and worse, altering what is there.

For Bradley does not, I think, in his innocence assume that words and scenes mean what they seem to mean, as Professor Charlton would have it. Shakespeare's characters are presented to us by their words and actions and by the interrelated words and actions of other characters. We have to accept what he offers us. When he does not want the audience to believe what a character says, he makes that fact absolutely clear by dramatic devises: the character says in soliloquy that he is lying, has lied, or is about to lie; or he confides his plans to another character; or the real event is acted out on the stage to prove him a liar. It is in such ways that Shakespeare makes us aware of what Iago and Falstaff and Richard III and all the other fabricators of lies are up to. But Bradley contradicts both honest men and liars at will in order to make them conform to his conception of them. Kent tells Lear that he is eight and forty, but, says Bradley, "it is clear that he is much older; not so old as his master, . . . but, one may suppose, three-score and upward." And then having deliberately changed Kent's age, he makes this newly adopted age the basis of his appreciation of Kent's character, for "If his age is not remembered, we fail to realize the full beauty of his thoughtlessness of himself." [4] There is certainly nothing improbable about Goneril's accusations against the hundred knights in the King's train, but Bradley arbitrarily decides that the charges were "probably" false.[5] And without any reason at all except that he thinks it would be better so, he decides that Lear's fool *must have been* "slightly touched in the brain" because otherwise the effective-

[4] A. C. Bradley, *Shakespearean Tragedy* (London, 1911), pp. 308-9.
[5] *Ibid.*, p. 283.

ness of the storm scenes is marred by there being two characters pretending to be insane instead of three characters presenting three different kinds of insanity (the king really insane, the fool "slightly touched," and Edgar pretending to be insane.)[6]

But these tamperings with the characters in *Lear* are probably not so destructive as are those offered in the discussions of the other great tragedies. Hamlet, at the end of the second act of the play, soliloquizes:

> The spirit that I have seen
> May be the devil; and the devil hath power
> To assume a pleasing shape; yea, and perhaps
> Out of my weakness and my melancholy,
> As he is very potent with such spirits,
> Abuses me to damn me.

Hamlet's uncertainties are quite consistent with the earlier emphasis on his desperate courage in following the ghost to another part of the platform in spite of the dangers of which Horatio warned him. They are also quite consistent, as I have pointed out before, with the various Elizabethan theories about ghosts.[7] But Bradley will not believe that Hamlet is telling the truth: "Evidently this sudden doubt, of which there has not been the slightest trace before, is no genuine doubt; it is an unconscious fiction, an excuse for his delay—and for its continuance."[8]

In Act III, Scene 3, in the soliloquy beginning "Now might I do it pat," Hamlet explains his reasons for not killing the king at prayer:

> and am I then revenged,
> To take him in the purging of his soul,
> When he is fit and season'd for his passage?
> No.

---

[6] *Ibid.*, pp. 311-12.

[7] See Note 1. I have used the English Arden texts throughout this paper.

[8] Bradley, p. 131.

> Up, sword, and know thou a more horrid hent;
> When he is . . . .
> . . . . about some act
> That has no relish of salvation in 't;
> Then trip him, that his heels may kick at heaven
> And that his soul may be as damn'd and black
> As hell, whereto it goes.

But Bradley decides:

The feeling of intense hatred which Hamlet expresses is not the cause of his sparing the King, and in his heart he knows this; but it does not at all follow that this feeling is unreal. . . . The reason for refusing to accept his own version of his motive in sparing Claudius is not that his sentiments are horrible, but that elsewhere, and also in the opening of his speech here, we can see that his reluctance to act is due to other causes.

He also adds that one of Hamlet's minor difficulties "probably was that he seemed to be required to attack a defenseless man; and here this difficulty is at its maximum." [9]

If Bradley refuses to believe what Hamlet says, it is not to be wondered at that he will not accept the word of Iago. But the rationalization of his refusal is different. He insists upon regarding Iago as a real instead of a dramatic character, and because Iago is an accomplished deceiver, he warns the audience to be on guard:

One must constantly remember not to believe a syllable that Iago utters on any subject, including himself, until one has tested his statement by comparing it with known facts and with other statements of his own and of other people, and by considering whether he had in the particular circumstances any reason for telling a lie or for telling the truth.

Accordingly, when Iago at the outset attests that he holds Othello in his hate and explains his reasons, telling the story of Othello's preferring Cassio to the military office he himself aspired to, and noting that Othello had acted in spite of the good offices of "three great ones of the city" in his behalf, Bradley comments:

[9] *Ibid.*, pp. 135-36.

It is absolutely certain that Othello appointed Cassio his lieutenant, and *nothing* else is absolutely certain. But there is no reason to doubt the statement that Iago had seen service with him, nor is there anything inherently improbable in the statement that he was solicited by three great personages on Iago's behalf. On the other hand, the suggestions that he refused out of pride and obstinacy, and that he lied in saying he had already chosen his officer, have no verisimilitude; and if there is any fact at all (as there probably is) behind Iago's account of the conversation, it doubtless is the fact that Iago himself was ignorant of military science, while Cassio was an expert, and that Othello explained this to the great personages.[10]

He even suggests that Iago did not hate Othello:

The only ground for attributing to him, I do not say a passionate hatred, but anything deserving the name of hatred at all, is his own statement, 'I hate Othello'; and we know what his statements are worth.[11]

Therefore, he concludes in judging all Iago's testimony:

He is the counterpart of Hamlet, who tried to find reasons for his delay in pursuing a design which excites his aversion. And most of Iago's reasons for action are no more the real ones than Hamlet's reasons for delay were the real ones. Each is moved by forces which he does not understand; and it is probably no accident that these two studies of states psychologically so similar were produced at about the same period.[12]

And having thus disposed of the motivation which Shakespeare gave to Iago, as well as that he gave to Hamlet, Bradley asks, "What then were the real moving forces of Iago's action?" and proceeds to find these forces in things Shakespeare did not mention at all: a desire to satisfy his sense of power, a pleasure in activity for its own sake, and a satisfaction in doing an artistic job.[13]

[10] *Ibid.*, pp. 211-12. It should be noted that Iago did *not* say that Othello was lying. Bradley has merely assumed that Iago must have thought so.

[11] *Ibid.*, p. 224.

[12] *Ibid.*, p. 226.

[13] *Ibid.*, pp. 226-31.

Any knowledge of dramatic literature, it would seem, should have prevented Bradley from commenting that "it is a curious point of technique" with Shakespeare "that the soliloquies of his villains sometimes read like explanations offered to the audience,"[14] for there is certainly nothing *curious* about this ancient device. What is curious is Bradley's idea that Shakespeare would have his characters speak directly to the members of the audience in order to confuse them and put them on a false scent by lying to them.

Lady Macbeth offers a full and complete analysis of her husband's character as she apostrophizes him after reading the letter which heralds his arrival, but Lady Macbeth "did not fully understand him," says Bradley.[15] Nor did Macbeth understand himself. The Thane of Cawdor contemplates murder in a soliloquy, the meaning of which seems plain:

> If it were done, when 't is done, then 't were well
> It were done quickly: if the assassination
> Could trammel up the consequence, and catch
> With his surcease success; that but this blow
> Might be the be-all and the end-all here,
> But here, upon this bank and shoal of time,
> We'd jump the life to come. —But in these cases,
> We still have judgment here; that we but teach
> Bloody instructions, which, being taught, return
> To plague the inventor: this even-handed justice
> Commends th' ingredients of our poison'd chalice
> To our own lips.[16]

Since Macbeth addresses no one but the audience here, it would generally be assumed that he says what Shakespeare wanted the audience to understand. But no, Bradley says, it is not fear but conscience that worries Macbeth:

Even when he *talks* of consequences, and declares that if he were safe against them he would 'jump the life to come,' his imagination

[14] *Ibid.*, p. 222.   [15] *Ibid.*, pp. 351-52.   [16] I.vii. 1-12.

bears witness against him, and shows us that what really holds him back is the hideous vileness of the deed.

In this same scene, Bradley continues, we feel pity as well as anxiety for Macbeth while Lady Macbeth "overcomes his opposition to the murder; and we feel it (though his imagination is not specially active) because this scene shows us *how little he understands himself.*"[17]

If Kent is to be understood only when we realize that he was an old man over sixty even though he himself states his age as forty-eight; if Hamlet's soliloquies are deceiving and Iago's deceitful; if Lady Macbeth and Macbeth as well give false analyses of Macbeth's character and motives—then surely Shakespeare must have been a wilfully obscure dramatist, or else he did not understand his own creations. Re-creating Shakespeare's characters as Bradley does by denying what they say even when they are alone with the audience seems to me to refute the claim of Professor Charlton that Bradley assumed that words and scenes mean what they seem to mean.

The second stumbling block that Bradley puts in the way of an understanding of Shakespeare's tragic characters comes from his failure to differentiate the tragic heroes from the hero-villains, and this failure, too, results from his refusal to heed what is explicitly stated by the characters on the stage. In his introductory lecture Bradley recognizes the fact that the hero need not be good, and he says that the "fatal imperfection or error" of the hero "is of different kinds and degrees," offering as examples "the excess and precipitancy of Romeo" and "the murderous ambition of Richard III." He points out that in most cases the tragic hero is doing what he thinks right, Richard and Macbeth being "the only heroes who do what they themselves recognize to be villainous." He thinks that Shakespeare had to give

[17] *Ibid.*, pp. 355, 357. (The italics are mine.) See also pp. 351, 369, 373-75.

Richard and Macbeth certain admirable characteristics in order that the audience might be compelled to "a horrified sympathy and awe which balance, at the least, the desire for the hero's ruin." [18] But these hesitant glimpses of the distinction between tragic hero and villain are not pursued in the subsequent detailed studies of character.

Actually it is necessary only to consider how the distinction between the tragic hero and the villain has been paralleled in both theology and jurisprudence to recognize how fundamental it is. In theology we see the traditional differentiation between venial and mortal sin, between the sin which may be expiated or forgiven and the sin which so alienates a soul from God that it cannot seek and find mercy and is therefore doomed to eternal punishment in hell. In jurisprudence there is likewise always a differentiation of those crimes which may be expiated or forgiven under the law and those crimes for which a man must pay with his life. Manslaughter and murder are different matters both before God and before the law. But to Bradley, Richard III and Hamlet, Othello and Lear, Macbeth and Romeo are all alike tragic heroes. "It makes no difference whether they mean well or ill," he says, for the men and women in the tragic world "fight blindly in the dark, and the power that works through them makes them the instruments of a design which is not theirs." [19] To him it is the greatness, the heroic size, of the tragic character that distinguishes him. "Dramas like *Cymbeline* and the *Winter's Tale*," he says, "which might seem destined to end tragically, owe their happy ending largely to the fact that the principal characters fail to reach tragic dimensions." [20] He carries this feeling for largeness as the hallmark of the tragic character

[18] *Ibid.*, p. 22.
[19] *Ibid.*, p. 27.
[20] *Ibid.*, pp. 20-21.

so far as to exclaim concerning Lady Macbeth that "she was too great to repent," [21]—a sentiment that would certainly horrify Shakespeare and every other Elizabethan, as it should doubtless horrify every good Christian of any age.

But let us look for a moment at the real tragic heroes and then consider how they differ from the villains of tragedy. Hamlet and Othello and Lear, as Bradley recognizes, never choose to do evil. They all, in fact, are trying to be the executors of justice. Yet Hamlet is not too great to repent his killing of Polonius and his wronging of Laertes. Othello dies to expiate the killing of Desdemona. Lear sorrows over his treatment of Cordelia and learns at last to be patient. All of them bring tragedy into their own lives and the lives of others because they allow themselves to be confused by passion, but none of them submits his will to his passion. Reason may be blinded by passion, so that it fails to direct the will. But reason does not "pandar will" in any of the tragic heroes. Their lives are turbulent because passion brings turbulence and disease to body and soul. Yet at the end each of the tragic heroes has passed through his period of turmoil to peace, and reason again rules.

Bradley affirms that "one end awaits Richard III. and Brutus, Macbeth and Hamlet," [22] but in so saying he surely overlooks the clear statement of the final reckoning which Shakespeare is careful to chronicle for both heroes and villains. In the case of all the tragic heroes we are made to see that their accounts have been settled, and that after life's fitful fever they sleep well. Laertes implores Hamlet:

> Exchange forgiveness with me, noble Hamlet;
> Mine and my father's death come not upon thee,
> Nor thine on me!

[21] *Ibid.*, p. 379.
[22] *Ibid.*, p. 32.

And Hamlet responds, "Heaven make thee free of it!" Bidding Horatio stay behind to tell his story, Hamlet gives his dying voice to Fortinbras in the election. Then, at peace, he departs while Horatio says farewell:

> Now cracks a noble heart.—Good night, sweet prince,
> And flights of angels sing thee to thy rest!

And Fortinbras commands for him a solider's honored burial:

> Let four captains
> Bear Hamlet, like a soldier, to the stage;
> For he was likely, had he been put on,
> To have proved most royally: and for his passage,
> The soldiers' music and the rites of war
> Speak loudly for him.

Othello asks pardon of Cassio and dies upon a kiss in expiating his murder of Desdemona. But before he dies, he asks Lodovico in his letters to the Venetian state to tell his story aright, and even at the moment of death Cassio pronounces his epitaph, "For he was great of heart," while Lodovico makes plans to go at once

> and to the state
> This heavy act with heavy heart relate.

Lear has been able to ask forgiveness of Cordelia and to have had a glimpse of happiness with her before the final catastrophe. At the end Albany would restore to him his kingdom and reward the virtue of his friends, but he cannot stay longer "upon the rack of this tough world," and there is a sense of peace at last when Kent proclaims:

> I have a journey, sir, shortly to go;
> My master calls me, I must not say no.

Each of the tragic heroes thus makes his peace with those he has wronged and settles his account with the living. Each is honored in death. We hear the *Pax vobiscum* that goes with each into his grave.

Professor C. V. Boyer was the first, I believe, to differentiate the villain from the tragic hero when he wrote in his study of *The Villain as Hero in Elizabethan Tragedy*: "when a character deliberately opposes moral law from wilfulness, and for the purpose of advancing his own interests, recognizing at the same time the sanction of the law he defies, we call him a villain." [23] It would be more accurate to say that the villain violates the moral law because he has let passion rather than reason determine the ends to be achieved and has made his reason the pandar to will, finding ways to procure what passion desires. But Professor Boyer emphasizes the two important characteristics of the villain: he recognizes the sanction of the moral order which he violates; and he violates that law deliberately to satisfy "his own interests," interests which are determined, I should add, by ambition or hate or whatever passion dominates him. Professor Boyer recognizes Macbeth as a villain on the basis of the same soliloquy in Act I, Scene 7, from which I have already quoted the earlier part. It is in this soliloquy that Macbeth reckons up the reasons why he should not commit the murder: he is the kinsman and the subject and the host of the king.

> Besides, this Duncan
> Hath borne his faculties so meek, hath been
> So clear in his great office, that his virtues
> Will plead like angels, trumpet-tongued, against
> The deep damnation of his taking off;
> And pity, like a naked new-born babe,
> Striding the blast, or heaven's cherubin, hors'd
> Upon the sightless couriers of the air,
> Shall blow the horrid deed in every eye,
> That tears shall drown the wind.—I have no spur
> To prick the sides of my intent, but only
> Vaulting ambition, which o'erleaps itself
> And falls on the other.

There would seem possible no more definite statement

[23] *Op. cit.* (London, 1914), p. 6.

of the claims of decency and morality as accepted by Macbeth himself, and there would seem possible no clearer statement than Macbeth's own that only ambition drives him to do what he accepts as a "horrid deed," yet Bradley, contradicting his earlier acknowledgment of Macbeth's having done what he knew to be villainous, now contends that Macbeth "has never, to put it pedantically, accepted as the principle of his conduct the morality which takes shape in his imaginative fears." [24]

To understand how clearly Macbeth belongs to the villain type it is well to compare him with King Claudius, even though Claudius is the antagonist rather than the protagonist in *Hamlet*. Like Macbeth, Claudius acknowledges his sin as a violation of eternal right, a sin that "hath the primal eldest curse upon 't, A brother's murder." And he counts "those effects for which I did the murder, My crown, mine own ambition, and my queen." He knows he has sinned and why. Both villains are made to point out to the audience that they have committed mortal sin, for both realize they have alienated their souls from God so that they cannot ask His mercy. Claudius cannot pray, and Macbeth cannot say "Amen" when the grooms cry "God bless us!" Macbeth does indeed respond to the knocking at the gates after the murder of Duncan with a sigh of "Wake Duncan with thy knocking: I would thou couldst!" But like Claudius he cannot repent in such fashion as to find God again without giving up those things for which he did the deed. Instead, he decides that "Things bad begun make strong themselves by ill." Macbeth's days accumulate evil as do those of Claudius. And at the end of the play he is not reconciled to God or man. It simply is not true, as Bradley says, that one end awaits Hamlet and Macbeth, for Hamlet dies as one who has come through tragic

[24] Bradley, p. 357.

error and tragic suffering to have angels sing him to his rest. And dead, he is honored with a soldier's burial. What Bradley could have said truly was that one end awaits Macbeth and Claudius. Macbeth goes unwept and without the comfort of friends or followers to his death. His dead body is mutilated, and Macduff brings in his head as a trophy of the final battle, proclaiming

> Behold, where stands
> The usurper's cursed head! the time is free.

But it is Malcolm who completes the judgment

> Of this dead butcher and his fiend-like queen,
> Who, as 't is thought, by self and violent hands
> Took off her life.

Similarly Hamlet pronounces judgment upon Claudius when, having stabbed him with the poisoned dagger, he also forces him to drink from the poisoned cup:

> Here, thou incestuous, murderous, damned Dane,
> Drink off this potion! Is thy union here?
> Follow my mother!

And Laertes affirms the judgment, "He is justly served." Like Macbeth, Claudius is ignominious in death. There is no preparation for an honorable burial. Always Sakespeare's villains, however great or however puny their characters, are marked as condemned by God and man. No analysis of the characters of tragedy which fails to take this fact into consideration can have a firm moral foundation.

Yet Bradley's purpose was to analyze Shakespearean tragedy by considering the moral nature of the tragic characters in relation to the moral universe. He paid no attention to the plot of the plays in this connection, and he assumed at the outset that the plays were "secular." Of these matters I propose to write in a later article. But before they can be considered, it is necessary to try to find the basis on which he made his analysis of the moral nature of the tragic characters.

It is at this point, it seems to me, that we encounter the third and greatest stumbling block to an understanding of Shakespearean tragedy, for I submit that Bradley, whom Professor Charlton would have to be a "psychological naturalist" or a "natural psychologist," actually makes his analysis of character on a foundation of a morality without morals and a psychology that could exist only in Wonderland. I am not objecting that his moral philosophy is not Elizabethan. I am not objecting that that part of moral philosophy which we call psychology is not with him what was current in Shakespeare's day. Rather I contend that Bradley's moral world is moral chaos, and that his psychology is something which could never have made sense in any period.

Listen to what Bradley says of the tragic heroes in general:

Some, like Hamlet and Cleopatra, have *genius*. Others, like Othello, Lear, Macbeth, Coriolanus, are *built on the grand scale*; and *desire, passion,* or *will* are in them a terrible force. In almost all we observe a marked onesidedness, a pre-disposition in some particular direction; . . . a fatal tendency to identify the whole being with one *interest, object, passion,* or *habit of mind.* . . . It is a fatal *gift*, but it carries with it a touch of *greatness*; and when there is joined to it *nobility of mind*, or *genius*, or *immense force*, we realize the full power and reach of the soul, and the conflict in which it engages acquires that *magnitude* which stirs not only sympathy and pity, but *admiration, terror,* and *awe*.[25]

I have italicized certain groups of words which represent Bradley's confused use of psychological terms. What is genius? Are Hamlet and Cleopatra, then, not built on the grand scale because they have genius? How are desire and passion differentiated? How can desire and/or passion be equated with will when their struggle is traditionally to gain control of the will? Are not interest and passion rather directed toward an object

[25] *Ibid.*, p. 20.

than equated with it? And what relation does a habit of mind bear to a passion? Nowhere does Bradley give definite meaning to these terms. Yet they are dictionary words. Linking them as Bradley does is like equating as driving forces driver, cart, horse, cargo, destination, and route.

Again what Bradley calls "spiritual force" means to him

whatever forces act in the human spirit, whether good or evil, whether personal passion or impersonal principle; doubts, desires, scruples, ideas—whatever can animate, shake, possess, and drive a man's soul.[26]

But can an impersonal principle shake or drive a man's soul unless he adheres to it with passion—personal passion, if you will? How can an idea shake a man's soul unless it rouses passion in him? This failure to delimit terms or to understand their interrelationships I find utterly confusing. And I doubt whether any system of psychology in any period would justify Bradley's use of these terms.

This confusion of terms is nowhere more bewildering than in the reference to passion and the passions. Passion gradually comes to occupy a great deal of Bradley's attention, for no one can read the plays as closely as he did without becoming aware of its dominant interest for Shakespeare. But he never tries to define it, he confuses passion and the passions, and he becomes utterly chaotic in his speech about it at times. Thus he says that Macbeth and Lady Macbeth "are fired by one and the same passion of ambition." A few paragraphs later he says that Macbeth was exceedingly ambitious and must have been so "by temper," but that this "tendency" must have been strengthened by his marriage. And then he adds that "When we see him, it has been further stimulated by his remarkable

[26] *Ibid.*, pp. 18-19.

success and by the consciousness of exceptional powers
and merit. It becomes a passion."[27] It would seem
that Bradley did not think of ambition, even exceedingly great ambition as a passion, though it "became"
a passion in Macbeth ultimately. Iago, he says, "has
less passion than an ordinary man." Arguing against
those critics who think Iago was impelled by hatred
and ambition because he says he was, Bradley comes
as near as he ever does to defining or at least describing
what he means by passion:

no ambition or hatred short of passion could drive a man who is
evidently so clear-sighted, and who must hitherto have been so
prudent, into a plot so extremely hazardous. Why, then, in the
Iago of the play do we find no sign of these passions or of anything
approaching to them? Why, If Shakespeare meant that Iago was
impelled by them, does he suppress the signs of them? . . . Passion,
in Shakespeare's plays, is perfectly easy to recognize. What vestige
of it, of passion unsatisfied or of passion gratified, is visible in Iago?
None: that is the very horror of him. He has *less* passion than an
ordinary man, and yet he does these frightful things.[28]

Light is thrown on his conception of passion also by his
comment on Othello:

there is no subject more exciting than sexual jealousy rising to the
pitch of passion; and there can hardly be any spectacle at once so
engrossing and so painful as that of a great nature suffering the
torment of this passion, and driven by it to a crime which is also a
hideous blunder. Such a passion as ambition, however terrible its
results, is not itself ignoble . . . But jealousy, and especially sexual
jealousy, brings with it a sense of shame and humiliation.[29]

And we can hear it again when he says of Lear that
"The force of his passion has made us feel that his
nature was great." [30]
The first confusion, then, in the use of the term
passion arises from the fact that sometimes Bradley
speaks of ambition and jealousy and hate and pride as

passions, but that again he speaks of them as becoming passions. The idea of passion superimposed on passions is always there. I have studied Bradley's analyses of character over and over again, and the nearest that I can come to understanding what he is saying is just that—that passion is something superimposed on the passions or the will or the genius or the idea or whatever it is that dominates the tragic hero. He has no understanding at all of the relation of mind and emotions— or reason and passions if you speak in terms that Shakespeare would have understood. Nor does he have any notion that the will is not something to be equated with reason and passion. *Passions* are something vaguely like ideas or desires or habits of mind or "genius." *Passion*, on the other hand, means greatness. It also means eloquence. Thus Hamlet is not passionate, though of course he is grief-stricken and melancholy, and he brings down his tragedy upon him when he acts to kill Polonius. Lady Macbeth's "will remains supreme," "even when passion has quite died away." Iago is cold by temperament. Othello and Lear and Macbeth are great because in them passion is tremendous.

Now I insist that this kind of analysis is not good character analysis, not because it fails to use the contemporary language of Elizabethan moral philosophy which Shakespeare used, but because it fails to understand the interrelationships of the things he talks about —will and passion and desire and genius and all the others. Bradley may use words that are to a certain extent the words of popular psychology in all periods, but he does not define them, and he does not use them in a way that would make sense in any generation.

I have said that Bradley's analysis of the characters of tragedy was made on a foundation of morality without morals as well as a psychology untrue to psychological thinking of any period. For instance, he speaks of this "tendency to identify the whole being with one interest, object, passion, or habit of mind, "as a "fatal gift" which "carries with it a touch of greatness." A little later he is more definite:

In the circumstances where we see the hero placed, his tragic trait, which is also his greatness, is fatal to him.[31]

What he seems to say is, therefore, that what we are accustomed to think of as the tragic flaw is the source of the greatness of the tragic hero. Othello's jealousy and Macbeth's ambition are thus the greatness of the characters. And conversely, Hamlet's and Cleopatra's *genius* must be not only their greatness but also the tragic flaw in each of them. Again Bradley states that *Julius Caesar* and *Hamlet* are tragedies of thought[32] and that their heroes must be considered separately:

The later heroes, on the other hand, Othello, Lear, Timon, Macbeth, Antony, Coriolanus, have, one and all, passionate natures, and, speaking roughly, we may attribute the tragic failure in each of these cases to passion. . . . All of the later tragedies may be called tragedies of passion.

Then he adds that

Antony and Coriolanus are, from one point of view, victims of passion; but the passion that ruins Antony also exalts him, he touches the infinite in it; and the pride and self-will of Coriolanus, though terrible in bulk, are scarcely so in quality; there is nothing base in them, and the huge creature whom they destroy is a noble, even a lovable, being.[33]

The conception of a tragic flaw in a character of heroic size, a flaw which may be as unheroic as the intemperate anger of Ajax, and which may yet undo all the good and all the greatness of a man and his works—this conception is one justification for the pity and terror of

[31] *Ibid.*, pp. 20-21.
[32] Bradley uses Hegel's phrase, applying it to *Julius Caesar* as well as *Hamlet*.
[33] *Ibid.*, 82-83.

tragedy. But when the flaw itself is the source of greatness, and when the character is judged by the sheer massiveness of the flaw, then there is nothing but moral chaos.

The "fatal tendency to identify the whole being with one interest, object, passion or habit of mind" is present, Bradley says, "in his early heroes, Romeo and Richard II., infatuated men, who otherwise rise comparatively little above the ordinary level." Only their tragic flaw, then, would seem to make them great. Indeed, Bradley says specifically: "It is a fatal *gift*, but it carries with it a touch of greatness." [34] And with this word *gift*, he raises a new problem. Whence comes this gift? Does the individual have no responsibility for identifying his "whole being with one interest, object, passion or habit of mind," and allowing himself to be fatally dominated by it?

It seems to me to project tragedy into moral chaos to make any such admission. But a little later in his first lecture Bradley goes on to say that the men and women in tragedy

fight blindly in the dark, and the power that works through them makes them the instrument of a design which is not theirs. They act freely, and yet their action binds them hand and foot. And it makes no difference whether they meant well or ill. [35]

Bradley fails utterly to identify the source of this fatal "gift," just as he fails to make clear what power works through these tragic characters to "make them the instrument of a design that is not theirs." In another paper I shall have more to say on this subject, but I want here to comment again that if that is a moral universe, as Bradley says it is, it is a moral universe without morals and without moral responsibility and without moral arbiter.

Bradley adds another disquieting comment when he

[34] *Ibid.*, p. 20.   [35] *Ibid.*, p. 27.

affirms that though these early heroes, Romeo and Richard II, rise comparatively little above the ordinary level except as their fatal "gift" lends them a touch of greatness, that fatal gift, when "nobility of mind or genius or immense force is added to it," enters into a conflict which acquires "that magnitude which stirs not only sympathy and pity, but admiration, terror, and awe." [36] Now admiration is an alien word in the description of the emotional response to the destroying force in a tragic character. Pity and terror and awe we expect when we witness a character carried into conflict with moral law. But admiration ought not to be part of a moral response to violations of moral law. However, once more we find that it is the magnitude of the conflict that elicits this response from Bradley. Actually it is apparent that Bradley does admire Shakespeare's villains and heroes alike if their sins or their passions are only great enough. Lady Macbeth was "too great to repent." It is no wonder that trying to orient his characters in such a moral universe he could only conclude that "tragedy would not be tragedy if it were not a painful mystery." [37]

[36] *Ibid.*, p. 20.   [37] *Ibid.*, p. 38.

INDEX